MW00453957

Innovators, Firms, and Markets

Innovators, Firms, and Markets

The Organizational Logic of Intellectual Property

Jonathan M. Barnett

OXFORD
UNIVERSITY PRESS

OXFORD
UNIVERSITY PRESS

Oxford University Press is a department of the University of Oxford. It furthers
the University's objective of excellence in research, scholarship, and education
by publishing worldwide. Oxford is a registered trade mark of Oxford University
Press in the UK and certain other countries.

Published in the United States of America by Oxford University Press
198 Madison Avenue, New York, NY 10016, United States of America.

© Oxford University Press 2021

All rights reserved. No part of this publication may be reproduced, stored in
a retrieval system, or transmitted, in any form or by any means, without the
prior permission in writing of Oxford University Press, or as expressly permitted
by law, by license, or under terms agreed with the appropriate reproduction
rights organization. Inquiries concerning reproduction outside the scope of the
above should be sent to the Rights Department, Oxford University Press, at the
address above.

You must not circulate this work in any other form
and you must impose this same condition on any acquirer.

Library of Congress Cataloging-in-Publication Data
Names: Barnett, Jonathan M., author.
Title: Innovators, firms, and markets : the organizational logic of
intellectual property / Jonathan M. Barnett.
Description: New York, NY : Oxford University Press, [2021] |
Includes bibliographical references and index.
Identifiers: LCCN 2020031298 (print) | LCCN 2020031299 (ebook) |
ISBN 9780190908591 (hardback) | ISBN 9780190908614 (epub) |
ISBN 9780190908607(UPDF) | ISBN 9780190908621(Digital Online)
Subjects: LCSH: Intellectual property. |
Patent laws and legislation—United States.
Classification: LCC K1401 .B375 2020 (print) |
LCC K1401 (ebook) | DDC 346.73048/6—dc23
LC record available at https://lccn.loc.gov/2020031298
LC ebook record available at https://lccn.loc.gov/2020031299

DOI: 10.1093/oso/9780190908591.001.0001

1 3 5 7 9 8 6 4 2

Printed by Sheridan Books, Inc., United States of America

For my mother, Queenie Barnett. May her memory be blessed.

I have seen with real alarm several recent attempts, in quarters carrying some authority, to impugn the principle of patents altogether; attempts which, if practically successful, would enthrone free stealing under the prostituted name of free trade, and make the men of brains, still more than at present, the needy retainers and dependents of the men of money-bags.

—John Stuart Mill, *Principles of Political Economy* ([1848] 1909, 933)

We must not lose track of the fact that inventions as such, important inventions, are made by individuals and almost invariably by individuals with very limited means.

—Philo T. Farnsworth, inventor of the first all-electronic television (Investigation of Concentration of Economic Power, *Hearings Before the Temporary National Economic Committee* 1939)

[N]either Courts [*sic*] nor treatise-writers have been radical enough in defending the legitimacy of the "monopoly" in a patent, as distinguished from the ordinary trade-monopoly.... I for one regard it as unfortunate that courts and treatise-writers have not stood up more boldly for the fundamental right-ness of the patent-right itself.

—John H. Wigmore, Dean of Northwestern University Law School (1942, vi–vii)

Contents

Figures and Tables

Figures

Tables

Preface

In this book, I have sought to develop a novel analytical framework for assessing the welfare effects of different levels of intellectual property (IP) protection. This framework is anchored in a seemingly mundane observation: certain types of firms can readily protect innovation without IP rights, but other types of firms cannot. This observation complicates, and in some cases overturns, the standard "incentives/access" trade-off that is typically used to assess the effects of making IP rights stronger or weaker. The trade-off, a mainstay of treatises, judicial opinions, and much of legal and economic analysis of IP law and policy, is straightforward. As IP rights increase in strength, innovators expect greater returns and invest greater resources in innovation but have greater capacities to impose access costs on intermediate and end users. As IP rights decline in strength, those effects are reversed. On both theoretical and empirical grounds, I argue that the conventional trade-off leads to false expectations in a substantial range of circumstances. These false expectations arise precisely in cases where certain firms, especially older, larger, and more integrated firms, have the ability to earn returns on innovation without recourse to IP rights, while other types of firms, especially younger, smaller, and less integrated firms, do not. Where the largest, most established, and most highly integrated firms can mimic and even outperform the IP rights delivered by the state, reducing IP rights can raise entry costs and shelter incumbents against the competitive threat posed by more efficient innovators. Counterintuitively, weak IP rights are often the best entry barrier the state can bestow on incumbents that are otherwise exposed to challenge by entrepreneurial entrants that are rich in ideas but poor in the capital required to commercialize those ideas. That may explain why some of today's largest technology firms support ongoing legal and policy changes to weaken patents (and IP rights generally), as did their predecessors in previous generations, while smaller R&D-specialist entities (and their financial backers) usually resist those changes.

The approach developed in this book seeks to build a bridge between the scholarly literature on IP and innovation law and policy, on the one hand, and the scholarly literature on contractual and organizational forms, on the other hand. Substantively, I pursue this convergence by importing into IP analysis the "positive-sum" perspective characteristic of business management and transactional legal scholars, who tend to examine how business arrangements create value by building relationships between firms and other entities. This contrasts with the "zero-sum" perspective characteristic of many economists and legal scholars on IP rights, who tend to examine how those rights block access and deplete value through actual or threatened litigation by IP owners against alleged infringers. While infringement litigation is an important part of the overall IP landscape, an inordinate focus on this adversarial context is akin to understanding the economic and social functions of contract law without examining the deal structuring, negotiation, and renegotiation activities through which contract law is actually implemented in real-world markets. Looking at innovation policy through a transactional lens shifts the analytical spotlight to the costly and complex tasks that real-world markets must undertake to assemble the financing and commercialization inputs required to convert an innovation into an economically viable product or service. With important exceptions,[1] academic and other discussions of IP law and innovation policy have not given a great deal of attention to these activities. Notably, the most famous commentator on the economics of innovation *did* recognize the importance of commercialization. In 1911, Joseph Schumpeter wrote:

> As long as they are not carried into practice, inventions are economically irrelevant. And to carry any improvement into effect is a task entirely different from the inventing of it, and a task, moreover, requiring entirely different types of aptitudes.... It is, therefore, not advisable, and it may be downright misleading, to stress the element of invention as much as many writers do.[2]

Prevailing scholarly approaches to IP and innovation law and policy generally focus on the use of IP rights to block imitators through litigation and then extract a supracompetitive premium in the market. This litigation-focused approach tends to overestimate the social costs, and underestimate the social gains, reasonably attributable to robust IP protections once situated within a broader timeline encompassing the full range of innovation, commercialization, and, in a minority of cases, dispute-resolution activities in technology and content markets. In particular, this approach overlooks how real-world technology markets deploy IP rights, together with contractual and organizational forms, to construct a rich variety of transactional structures so that innovation can be efficiently financed and commercialized by specialized firms situated at different points on the technology supply chain. IP rights enable these value-creating relationships by embedding informational assets in a "property envelope" that mitigates the threat of expropriation inherent to information-intensive transactions among sophisticated parties with potentially adverse competitive interests. By mitigating those transactional hazards, IP rights can lower entry barriers for innovator-entrepreneurs that lack an internal commercialization infrastructure and therefore rely on contractual relationships with third parties to extract a positive return from their R&D investments. By implication, reducing IP strength restores expropriation risk, raises entry barriers for innovator-entrepreneurs, and shifts the innovation and commercialization process to vertically integrated entities that maintain an end-to-end pathway from idea conception through market release.[3] More generally, secure IP rights support the formation of markets in financing, licensing, and trading technology assets, while the absence of those rights restores expropriation risk and causes those markets to shrink. This does not necessarily mean that innovation comes to a halt in a weak-IP environment. However, it does mean that the organizational mechanisms through which innovation is financed and commercialized look substantially different, which in turn may inefficiently distort firm and market structures in a manner that favors large, integrated incumbents and runs counter to the public interest in a dynamically efficient innovation economy.

This book builds upon the work of other scholars in law, economics, and business management who have explored various points of interaction between IP rights, transactional structures, and organizational forms. More specifically, the organizational approach to IP law and policy set forth in this book contributes to, and seeks to extend, a growing literature among legal academics, economists, and business management scholars on the transactional functions of IP rights and, more generally, the interaction between IP rights and the scope of the firm.[4] In particular, I develop a theoretical account of the transactional and organizational functions of the patent system (encompassing patent-relevant portions of antitrust law), which in turn provides a tool for assessing how changes in the strength of formal IP protections influence the market's selection of organizational forms for executing the innovation and commercialization process. This theoretical framework anticipates that weak-IP regimes will tend to favor large integrated firms that can monetize innovation through integrated commercialization structures, while strong-IP regimes will enable a broad range of organizational forms that encompass interfirm commercialization arrangements governed by contract. Largely consistent with these expectations, I identify historical patterns in the organization of innovation and commercialization activities in U.S. technology markets in apparent response to changes in the strength of formal IP protection during an almost 120-year period starting in 1890 and ending in 2006. In general, periods of strong IP protection tend to be characterized by vertically disintegrated market architectures characterized by venture-funded innovators and the development of licensing and trading markets in intellectual assets. By contrast, a long period of weak IP protection from the late New Deal through the 1970s coincides with substantially vertically integrated market architectures in which innovation and commercialization were mostly undertaken by large integrated firms, often directly or indirectly supported by government funding. The proposed relationships between organizational form and the "demand for IP" are further confirmed by entity-specific differences in IP advocacy behavior, as illustrated primarily through lobbying behavior in connection with the America Invents Act of 2011 and amicus brief filings in Supreme Court patent-related litigation during 1986–2016. Larger and more integrated firms (outside the pharmaceutical industry) tend to lobby for weaker patent rights, while smaller, R&D-intensive, and less integrated firms (and investors in those firms) tend to express the opposite preference. This runs counter to conventional intuitions that strong IP rights protect the market positions of dominant incumbents.

This organizational approach not only provides a positive tool of IP analysis but also has normative implications that challenge much of what has become conventional thinking on IP (and IP-related antitrust) law and policy. It is common to argue today that strong IP rights "tax" the flow of knowledge assets,[5] raise entry barriers that protect incumbents, and ultimately harm consumers through inflated prices and reduced innovation. This view has motivated more than a decade's worth of actions by the Supreme Court, Congress, and, with some recent exceptions, the antitrust agencies to weaken the strength of patent protections. Robust IP rights certainly can give rise to social costs in the form of opportunistic litigation and licensing strategies. These unwelcome side effects deserve serious scrutiny and, when appropriate, targeted legal responses. Yet it is important to appreciate how IP rights generate social gains by mitigating the financing and transactional obstacles that an innovator-entrepreneur encounters in the process of converting an innovation into a product that can deliver returns for inventors (and investors) and value for consumers. Relatedly, it is important to appreciate that, outside the pharmaceutical market, weak-IP regimes tend to advantage larger and more integrated firms that can deploy size, scale, and other non-IP mechanisms to capture returns on R&D, while disadvantaging smaller and less integrated firms that have strong innovation capacities but meager capital and other commercialization resources. Strengthening IP rights reverses those effects, providing the small-firm innovator—and, more generally, R&D-intensive and substantially unintegrated entities—with the tools necessary to extract returns from R&D through contractual relationships with the suppliers of capital and other commercialization inputs required to move an innovation from lab to market. Relatedly, secure IP rights provide the necessary property-rights foundation for forming secondary markets in intellectual assets divorced from any particular product or service, which in turn facilitates disaggregated supply chains in which upstream R&D-specialist entities broadly disseminate technology inputs to a large pool of intermediate users. As suggested by past and present IP-skeptical advocacy efforts of large technology firms, weakening patents can raise an implicit entry barrier to innovative entrants that can potentially challenge incumbents that are otherwise well protected by a difficult-to-replicate financing, production, and distribution infrastructure. This book explores the reasons behind these and other unexpected outcomes, which in turn have surprising implications for IP and innovation law and policy.

Plan of Organization

This book consists of three parts. For purposes of a brief reading guide, I summarize each part here.

Part I. Theory: Rethinking Intellectual Property

The conventional approach to IP analysis has a critical oversight; namely, it does not take into account that any reduction in formal IP rights induces firms to shift to IP-like alternatives in order to continue to capture gains from R&D investments. Depending on a firm's costs of adopting these non-IP mechanisms, the supply or withdrawal of IP coverage can give rise to an indeterminate range of positive, neutral, and negative effects on returns for innovators and costs for users. Critically, different entity types incur different costs in deploying non-IP-based strategies, mostly as a function of size, level of integration, and time in the market. In general, a large, vertically integrated, and well-established firm can deploy the efficiencies and goodwill associated with its existing financing, production, and distribution infrastructure in order to erect implicit entry barriers that protect the firm's ability to secure returns on innovation. By definition, those non-IP mechanisms for capturing returns on R&D are foreclosed from entrants that excel in innovation but do not have and cannot easily establish a comparable commercialization infrastructure. Given this fundamental divergence in substitution costs, the effects of changes in the level of IP protection can differ considerably across entity types. This has a further implication. Everything else being equal, innovators will select the entity type—or precisely, a form of organization that has a certain mix of attributes of more and less integrated entity types—that maximizes returns on R&D investment, given the existing level of IP coverage. As a result, the firm-level organizational effects of changes in the level of IP protection translate in the aggregate into market-level organizational effects by influencing the transactional choices of innovators, investors, and other parties along the commercialization pathway from lab to market.

Part II. History: Intellectual Property and Organizational Forms

The proposed relationship between the level of IP protection and organizational form suggests that changes in the level of IP protection can significantly impact the manner in which firms elect to organize the innovation and commercialization process. In particular, it suggests that zero- or weak-IP regimes should generally result in a skewed mix of organizational forms dominated by large integrated firms, whereas strong-IP regimes enable an unconstrained range of organizational forms, including R&D-specialist entities that fund innovation through IP-based licensing relationships with producers and other holders of complementary commercialization inputs. This hypothesis is broadly consistent with a novel organizational history of the U.S. patent system since the late nineteenth century through the mid-2000s. Based on evidence relating to certain indicators of patent strength (including patent-related enforcement of the antitrust laws), I identify three "grand" periods in U.S. patent history: (i) a mostly strong-patent period, during the late nineteenth and early twentieth centuries; (ii) a mostly weak-patent period, extending from the late New Deal through the 1970s; and (iii) a mostly strong-patent period, extending from the early 1980s through the mid-2000s. The proposed relationship between IP rights and organizational form is consistent with the observation that smaller and less integrated entities, supported by private sources of risk capital, were a principal source of innovation during the two periods of robust patent protection (the late nineteenth century to the early twentieth century and the late twentieth century to the early twenty-first century). This relationship is similarly consistent with the fact that larger and more integrated entities (supported by public sources of risk capital in the form of government grants and procurement contracts) drove innovation during the long period of weak patent protection from the late New Deal through the 1970s. In short, as IP strength increases, firm scope tends to shrink, demand for government-supplied risk capital decreases, and markets in IP assets develop; as IP strength weakens, those effects tend to be reversed.

Part III. Politics: The Market Rents of Weak Intellectual-Property Rights

It is common to assume that large incumbents prefer stronger IP rights in order to impede entry by potential competitors. Yet the organizational approach to IP rights anticipates precisely the opposite. Larger and more integrated firms should either be indifferent to robust patent protection given the ability to adopt non-IP mechanisms for capturing returns on R&D or oppose robust patent protection in order to erect an implicit entry barrier to smaller and less integrated firms. Given these entity-specific differences in adopting non-IP mechanisms for capturing returns on innovation, incumbents may enjoy stronger entry protection and increased pricing power under weak-IP regimes. Evidence from the late nineteenth century through the present largely confirms this prediction. With the exception of the pharmaceutical industry, larger and more integrated incumbents tend to lobby for weaker patent rights or oppose the extension of these rights to new industries. By contrast, smaller and less integrated entities that specialize in innovation but lack downstream production and distribution capacities support stronger patent protection. This is true of debates over patent protection in the nineteenth-century railroad industry, the extension of IP protection to the software industry in the 1960s and 1970s, debates over "patent reform" legislation enacted in the 2000s, and trends in amicus briefs filed in Supreme Court patent-related decisions during 1986–2016. Finally, I apply this book's organizational approach to the IP-skeptical policy actions taken by judges, legislators, and the antitrust agencies since 2006 (including an extension of this approach to copyright law and policy since the onset of the "digital revolution" in content markets). This analysis shows that weakening IP protection is likely to induce an organizational bias that favors substantially integrated entities that leverage size and scale to extract returns from technological innovation while disadvantaging substantially disintegrated R&D specialists that have been among the key sources of breakthrough innovation in U.S. technology markets.

Acknowledgments

This book coalesces, refines, and extends arguments and concepts that I have pursued since having the fortune to enter academia more than a decade ago. Those arguments and concepts have been enriched by valuable comments at workshops and conferences at which I presented earlier versions of certain chapters or prior related papers. I am grateful for comments from participants at workshops at Harvard Law School, the Hoover Institution at Stanford University, New York University School of Law, Stanford Law School, Tel Aviv University Faculty of Law, UCLA School of Law, the University of Chicago Law School, the University of San Diego School of Law, the Center for the Protection of Intellectual Property at the Antonin Scalia Law School at George Mason University, the Brigham Young University Winter Deals Conference, and annual conferences of the American Law and Economics Association and the Society for Institutional and Organizational Economics. I am especially grateful for comments and suggestions from my colleagues at the University of Southern California Gould School of Law, my editors David Pervin and James Cook at Oxford University Press, and the anonymous referees on the book manuscript. I would like to thank in particular Richard Epstein, Bo Heiden, and Adam Mossoff, who took the initiative to organize a symposium on the book manuscript, held by the Classical Liberal Institute of New York University School of Law in collaboration with the Hoover Institution at Stanford University. This was truly an unexpected honor.

This book would not have been possible without the research support provided by the USC Gould School of Law. I am grateful for the exceptional assistance provided on this book and prior related papers by the dedicated librarians of the USC Gould School of Law, including Cindy Guyer, Diane Jaque, Paul Moorman, Anahit Petrosyan, Brian Raphael, and especially Karen Skinner. I am also grateful for the contributions of student research assistants on this project or prior related papers, including Alina Aghankhani, Natalie Amsellem, Daniella Barnett, Vanand Baroni, Justin Bongco, Jinmin Chen, Quincy Chuck, Taylor Francis, Daniel Fullerton, Blake Horn, Aman Joea, Kate Lee, Kawon Lee, Hannah Nachef, Ingrid Newquist, Viet Nguyen, Kaitlyn Pangburn, Jose Rodriguez, Daniel Ross, Paul Watanabe, and Mingmei Zhu.

I owe my greatest debt to my family. I am grateful to my mother, Queenie Barnett, who passed away too early to see this work, and my father, Alan Barnett, for the limitless support that they have given me in my academic pursuits. I thank my wife, Yael, and our children, Daniella, Shira, and Lia, for constant encouragement and endless patience while I have devoted so much time to this project. I can only hope that I have made a contribution worthy of your expectations.

Introduction

Conventional wisdom assumes that IP rights intervene in a pristine public domain that is otherwise free of constraints on access. Without patents and other IP rights, new ideas, knowledge, and information would flow freely. In an often-quoted dissent in *International News Service v. Associated Press*, Supreme Court Justice Louis Brandeis wrote in 1918 that "knowledge, truths ascertained, conceptions and ideas ... become, after voluntary communication to others, free as the air to common use."[1] This assumption is illusory. Even if the state fails to supply IP rights, or does not enforce them reliably, markets do not sit still. Innovators, and the various entities that undertake or fund the complex tasks required to commercialize innovations, adopt alternative non-IP mechanisms to regulate access and generate returns. So the "pristine" public domain is "blemished" by other mechanisms that seek to mimic—and, in some cases, outperform—"missing" IP rights. This is a simple outcome of the competitive process of market survival. Exclusivity must be secured to some extent in order to generate the profit streams required to cover costs and earn a positive return. That curiously neglected principle explains why robust self-sustaining innovation environments are virtually never free of access constraints at *some* point on the total relevant package of products and services. Markets are adept at using various combinations of technological and contractual instruments to extract value from innovations that would otherwise be free for all to take without compensation. That should be viewed as a fortunate circumstance—that is, *not* a blemish at all. Without those instruments, privately funded innovation would dwindle without the familiar market-making mechanisms that are used to price access, generate revenues, cover costs, and leave innovators—and, critically, investors that fund the commercialization of innovation assets—with something more than could have been earned from a well-diversified mutual fund portfolio. So long as it is believed that markets, and not the state alone or primarily, are best positioned to allocate resources for purposes of funding and executing innovation and commercialization activities, there must be some feasible exclusivity mechanism on hand.

This book is guided throughout by a simple principle. The state supply of IP rights always operates together with the market's supply of IP-*like* instruments. The "real" effect of any "nominal" change in IP rights in the statute books or case law reporters cannot be anticipated without taking into account the market's capacity to deploy alternatives that partially or entirely substitute for those rights. If the state withdraws or weakens IP rights, the market will move to the next-best alternative device for capturing returns on innovation. This dynamic approach to IP analysis, in which the state supply of IP rights interacts with the market supply of IP-like mechanisms, produces

Innovators, Firms, and Markets. Jonathan M. Barnett, Oxford University Press (2021). © Oxford University Press.
DOI: 10.1093/oso/9780190908591.003.0001

a diverse range of scenarios that sometimes violate the standard assumption that decreases in IP strength always expand the open-access public domain and increases in IP strength always reduce it. Decreasing IP strength might increase access, as would be conventionally expected, but it might leave access unchanged or perversely decrease it once market responses are taken into account. Conversely, increasing IP strength can generate the same unbounded range of outcomes. In general, the aggregate effects of changes in formal IP rights on access to the relevant pool of knowledge assets are more complex and varied than has commonly been assumed.

The basic intuition can be easily illustrated. Suppose the state abolishes the patent system—something that was done in Switzerland in 1850 (and then reintroduced in 1907) and the Netherlands in 1869 (and then reintroduced in 1912).[2] Standard analysis anticipates that an open-access commons obviously results. But nothing is obvious—or rather, everything depends on the market response to the state's action. If the market adopts alternative strategies that cover any shortfall in coverage, and there are no additional costs involved in moving to those alternatives as compared to the costs that would have been incurred to enforce the withdrawn IP right, then the state's action would have no effect on the aggregate constraints that govern access to the relevant pool of knowledge assets. That is, a nominal reduction in IP rights (up to and including total abolition) translates into no *real* change in the total access costs borne by intermediate and end users. But this does not mean that everything else remains the same. In that weak-IP environment, innovation proceeds but must do so under a different set of feasible mechanisms for extracting revenues from innovation, which in turn implies that firms will elect to operate under a different mix of organizational structures and to invest resources in a different mix of R&D projects. Consistent with these theoretical expectations, Petra Moser found that in the late nineteenth century, innovators in European countries without patent protection, or with highly incomplete forms of patent protection, responded by shifting resources toward sectors in which secrecy could be most easily maintained. This adaptive strategy in a weak-IP environment frustrated imitation of certain innovation assets in a manner akin to the formal IP right that had been withdrawn.[3] That is, innovators substituted technological opacity for IP rights, which enabled firms to impede free-riding as a practical matter and extract a positive return on innovative efforts absent any legal capacity by which to impede imitation.

It might therefore be argued that IP rights do not matter. The market simply "makes up the difference" by shifting toward alternative mechanisms for extracting returns from innovation or shifting resources toward innovation fields in which those alternative mechanisms can be most easily deployed. Of course, IP rights *do* matter— otherwise, firms would not invest resources in obtaining and enforcing them or attempting to influence courts, legislators, and regulators to adjust the terms of those rights. But now we must confront a puzzle. Why do IP rights matter if there are so many other mechanisms that firms can use to earn returns on innovation? The reason is that different types of entities bear different costs in shifting from formal IP toward IP-like equivalents for the purpose of capturing returns on innovation investments.

Those entity-specific differences in the costs of adopting non-IP alternatives generate entity-specific differences in the value placed on IP instruments relative to non-IP instruments for extracting returns on innovation. Some entity types—typically, the largest, most integrated, and most well-established firms—can move quickly and at a low cost toward IP-like equivalents. However, other entity types cannot easily do so. More specifically, certain types of entities cannot feasibly construct an integrated R&D, production, and distribution supply chain that acts as an IP-like umbrella that captures returns from innovation even in the absence of formal property rights.

Any entity's or individual's response to changes by the state in IP strength depends on the costs borne by that entity or individual in adopting alternatives to IP rights. If those adoption costs are high, then changes in IP strength will have a significant effect on the firm's ability to regulate access to, and therefore earn a return on, innovation. Everything else being equal, that type of firm will reduce its investments in innovation in response to a reduction in the strength of formal IP rights. By contrast, if those adoption costs are low to nominal, then changes in IP will have little to no effect. Those types of firms will have little reason to reduce investment in innovation in response to reductions in the strength of formal IP rights. Hence, in general, different firms will be impacted in different ways—and some not at all—by different levels of formal IP protection.

If we add some more detail, this principle can be stated more concretely and in a form that potentially lends itself to some degree of empirical scrutiny. Changes in IP strength will tend to have the weakest effect on larger, more established, and more integrated entities—which I will call "hierarchical" entities. That is because those entities tend to have low adoption costs (with the important exception of the biopharmaceutical markets) in response to weak-IP environments. In general, a large integrated entity can cover shortfalls in formal IP coverage by relying on economies of scale and scope, reputational capital, internal financing, and accumulated know-how (among other non-IP advantages). As a result, those firms often do not expect to suffer any reduced return on innovative effort in the absence of IP rights. Conversely, changes in IP rights will tend to have the strongest effect on smaller, less established, and less integrated entities—which I will call "entrepreneurial" entities. That is because those entities tend to have higher adoption costs in response to weak-IP environments. A smaller or weakly integrated entity will often bear higher costs in accessing non-IP alternatives and therefore often *does* expect to suffer a reduced return on innovation in the absence of IP rights. If the state reduces IP strength, then entrepreneurial entities bear escalating costs in regulating access through alternative mechanisms, expect reduced returns on innovation, and may withdraw from the market or elect not to attempt entry in the first place. By contrast, hierarchical entities can adopt alternative mechanisms at no or little cost, expect relatively unchanged returns, and therefore are largely impervious to reductions in IP strength. If adoption costs are too high even for hierarchical entities (almost certainly the case in most segments of the biopharmaceutical industry), then economically and technologically feasible non-IP instruments are insufficient to capture returns on innovation, and innovators either exit or seek funding from state or private patronage. The result: the market allocation of resources to innovation activities is displaced by bureaucratic allocation driven by rent-seeking behavior, reputational prestige, and philanthropic goodwill. In short, without IP rights, the state or the patron displaces the market in funding and supporting innovation.

The costs of adopting non-IP alternatives are the conceptual link that ties together IP rights and organizational forms and, ultimately, market structure. A dynamic approach to IP analysis anticipates innovators' responses to changes in IP rights as a function of innovators' costs of adopting IP-like equivalents. Those costs are in turn a function in substantial part of the organizational forms—specifically, an entity's size and level of integration—through which entities execute innovation and commercialization functions in the relevant market. A fully dynamic approach to IP analysis requires one further step to draw the full picture. Organizational forms are not fixed. An individual or entity that wishes to develop, produce, and distribute a new technology can elect to undertake any part of the innovation and commercialization process through various organizational forms, ranging from an academic research department to a small start-up to a large multinational conglomerate and various permutations that mix and match attributes of those entity types. Changes in IP strength have different effects on the expected returns to innovation depending on the type of entity that executes the innovation and commercialization process. For entrepreneurial entities, those effects can be substantial and even existential; for hierarchical entities, those effects may be moderate or even trivial. By anticipation, innovators respond to changes in IP strength by selecting organizational forms that maximize expected net returns on innovation, *given* the anticipated level of IP strength. This is the transmission mechanism through which the level of IP protection provided by the state has an effect on the mix of organizational forms observed in the market.

Subject to appropriate qualification for other contributing factors in particular market segments, the connection between IP strength and organizational form can be extrapolated from the level of the firm to the level of the market. In the aggregate, innovators' micro-level organizational selections play an important part in determining the macro-level "architecture" of the relevant innovation market. Again, take the extreme case in which IP is abolished or widely unenforced. The total bundle of access constraints will remain roughly constant so long as there exist cost-equivalent non-IP alternatives that innovators can adopt in lieu of formal IP rights. But the transactional forms selected to conduct and commercialize innovation—and, as a consequence, the higher-level market structure generated by the aggregation of those transactional choices—may look substantially different. Innovators will anticipate low expected returns using entrepreneurial forms (e.g., the start-up) and will migrate toward hierarchical forms (e.g., the large incumbent) protected by the non-IP-dependent advantages of scale, access to capital, and reputational goodwill. The potential result: a hierarchical environment that supports integrated entities that deploy capital-intensive advantages in production and distribution capacities to erect entry barriers and capture returns on innovation. Now, suppose IP strength is restored and enforced. Innovators can now capture returns using any combination of organizational forms and, by the trial-and-error process of market interaction, will converge toward those forms that maximize expected returns to innovation. The potential result: an entrepreneurial environment that supports weakly integrated entities that primarily engage in R&D and rely on contractual relationships with third parties to achieve commercialization and capture returns on innovation.

The dynamic approach to IP analysis presented in this book provides an analytical framework that shifts empirical and normative analysis of IP rights away from its traditional concern with the causal relationship between IP rights and innovative output. Unlike the conventional incentive-based approach to IP rights, this dynamic approach does not uniformly envision significant declines in R&D investment under weak-IP regimes given the ability of large integrated firms to capture returns on R&D through non-IP alternatives. However, this approach does anticipate that changes in IP rights will influence how markets *organize* the innovation and commercialization processes that deliver new products and services to market. These organizational effects can in turn impact the efficient allocation of resources across the total feasible universe of innovation projects—which, from an economic perspective, is the core function of any IP system. Viewed through this organizational lens, the net efficiency effects of changes in the strength of IP rights are often counterintuitive. In particular, this analysis identifies an important set of circumstances in which reducing IP strength can raise entry barriers for vertically disintegrated firms that excel in R&D but lack the financing, production, and distribution capacities to monetize innovation independently. Hence, even if total R&D investment in certain markets remains robust under weak-IP regimes, there is nonetheless a potentially significant efficiency loss in the form of an organizational bias that favors large integrated firms, which can deploy difficult-to-replicate financing, production, and distribution capacities to offset shortfalls in formal IP coverage. In turn, this organizational bias may result in adverse welfare effects by skewing the allocation of innovation capital toward incremental projects that "tweak" the existing technological paradigm (often favored by incumbents) and away from breakthrough projects that challenge the existing paradigm (often favored by R&D-specialist entrants). Unlike the conventional economic case for IP rights, the dynamic approach supports a presumption in favor of secure IP protection, not because it is always a necessary predicate for robust innovation but because it is a necessary predicate for maximizing the likelihood that the market will efficiently organize the innovation and commercialization process.

PART I

THEORY

Rethinking Intellectual Property

1
Dynamic Analysis
of Intellectual Property

In this chapter, I develop a dynamic framework for analyzing IP rights that takes into account firms' ability to adopt alternative non-IP mechanisms to secure returns on innovation. Firms' ability to shift toward IP-like alternatives to fill in gaps in formal IP coverage may seem like a mundane observation. It is well known that firms always have the choice between patenting the "secret sauce" (and thereby disclosing it) or just continuing to keep it secret. Merck chooses the former strategy, Coca-Cola the latter. But these everyday choices among IP and non-IP instruments facing real-world firms—the patent/secrecy choice being only the most obvious example—are the key to understanding how *real* changes in the costs of accessing intellectual assets, and the resulting change in the size of the public domain, can diverge from *nominal* changes in IP rights by the state. (By "public domain," I mean the set of intellectual assets to which there are no legal or technological barriers to access by intermediate or end users.) The key observation is that the aggregate effect of changes in IP rights supplied by the state cannot be assessed without anticipating firms' ability to adopt functional equivalents supplied by the market. This dynamic interaction between publicly and privately supplied instruments for regulating access to informational assets can yield outcomes that run counter to conventional intuitions that increases in IP strength always imply increases in access costs and a reduction in the size of the public domain. Precisely the opposite is sometimes the case.

1.1 Expanding the Menu: IP and Non-IP Instruments

Conventional analysis follows the natural intuition that increases in IP strength always increase access costs for intermediate and end users and therefore reduce the size of the public domain, while decreases in IP strength always achieve the opposite outcome. This assumption underlies the textbook "incentives/access" trade-off that drives conventional analysis of IP law and policy, whether by scholars, judges, or policymakers. The logic is well known. When the state increases IP strength, this enhances innovation incentives by increasing innovators' expected pricing power and therefore economic returns on successful innovation investments. For the same reason, increasing IP strength reduces access by raising the costs borne by intermediate and end users of the relevant pool of IP-protected assets. The opposite outcome prevails when the state reduces IP strength: incentives decline, but access increases.

Innovators, Firms, and Markets. Jonathan M. Barnett, Oxford University Press (2021). © Oxford University Press.
DOI: 10.1093/oso/9780190908591.003.0002

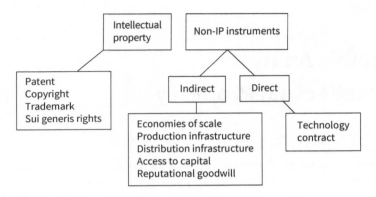

Figure 1.1 IP and non-IP instruments

This analytical framework is only reliable if we assume that the access constraints *nominally* delineated by formal IP rights—patents, copyright, and other variants—are indicative of the total bundle of *real* access constraints under which innovators actually operate. That assumption is contestable as soon as we recognize that formal IP rights are not the only mechanism by which firms can regulate access and extract returns from R&D. A large, vertically integrated incumbent like Intel may have means other than IP rights to delay or block cost-competitive imitation of its semiconductor innovations, especially by smaller competitors that may be able to reverse-engineer Intel's technology but cannot feasibly secure the capital and expertise required to match Intel's production and distribution infrastructure. As depicted in Figure 1.1, firms can typically select from an abundance of *non*-IP mechanisms by which to regulate access to, and extract value from, an informational asset even if formal IP rights are weak or nonexistent. This simple observation complicates the typically assumed relationships between the strength of formal IP rights, innovation incentives, and the access costs borne by intermediate and end users.

1.1.1 Direct Non-IP Instruments

Firms can use technological and contractual mechanisms that secure practically effective exclusivity over a knowledge asset and extract value by directly regulating access to it. There are three basic strategies. First, existing technological constraints may sufficiently increase the cost of copying such that legal protection is immaterial. This can explain why Congress only extended copyright protection to sound recordings (as distinguished from musical compositions) starting in 1972.[1] Prior to that time, the costs incurred by "bootleggers" to match the quality and volume of legitimately produced vinyl records were probably sufficiently high that unauthorized copies did not generally pose a competitive threat. Second, a firm can affirmatively deploy technologies that sufficiently increase the copying and distribution costs incurred by most nonpaying users. For example, a software firm can regulate access to its product by delivering it in a form that makes it difficult to copy or disables the product in the event the user attempts to copy and distribute it to others. This type of technological solution is likely to be effective at least against the large pool of "unsophisticated" users. Third, even if there is no effective anti-copying technology available, a firm may still be able to regulate and therefore price usage to some meaningful extent by delivering its product subject to a contract that restricts users' ability to copy or distribute the product. This is a widely used tool in the software industry, which typically distributes software subject to a user license agreement that specifies authorized and unauthorized uses in great detail. While contractual constraints are less effective than technological constraints, since breach of the license may be difficult to detect, legal enforcement is costly, and individual infringers may be judgment-proof, a license may be effective against institutional users (that is, large commercial, governmental, or nonprofit entities) against whom the IP holder can credibly threaten to litigate or withhold valuable updates and support services.

1.1.2 Indirect Non-IP Instruments

Suppose a market in which an innovation is exposed to imitation due to weak or zero IP rights and innovators have no reliable technological or contractual mechanism by which to regulate and therefore price usage. Will all returns on innovation then flow to free-riding second movers? Surprisingly, not always. In his landmark 1986 paper,[2] David Teece made a simple but powerful observation. A firm can sometimes use indirect mechanisms that extract value from innovation by exploiting a competitive advantage in certain complementary assets without which the innovation loses much of its value to the user. Complementary assets are broadly defined and can include (among others) economies of scale in production, marketing, and distribution; complementary products and services (which encompasses firm-specific ecosystems and platforms); accumulated know-how; cost-of-capital advantages (through either internal or external financing); network effects (when combined with switching costs); and brand name and associated goodwill. Those assets effectively act as an entry barrier (and therefore enable the innovator to earn a positive return) because, if they are not replicated at least approximately and at a comparable cost, a competitor will be unable to deliver a quality-comparable and cost-comparable package of goods and services to the target consumer.

To illustrate, suppose a home hobbyist produced an exact copy of a particular model of a Mercedes-Benz and resided in a jurisdiction that did not recognize IP rights. Mercedes-Benz would be legally powerless to stop the "car pirate." However, it would not be commercially threatened. Without a comparable production, marketing, and distribution infrastructure; accumulated know-how; dealership, financing, and leasing network; and post-purchase warranty, support, and repair system, the hobbyist would be unable to deliver to a mass consumer population a package with comparable product and service attributes at a comparable price point. Hence, the competitive threat to Mercedes-Benz would be approximately nil.[3]

This stylized example illustrates a more general principle. To appreciate the extent to which a firm's technology is protected against imitation, it is necessary to consider the full menu of IP and non-IP mechanisms by which the firm can raise third parties' imitation costs (which include the costs of imitating the total relevant bundle of products and services), delay entry, and capture a premium on its innovative efforts. Even if a firm's technology can be copied at a comparable quality level and cost, the firm will still be significantly protected against entry, and therefore it will still be able to capture some premium on its innovative efforts, so long as competitors cannot replicate at comparable quality and cost the complementary suite of products and services, and the associated distribution and post-purchase servicing infrastructure, in which that technology is embedded. For such firms, formal IP protection may not be the most critical mechanism by which they establish practically effective (even if not legal) exclusivity, delay entry by competitors, and earn a premium on innovative effort.

This proposition is not mere theory. Extensive survey studies of large firms' views on the relative value of patent protection in extracting returns from R&D indicate that in many industries, patents are not the most highly valued instrument for appropriating returns from R&D. With the important exception of the pharmaceutical and certain chemicals industries, those studies, conducted in the 1980s (the Mansfield and "Yale" survey studies) and early 2000s (the "Carnegie Mellon" survey study), found that managers at large firms reported that they rely primarily or more substantially on mechanisms *other* than patents to earn returns on innovation.[4] This is not to say that patents are necessarily irrelevant for these firms. However, it does indicate that for the Mercedes-Benzes of the world, patents often do not rank highly in the pecking order of mechanisms by which to raise entry costs and earn a return on innovation. Alternative IP-like instruments can also plausibly explain why, for several decades, R&D investment remained relatively robust in the U.S. automotive industry even though manufacturers adhered to industry norms that discouraged patent litigation and encouraged "below-market" royalty rates in license agreements.[5] Even in the absence of strong IP protection, it appears that at least large and vertically integrated firms in certain industries can capture returns from R&D through non-IP-based strategies and, hence, rationally continue to invest resources in innovation. Surprisingly, as I will argue, the diminished necessity of IP rights among large dominant firms in certain industries provides the basis for identifying the economic rationale for IP rights in general.

1.2 Diverse Effects of IP Protection

Conventional analysis of IP rights assumes that providing IP protection always increases incentives for innovation at the price of raising access costs for intermediate and end users, resulting in a decrease in the size of the public domain. Conversely, withdrawing IP protection always reverses those outcomes, resulting in an increase in the size of the public domain. If firms can select from a broad menu of IP and non-IP mechanisms to regulate access by users, and will do so in order to maximize returns on innovation at the lowest cost, this conventional scenario becomes only one of multiple outcomes that may result from the supply or withdrawal of formal IP protection. Even if the state fails to supply IP rights, the market will sometimes effectively cover the gap in property-rights coverage. In some cases, market-supplied IP-like instruments may even outperform the IP instruments made available by the state. The interaction between privately and publicly supplied instruments for capturing value from innovation disrupts the standard positive relationship between IP protection and access costs. As I will discuss in the remainder of this chapter, any increase in IP protection can, in general, increase access costs (as expected conventionally), leave those costs unaffected, or even decrease access costs. The same range of conventional, indifferent, and "inverted" effects—and corresponding expansions and contractions in the size of the public domain—may in general result from any decrease in IP protection.

A multiplicity of effects from changes in IP protection does not mean, however, that those effects are random in any particular case. I will propose an analytical framework in which those effects can be anticipated at some reasonable approximation within a structured population of reasonably well-defined entity types. This discussion is based on simplified scenarios, and therefore, like any theoretical discussion, the extent to which it is applicable to real-world markets is still an open question. However, it will provide the theoretical foundation on which I will add progressively more granular detail and empirical evidence throughout the rest of the book. As I do so, it will be possible to develop some level of confidence in the explanatory reach of this theoretical framework and refine it as suggested by particularized evidence drawn from more complex real-world environments.

1.2.1 Analytical Framework

I will analyze the effects of changes in IP protection in two hypothetical settings, a "simple" and "complex" setting populated in each case by some combination of two idealized firm types, designated as "I-Firm" and "U-Firm." As reflected in Table 1.1, each firm type is identical in all respects, except that I-Firm is an older, larger, and substantially integrated firm, and U-Firm is a younger, smaller, and substantially unintegrated firm. To make the analysis more concrete, I-Firm is analogous to an established incumbent that maintains an end-to-end innovation, production, and distribution infrastructure; U-Firm is analogous to a start-up that focuses on R&D and has few other capacities in the technology supply chain. Each firm invests resources in IP or non-IP instruments, or some combination thereof, in order to secure the capacity to regulate access to its innovation assets, which enables it to price usage and capture returns on the R&D investment made to produce those assets. Consistent

Table 1.1 Firm types and characteristics

Firm Type	Size	Level of Integration	Time in Market
Integrated firm (I-Firm)	Large	High	Long
Unintegrated firm (U-Firm)	Small	Low	Short

with standard models of economic behavior, I assume that each firm type allocates resources to adoption and use of any selected IP or non-IP instrument subject to a marginal cost-benefit constraint. That is, the firm will allocate resources to a particular instrument (for example, filing a patent application or undertaking secrecy precautions) just up to the point at which the incremental cost of securing additional capacity to regulate access through that instrument equals the incremental returns from doing so. This decision rule is constrained in turn by the opportunity cost of capital: that is, each firm will shift resources away from the use of both IP and non-IP instruments if those resources will yield higher expected returns in an alternative investment opportunity.

By construction, the two idealized firm types exhibit stark differences in the preferred instrument for securing returns on innovation. For I-Firm, it is always the case that capturing returns on innovation through IP instruments is more costly than doing so through any non-IP alternative. That is, each dollar invested in an IP instrument will yield lower returns than the same dollar invested in a non-IP instrument. For U-Firm, those relationships are reversed; it is always the case that capturing returns on innovation through IP instruments is less costly than doing so through any non-IP alternative. Based on these entity-specific cost differences in (or, equivalently, differences in net expected returns from) adopting non-IP-based strategies for regulating access to an innovation asset, we can anticipate how changes in IP protection elicit different responses from each firm type and, consequently, different effects on the access costs borne by users and the implied size of the public domain in which access constraints are absent.

In this stylized environment, I will analyze these entity types' anticipated responses to different levels of IP protection, which will be limited for analytical purposes to (i) a positive-IP regime, in which the state makes available a certain positive level of IP protection for a relevant class of innovation assets, and (ii) a zero-IP regime, in which the state declines to provide any such protection.[6] Three scenarios will then be analyzed. First, I will address a simple scenario in which a firm must choose between using either an IP or a non-IP instrument to regulate access to its innovation asset. Second, I will address a more complex scenario in which a firm can use a combination of IP and non-IP instruments to regulate access and extract returns from its innovation investment. Third, I will address a somewhat more complex environment populated by firm types that exhibit attributes reflecting some mix of the idealized I-Firm and U-Firm types. Each increase in analytical complexity moves closer to real-world innovation environments.

1.2.2 The Simple Setting

Suppose a firm has developed a valuable new technology at some positive cost and must elect between using either an IP or a non-IP instrument to extract returns from its investment. For example, a firm might face a binary choice between protecting its technology through secrecy or the patent system (which requires disclosure), each of which in turn delivers certain units of return to the firm. Either protection strategy necessitates that the firm incur costs to implement it. To maintain secrecy, the firm must install a security system and undertake certain precautions. To apply for and enforce a patent, the firm must retain legal representation, pay application fees at the patent office, disclose valuable information to competitors, continue to pay maintenance fees to keep the patent in force, and periodically monitor and take action against infringers. The firm will only adopt the IP instrument (in this case, a patent), and will only continue to invest resources to enforce it, provided the cost of doing so yields an expected net positive gain relative to using the non-IP instrument (in this case, secrecy), and vice versa.

Critically, each firm type incurs different costs to regulate access and thereby "purchase" a unit of return through each instrument. I denote the per-unit cost of using the IP instrument as C_{ip} and the per-unit cost of using the non-IP alternative as C_{nip}. For I-Firm, $C_{ip} > C_{nip}$, and therefore it can always earn higher net returns for the same expenditure through the non-IP instrument. For U-Firm, $C_{ip} < C_{nip}$, and therefore it can always earn higher net returns for the same expenditure through the IP instrument. In both cases, I assume that marginal returns per dollar expended on an IP or non-IP instrument are constant (subsequently, I relax this assumption).

Individual selections by I-Firm and U-Firm between IP and non-IP instruments for capturing returns on innovation impact the access costs borne by users and the implied size of the public domain. Table 1.2 presents the full range of possible effects on access costs and innovation incentives of a positive-IP or zero-IP regime in markets populated by I-Firm only, U-Firm only, and I-Firm and U-Firm simultaneously. Those effects vary depending on (i) firm type and (ii) whether both firm types are in the market simultaneously. Each case is explained in the discussion that follows.

Conventional Cases (A, D)

For U-Firm, higher net returns on innovative effort are always expected by using IP, relative to non-IP, mechanisms ($C_{ip} < C_{nip}$). If the state supplies an IP right (case A), then the innovator firm will abandon non-IP mechanisms and adopt the IP right, which delivers returns on innovation at a lower cost, resulting in a net gain relative to the previously existing environment in which IP rights were absent. The innovator firm will shift resources to the IP right and will now be able to "purchase" stronger access-regulation capacities and enjoy higher returns on innovation. This bolsters innovation incentives but increases the access costs borne by users and curtails the size of the public domain, as would be conventionally expected following an increase in IP

Table 1.2 Diverse effects of different levels of IP protection

Case	Firm(s): Cost Characteristics	Change in Access Costs	Change in Innovation Incentives
Positive-IP Regime			
A	U-Firm: $C_{ip} < C_{nip}$	+	+
B	I-Firm: $C_{ip} > C_{nip}$	None	None
C	I-Firm: $C_{ip} > C_{nip}$ U-Firm: $C_{ip} < C_{nip}$	−	+
Zero-IP Regime			
D	U-Firm: $C_{ip} < C_{nip}$	−	−
E	I-Firm: $C_{ip} > C_{nip}$	None	None
F	I-Firm: $C_{ip} > C_{nip}$ U-Firm: $C_{ip} < C_{nip}$	+	−

protection. Conversely, if the state withdraws the IP right (case D), then the innovator firm is forced to make up the shortfall in coverage by shifting resources to more costly non-IP alternatives. Even if the innovator firm could cost-feasibly recover its "lost" access-regulation capacities through non-IP instruments, it would nonetheless incur more costs to do so relative to using the IP instrument, expect lower net returns, and may therefore shift resources to non-innovation opportunities. In a more extreme (but typically assumed) case, C_{nip} is so large that U-Firm would exit the market if it had to bear that cost—that is, there are no cost-feasible non-IP alternatives to make up any portion of the shortfall in IP coverage and still earn a positive return on investment. In that case, the public domain is pristine, but it contains nothing—the classic dynamic efficiency loss anticipated by the conventional economic case for IP rights.

Indifference Cases (B, E)

For I-Firm, higher net returns on innovative effort are always expected by using non-IP, relative to IP, mechanisms ($C_{ip} > C_{nip}$). I-Firm is indifferent to whether or not the state provides IP rights, since it will always prefer to use non-IP alternatives. Even if the state provides IP rights (case B), I-Firm will decline to adopt the IP instrument, and total access costs therefore remain the same. By the same rationale, I-Firm is indifferent to the withdrawal of IP rights (case E) given that it can always employ a lower-cost non-IP alternative. In this case, whether or not the state provides IP rights does not matter; innovation incentives, access costs, and the size of the public domain remain constant.

"Inverted" Cases (C, F)

So far, I have identified (i) a conventional case where, for U-Firm, innovation incentives and access costs move in tandem with the supply or withdrawal of IP protection (cases A and D), since the firm relies on IP protection as its lowest-cost access-regulation mechanism, and (ii) an indifference case where, for I-Firm, innovation incentives and access costs remain constant irrespective of the supply or withdrawal of IP protection (cases B and E), since the firm always enjoy higher returns by employing non-IP alternatives for regulating user access. Under certain circumstances, a third "inverted" case is realized: access costs fall when IP rights are provided and rise when IP rights are withdrawn.

This result can arise when I-Firm and U-Firm occupy the market simultaneously. The logic is as follows. Suppose the state withdraws IP rights (case F), and, due to the absence of any cost-feasible non-IP alternative, U-Firm (for which $C_{ip} < C_{nip}$) is compelled to exit the market, while I-Firm (for which $C_{ip} > C_{nip}$) is unaffected, due to its lower-cost access to non-IP alternatives. Assuming no other potential entry threats, I-Firm will then occupy the entire market. Given its dominant position, I-Firm might elect to raise prices to access its innovation asset or do so implicitly through increased technological or contractual constraints, in both cases effectively reducing the size of the public domain. Conversely, if the state restores IP (case C), then U-Firm can re-enter, restoring competitive discipline and compelling I-Firm to lower prices to access its innovation asset or to do so implicitly by relaxing technological or contractual constraints, thereby effectively increasing the size of the public domain.[7] At the same time, total innovation incentives likely increase due to the re-entry of U-Firm into the market and the consequently renewed competitive pressure on I-Firm. In this case, I-Firm is no longer indifferent whether or not the state supplies IP rights. It strategically prefers a market without IP rights, since this erects an implicit barrier to U-Firm, thereby protecting I-Firm's market position and enhancing its pricing power.

1.2.3 The Complex Setting

In some industries, innovators face a choice between patent-based and secrecy-based protection strategies that approximates the simple "either/or" choice between IP or non-IP instruments described above. This is often the case in the pharmaceutical market. More typically, however, firms construct a mixed portfolio of IP and non-IP instruments to protect their innovation assets at the lowest cost, yielding the highest net expected return. For example, Microsoft protects its Windows operating system through copyright but also relies on non-IP instruments, including end-user license agreements, technological constraints, a difficult-to-replicate portfolio of accumulated goodwill, distribution and marketing relationships, support services, and a large pool of software developers that produce applications compatible with Windows.

With limited modification, this scenario can be incorporated into the existing analytical framework by making two additional assumptions that are consistent with real-world environments: (i) an innovator firm can deploy *both* IP and non-IP instruments concurrently with respect to the same innovation asset, and (ii) expenditures on any particular IP or non-IP instrument deliver diminishing marginal returns. For analytical purposes, it is helpful to suppose that an innovator firm allocates resources to the adoption and enforcement of IP and non-IP instruments in succession. For I-Firm, it initially invests resources in the lower-cost non-IP instrument (recall that for this firm type, $C_{ip} > C_{nip}$); however, as marginal returns earned through the non-IP instrument diminish sufficiently, then the inequality is reversed, and the firm shifts resources to the IP instrument. For U-Firm, it initially invests resources in the lower-cost IP instrument (recall that for this firm type, $C_{ip} < C_{nip}$); however, as marginal returns earned through the IP instrument diminish sufficiently, then the inequality is reversed, and the firm shifts resources to the non-IP instrument. In either case, the firm ultimately achieves the maximally efficient allocation of resources to a portfolio of IP and non-IP instruments for purposes of regulating access to the firm's innovation assets.

The conventional framework (cases A and C) would now appear to apply without qualification across all entity types. Both firm types would seem to prefer a positive-IP regime, which would enable I-Firm or U-Firm to maximize total net returns through an efficient portfolio of IP and non-IP instruments. Consistent with standard assumptions, providing IP rights would then always raise access costs and reduce the size of the public domain, while those effects would be reversed if IP rights were withdrawn.

That conclusion is too simple. Even in the complex case, which contemplates the complementary use of IP and non-IP instruments with respect to the same innovation asset, the value that firms place on the IP instrument will still depend on the relative costs any firm incurs to secure returns on innovation through IP as compared to non-IP instruments. Where $C_{ip} > C_{nip}$, as in the case of I-Firm, it will initially secure returns though non-IP instruments and then, subject to the rate at which marginal returns earned through the non-IP instrument diminish, will shift to the IP instrument once it will earn higher net returns by doing so. In this case, even I-Firm may either (i) advocate for the state to provide IP rights as a supplement to non-IP instruments, or, (ii) if marginal returns from the non-IP instrument do not diminish rapidly (and hence it does not contemplate making extensive use of the IP instrument), prefer zero IP rights in order to disadvantage and impede entry by U-Firm. In the case where $C_{ip} < C_{nip}$, as in the case of U-Firm, it will initially secure returns though the IP instrument and then, subject to the rate at which marginal returns earned through the IP instrument diminish, shift to non-IP instruments once it expects to earn higher net returns by doing so. As in the "simple" case, U-Firm would resist the withdrawal of IP rights, since it would then bear higher costs to acquire capacities to regulate access—that is, it would be forced to shift "too soon" to non-IP instruments—and hence would expect to earn lower net returns on its innovation investment. In the extreme (but not atypical) case in which using the non-IP instrument is not a cost-feasible protection strategy, U-Firm is compelled to exit the market.

Even in this more complex case, there will be significant, although more graduated, differences in the sensitivity of firm types to the provision or withdrawal of IP protection. This will be reflected in the varying proportions of IP and non-IP instruments used by each firm to regulate access to its innovation assets. Given the assumed entity-specific differences in capturing returns through IP and non-IP instruments, all firms will continue to exhibit some sensitivity to the supply or withdrawal of IP protection, and the degree of sensitivity will continue to correlate inversely with firms' costs of capturing returns through non-IP relative to IP instruments. As the costs of adopting non-IP instruments become larger (as in the case of U-Firm), a firm will tend to place a higher value on IP rights, which would represent the highest-net-return instrument in its portfolio of IP and non-IP instruments. As those costs become smaller and non-IP instruments represent the highest-net-return instrument in the firm's portfolio (as in the case of I-Firm), the opposite result applies, up to and including the case in which I-Firm strategically disfavors IP rights in order to raise entry costs for U-Firm.

1.2.4 Putting It All Together

We are now in a position to replace the binary distinction between I-Firm and U-Firm with a realistic continuum of firm types bounded on each end by the two idealized types, as shown in Figure 1.2. The intermediate range between these "pure" forms encompasses a variety of intermediate entities, designated as semi-integrated firms, or "S-Firms," which incur different costs of adopting non-IP instruments and, as a result, different levels of sensitivity to the availability of (and therefore different intensities of demand for) IP rights.

The sensitivity of any particular S-Firm to the availability of IP protection (and hence its location on the continuum depicted in Figure 1.2) will depend on two factors: (i) the difference in costs between using IP or non-IP instruments to capture returns on innovation and (ii) the rate at which marginal returns diminish using each IP or non-IP instrument. If the per-unit cost of using non-IP instruments is not substantially lower than IP instruments and marginal returns diminish rapidly under non-IP instruments, then S-Firm will be closer to the U-Firm bound on the continuum and therefore sensitive to the level of IP protection. That is because S-Firm will exhaust rapidly the net positive returns available through non-IP instruments and will need to shift to use of the IP instrument to capture a positive return on its innovation investment. If those variables are reversed (non-IP instruments are much less costly and yield marginal returns at a slowly diminishing rate), then S-Firm will be closer to I-Firm on the continuum and will not be especially sensitive to the availability of IP protection. In that case, S-Firm may strategically prefer zero IP protection in order to frustrate entry by other S-Firm types that have higher costs of adopting non-IP instruments, which may then confer on S-Firm some degree of pricing power. Hence, even in this more complex scenario, there remains the possibility of

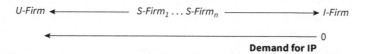

Figure 1.2 Continuum of firm types and demand for IP

an inverted case in which competitive discipline is reduced and total access costs increase even though IP rights have been withdrawn.

1.2.5 A Somewhat Special Case: Pharmaceuticals

The dynamic approach to IP analysis anticipates that firms that exhibit large size and high levels of integration (designated as I-Firms and the broader population of S-Firms that are closer to the end of the organizational continuum occupied by I-Firms) will in general prefer non-IP instruments and, depending on certain factors, exhibit weak demand for, or indifference or opposition to, the supply of IP rights by the state. That proposition, however, is unlikely to hold true in the case of any firm type that operates in markets that are characterized by the following factors: (i) a substantial difference between innovation and imitation costs, (ii) long lag times between product innovation and market release, and (iii) a high rate of project failure. The first factor will be exacerbated in cases where the innovation costs are especially high in absolute terms. In that challenging innovation environment, it may be that even in the case of a large integrated firm, non-IP instruments are ineffective in blocking entry and enabling firms to recover the substantial costs expended on the innovation and commercialization process. That is, this is a case in which, even for I-Firm, C_{ip} < C_{nip}. Even a firm that exhibits large size and a high level of integration may qualify as an S-Firm that is located close to the U-Firm end of the continuum and therefore devotes a substantial share of its enforcement resources to IP instruments. It would therefore be expected that this firm would express a policy preference in favor of some positive level of IP protection.

The pharmaceutical industry (excluding firms that exclusively or primarily produce generic products) operates in this type of innovation environment. There are at least three challenging features in this environment that correspond to the factors indicated above. First, total innovation and commercialization costs are exceptionally high, currently estimated to exceed $2 billion on average (including the capitalized costs of failed projects).[8] The costs incurred by generic firms to enter a particular market are nominal by comparison (reflecting low reverse-engineering costs and a regulatory scheme that lowers imitation costs by enabling generic firms to avoid replicating the testing efforts of the pioneer firm). Second, there is an approximately ten-year lag on average from product conception through product release. Third, a large majority of R&D projects in the industry fail to achieve market release, with a considerable number failing during the testing phase after considerable investments have been sunk into the project.[9] These factors probably explain why the pharmaceutical industry has consistently exhibited strong demand for formal IP rights despite being characterized historically by large size and high levels of integration. Even in this IP-dependent environment, however, as I will show in Chapter 6, pharmaceutical firms rely to a substantial extent on their capital-intensive testing, production, and distribution infrastructure in order to extract returns from R&D, providing a real-world illustration of an S-Firm that deploys a mixed portfolio of IP and non-IP instruments to extract a positive return on its internal R&D investment. The pharmaceutical firm's extensive portfolio of capital-intensive non-IP-based instruments in turn poses an entry barrier for smaller R&D-focused biotechnology firms that occupy a position closer to the U-Firm endpoint on the organizational continuum. Hence, the pharmaceutical industry only partially deviates from the proposed relationship between the demand for IP rights and organizational type.

1.3 Review

In this chapter, I described two idealized firm types that respond differently to the availability of IP rights based on cost differences in using non-IP alternatives: U-Firm, which is characterized by high-cost access to non-IP instruments, and I-Firm, which is characterized by low-cost access to those same instruments. I-Firm corresponds to larger, more integrated, and more established firms that have access to a wealth of non-IP instruments for extracting returns from innovation. U-Firm corresponds to smaller, less integrated, and less established firms that do not have comparable access to non-IP instruments. Comparative differences in the costs of accessing non-IP instruments generate different levels of sensitivity to the availability of IP protection. In the conventional case, firms that exhibit characteristics close to the idealized U-Firm type are highly sensitive to the availability of IP protection and behave just as conventional IP analysis anticipates: the availability of IP protection increases firms' ability to regulate access, which expands expected profits and incentivizes firms to invest in innovation. In the indifference case, firms that exhibit characteristics close to the idealized I-Firm type are insensitive to the availability of IP protection, because non-IP alternatives are always available at a lower cost. Alternatively, those firms may be strategically sensitive to the availability of IP protection—that is, they may favor zero IP protection in order to frustrate entry by weakly integrated, smaller, and younger firms that have no viable non-IP alternative. This corresponds to what I called the "inverted" case, in which withdrawing IP rights increases entry barriers for smaller and less integrated competitors, enhances the market power of larger and more integrated incumbents, and therefore raises access costs for intermediate and end users. Finally, I explored a more realistic scenario in which firms can use both IP and non-IP instruments to protect an innovation asset. Even in this more complex setting, I anticipated similar relationships between firm type, sensitivity to the availability of IP protection, and access costs, although in a more graduated fashion, reflecting the fact that this scenario contemplates a continuum occupied by S-Firms exhibiting a mix of characteristics (in varying proportions) associated with the idealized I-Firm and U-Firm types. This last scenario starts to approach the complexity of real-world innovation environments, to which I turn in the next Chapter 2.

2
Organizational Effects of Intellectual Property (Micro Level)

In this chapter, I start to operationalize the dynamic analysis of IP rights by situating the analytical framework developed in Chapter 1 in environments that exhibit certain features characteristic of real-world innovation markets. In particular, I examine how the effects of IP rights on firms' capacities to regulate access are expected to differ as a function of firms' organizational structure, which roughly proxies for firms' costs of adopting non-IP alternatives for extracting returns from innovation. To do so, I provide particularized illustrations of firms and other entities that correspond to S-Firm entities that exhibit a mix of characteristics associated with the idealized I-Firm or U-Firm types presented in Chapter 1. Any particular entity will exhibit some mix of relevant characteristics that situates any such entity at a particular point on the organizational continuum, which will in turn provide insight into that entity's likely sensitivity to the strength of formal IP rights provided by the state. Entities that exhibit characteristics mostly associated with the idealized I-Firm type will be known as "hierarchical" entities; entities that exhibit characteristics mostly associated with the idealized U-Firm types will be known as "entrepreneurial" entities. Based on the proposed relationship between the "demand for IP" and organizational form, this discussion identifies typical real-world circumstances in which IP rights can be a critical tool, if not a necessary precondition, for entry by younger, smaller, and less integrated firms—entrepreneurial types—that rely on contractual relationships to assemble the commercialization inputs required to reach market. By implication, the absence of IP rights in those circumstances erects an implicit entry barrier that protects integrated incumbents—hierarchical types—that have low-cost access to a rich suite of complementary assets by which to extract returns from innovation. Contrary to conventional intuitions, it is sometimes the lack of IP rights that enables dominant firms to mitigate or eliminate the competitive threat posed by smaller but more innovative entrants.

2.1 The Incumbent's Advantage

Conventional discussions assume that a world without IP lowers entry barriers by making knowledge assets available to all interested parties. Put simply: less IP, more access. That intuitive assumption does not universally hold true under a dynamic analysis that takes into account the existence of non-IP instruments and the

Innovators, Firms, and Markets. Jonathan M. Barnett, Oxford University Press (2021). © Oxford University Press.
DOI: 10.1093/oso/9780190908591.003.0003

fact that different entities incur different costs in accessing those instruments. Non-IP instruments are ubiquitous and often effective. But those instruments are not always available at the same cost to all firms. Non-IP instruments are often most easily available to hierarchical firms that are large in size and highly integrated and, as a simple function of time in the market, hold abundant reputational capital. To the extent that an entrant cannot easily replicate or acquire the complementary package of goods and services in which a particular technology is embedded (recall the home hobbyist's Mercedes-Benz replica discussed in Chapter 1), a hierarchical firm can extract returns on innovations that are otherwise exposed to second-mover imitation. Entrepreneurial firms inherently tend to lack these complementary assets and therefore are often uniquely exposed to imitation. Consider some of the most powerful forms of non-IP instruments: scale economies in production, testing, marketing, and distribution; accumulated know-how; cost-of-capital advantages; and brand name and associated goodwill. These all tend to be characteristics that are inherent to firms that have achieved a certain size or level of integration, acquired ample internal capital (or hold collateralizable assets or existing revenue streams that reduce lender risk and therefore reduce the cost of external capital), attracted a dedicated user base (especially if users would incur costs in switching to another vendor), accumulated a broad portfolio of goods and services, or have been in the market for a substantial amount of time.[1] This is not to say that smaller firms do not sometimes have access to effective non-IP instruments—in particular, even smaller firms can enjoy a first-to-market timing advantage in markets characterized either by low capital requirements and rapid product obsolescence (for example, the fashion industry) or low capital requirements and network effects protected by switching costs (for example, certain software industries). (Note that even in these cases, IP rights remain critical: the fashion industry relies on trademark protection for names and logos, and the software industry relies on copyright to protect the source code and other copyrightable aspects of a computer program, even when operating under "open-source" licenses.)[2] However, non-IP instruments—or, at least, the most potent non-IP instruments—tend in general to be assets that are most easily accessible to firms that are characterized by high levels of integration, large size, and longevity or some combination of those characteristics.

2.1.1 The "Fast Second" Strategy

The differential distribution of non-IP instruments across the total population of firm types (structured by the characteristics of integration, size, and age) complicates the standard assumption that less IP always implies more access. A dynamic analysis anticipates that weakening or removing formal IP rights can raise entry barriers by advantaging incumbents or other integrated firms that have the lowest-cost access to non-IP alternatives. This scenario is most dramatically illustrated by the "fast second" business strategy often ruefully observed by small innovators in technology markets. Large incumbents can imitate successful innovations and then outmatch smaller first movers by deploying the downstream production, marketing, financing, distribution, and post-purchase support functions required to move down the commercialization pathway.

One of the foremost writers on innovation and entrepreneurship, Peter Drucker, identified IBM as the leading practitioner of the "fast second" strategy, observing as of 1985: "It has successfully imitated every major development in the office-automation field. As a result, it has the leading product in every single area."[3] To be clear, Drucker was not claiming that IBM was a free rider; rather, he was observing that IBM excelled in using complementary *non*-innovation capacities to integrate technologies pioneered by others into a cost-competitive and user-friendly product and services bundle. Drucker's observation would not have found disagreement among IBM management. Thomas J. Watson Jr., IBM's famous CEO for several decades, candidly described these complementary capacities as the firm's core competitive advantage:

> In the history of IBM, technological innovation wasn't the thing that made us successful. Unhappily there were many times when we came in second. But technology turned out to be less important than sales and distribution methods. We consistently outsold people who had better technology, because we knew how to put the story before the customer, how to install the machines successfully, and how to hang on to the customers once we had them.[4]

Watson's description of IBM's "fast second" strategy is best illustrated by one of the greatest of all modern inventions: the electronic general-purpose computer.[5] The first working model of a general-purpose electronic computing device (as distinguished from mechanical devices that had relied on punch-card technology), the ENIAC, was developed by J. Presper Eckert and John Mauchly, professors at the University of Pennsylvania in the early 1940s. Eckert and Mauchly formed a firm to commercialize their invention for the private market. The firm was acquired by Remington-Rand, then a large business-machines manufacturer, which successfully marketed the computer to the U.S. Census Bureau in 1951. In response, IBM moved decisively into the market and secured a dominant position, largely due to its substantial internal capital, production, distribution, and sales infrastructure, and deep technical capacities. Within four years, IBM had secured its place as the market leader.[6] Even though IBM did not initially replicate the ENIAC's technical functionalities, it had far outperformed the innovators with respect to the nontechnical capacities that were necessary to produce, market, and support the new technology for the target business-user market. While other firms continued to pose meaningful competition for IBM in certain segments of the industry, IBM retained a dominant market share in the computing hardware market throughout the postwar period, estimated at approximately two-thirds of the global market as of the mid-1960s.[7] Neither Eckert nor Mauchly achieved the same good fortune.

2.1.2 "Fast Second" Wins

The innovator's fears of large-firm imitation are not without foundation. Business management scholars have identified multiple cases in which small entrepreneurial firms with innovative technologies failed to achieve commercial success while incumbents with weaker innovative capacities imitated the entrepreneur and captured the market. An underdiscussed body of research by Steven Schnaars and other scholars identifies a string of cases in which the winner in the market was the well-endowed second mover who lay in wait for the first mover to introduce and prove the technical feasibility and commercial value of a new technology and then imitated and commercialized it using its superior production, financing, and distribution capacities. Some of these cases are described in Table 2.1.

The case of the internet browser can illustrate in more detail the mechanism behind the repeated success of incumbent second movers in innovation markets. Founded by Marc Andreessen, Netscape pioneered the browser market in the mid-1990s, and its browser, the Netscape Navigator, initially captured a dominant market share (79 percent as of 1996). Following Microsoft's entry into the market in 1995, Netscape began to lose market share, and Microsoft's Internet Explorer browser represented 90 percent of the market by 2004.[8] Netscape lost the market for two simple reasons: its browser was not sufficiently protected by IP rights, and it could not compete with Microsoft on price. As the provider of the dominant operating system in the desktop PC market, Microsoft could outcompete Netscape by providing its Internet Explorer browser at no incremental charge and capturing revenues through the complementary goods and services embodied by the Windows operating system and associated suite of applications. Microsoft's zero-price policy compelled Netscape to do the same, effectively lifting all pricing constraints on consumers' access to this technology and, as a consequence, undermining the financial viability of Netscape, which was mostly a stand-alone browser provider. This led Netscape to take desperate measures: in 1998, it announced that it would release the source code for Netscape through the newly established Mozilla Foundation, and in 1999, it was acquired by AOL,[9] which might have enabled a giveaway model in which a zero-priced browser drove sales of complementary excludable assets. None of these strategies was effective, however, and Navigator's share of the browser market plummeted to negligible percentages. In two respects, the absence of IP rights promoted dominance of the browser market by the far larger second mover. First, the absence of IP rights enabled Microsoft to largely replicate the functionality of the first mover's innovation. Second, Microsoft's partial waiver of its IP rights over its imitation product compelled Netscape to undertake a zero-pricing strategy that was unsustainable in the absence

Table 2.1 Selected innovations imitated and captured by second movers

Innovation	Innovator ("Loser")	Imitator ("Winner")
(1) 35mm camera	Leica (1925) Contrax (1932) Exacta (1936)	Canon (1934) Nikon (1946)
(2) Ballpoint pen	Reynolds (1945) Eversharp (1946)	Parker (1954) Bic (1960)
(3) Mainframe computer	ENIAC/UNIVAC (1946)	IBM (1953)
(4) Credit card	Diner's Club (1950)	American Express (1958) Visa/Mastercard (1966)
(5) Commercial jet aircraft	De Havilland (1952)	Boeing (1958) Douglas (1958)
(6) Diet soft drink	No-Cal (Kirch) (1952) Diet Rite Cola (Royal Crown) (1962)	Patio Cola (Pepsi) (1963) Tab (Coca-Cola) (1963) Diet Pepsi (1964); Diet Coke (1982)
(7) ATMs	DeLaRue (1967) Docutel (1969)	Diebold (1971); IBM (1973) NCR (1974)
(8) Caffeine-free soft drink	Sport (Canada Dry) (1967); RC100 (Royal Crown) (1980)	Pepsi Free (1982) Diet Coke, Tab (1983)
(9) CAT scanner	EMI (1972)	Pfizer (1974); Technicare (1975); GE (1976) Johnson & Johnson (1978)
(10) Money-market mutual fund	Reserve Fund of New York (1973)	Dreyfus (1974); Fidelity (1974) Merrill Lynch (1975)
(11) Pocket calculator	Bowmar (1971)	Texas Instruments (1972)
(12) Food processor	Cuisinart (1973)	Black & Decker (late 1970s); Sunbeam (1984)
(13) MRI	Fonar (1978)	Johnson & Johnson (1981) GE (1982)
(14) Browser	Netscape (1994)	Microsoft (1995)

Note: Each year refers to the year in which the relevant product was commercially released or a patent was issued relating to the product.

Sources: All examples, except 1 and 14, are drawn from Schnaars (1994, 38–43, tab. 3.1). Example 3 is also discussed in Jewkes, Sawers, and Stillerman (1969, 341–41). Example 5 is also discussed in Drucker (1985, 245–46). Examples 5, 6, 8, and 9 are also discussed in Ceccagnoli and Rothaermel (2008, 21, tab. 1). Examples 5, 8, 9, and 11 are also discussed in Teece (1986, 287; 1988: 47–48). Examples 9, 11, and 14 are also discussed in Pisano and Teece (2007, 280).

of a revenue-generating complementary asset. Contrary to standard intuitions, it was the absence of IP rights that enabled the incumbent to overcome a more innovative entrant, ultimately resulting in the pioneer's exit from the market once AOL ceased support for Navigator in 2008.[10]

2.2 The Entrant's Predicament

The incumbent's advantage implies that IP rights often level a playing field that is otherwise tilted in favor of large integrated firms with lower-cost access to non-IP alternatives for capturing revenue from innovation investments. This proposition is consistent with the aforementioned Yale and Carnegie Mellon surveys (see Chapter 1, section 1.1.2) of firm managers concerning the relative importance of patents as compared to other mechanisms by which to capture value on innovation. Outside of pharmaceuticals and certain chemical markets, those studies showed that large-firm managers tend to assign a relatively low ranking to patents as compared to non-IP mechanisms. This survey result is often cited in support of the proposition that patents *in general* are not a critical precondition for supporting innovation incentives. But that interpretation of the evidence overlooks a critical point: these studies do not survey the value placed on patents by managers at smaller firms, including start-ups and other emerging firms that are often key sources of the most innovative technologies. Hence, as two of these studies specifically cautioned,[11] these findings have nothing necessarily to say about the relative value that smaller firms might place on patents as compared to non-IP alternatives (and expressly support the value of patents for large firms in the pharmaceutical and certain chemical markets).

The 2008 "Berkeley Patent Survey," which obtained survey information on the value that start-ups and other smaller firms place on patents, has partially filled this gap in our knowledge.[12] The results are more complex than the large-firm survey studies but ultimately converge on a fairly straightforward conclusion: "[O]ur chief finding is that, outside of the software and Internet sector, patenting plays a substantial role in helping early-stage technology companies compete."[13] To be clear, this is not to say that the Berkeley study found that, across the board, patenting is a critical value-appropriation strategy for all start-ups in all sectors. In particular, the study (which encompassed responses from 1,332 small-size firms founded during 1998–2008, drawn from a larger sample of more than 15,000 firms) reported that patents were ranked highly as a means for capturing value from innovation by managers of biotechnology, medical device, and information-technology hardware firms but were assigned a low ranking by managers of internet and software firms.[14] These reported preferences largely track revealed preferences: the study found that small firms in internet and software markets do not patent regularly (other than software firms backed by venture capital (VC) funding, while high patenting rates are observed among small firms in the biotechnology, medical devices, and information-technology hardware markets.[15] Consistent with other non-survey-based empirical studies,[16] the Berkeley study also found that securing outside capital is an important motivation behind smaller firms' decision to invest resources in patenting. Firms that reported filing for patents identified the ability to secure outside capital as a key motivation,[17] while a broader sample of firms that did and did not file for patents reported that potential funding sources valued patents highly (with larger percentages observed in the biotechnology and medical-device industries).[18] This nicely explains why patenting was substantially more common among VC-backed firms: the study found that 63 percent of VC-backed software and internet start-ups and 86 percent of VC-backed biotechnology start-ups held patents or had filed patent applications.[19]

Survey studies are inherently subject to methodological limitations insofar as any respondent sample may not be fully representative of the target population.[20] It is therefore comforting that the different valuations of patents expressed by managers at larger and smaller firms (with the exception of non-VC-backed smaller firms in internet and software markets) in the body of survey-based evidence is consistent with non-survey-based empirical studies identifying differences in the resources invested by larger and smaller firms in applying for and enforcing patents. In general (and making necessary adjustments for differences in firm size), small firms invest more intensively in these activities as compared to large firms. In particular, researchers have found that small firms generate more patents per R&D dollar than large firms[21] and more patents per employee than large firms[22] and have a higher propensity to litigate patents as compared to large firms.[23] Smaller firms' proclivities toward more intensive patent application and enforcement suggest that these firms tend to place a high value on patents, given the substantial costs involved, which are especially burdensome for a small to medium-size firm. Although patent application fees at the U.S. Patent and Trademark Office (USPTO) are unlikely to exceed several thousand dollars,[24] average estimated legal fees are substantial. According to a study by the American Intellectual Property Association, legal fees relating to the patent-application process range (depending on the complexity of the invention) between $10,000 and $15,000 (excluding the substantial additional costs relating to amendments and appeals), while average estimated legal fees in a fully adjudicated patent litigation range (depending on the amount at risk) from approximately $1 million to more than $7 million.[25] The Berkeley study reported significantly higher estimates, finding that average out-of-pocket patent-application expenses (including legal fees) exceeded $30,000.[26] Given the significant size of these costs, the fact that small firms in many industries regularly invest in applying for, and enforcing, patents provides a strong indication of the value placed by those firms on IP rights.

In the aggregate, there is considerable evidence to suggest that the demand for IP rights in a substantial number of commercially significant markets varies approximately inversely with firm size (setting aside the biopharmaceutical industry, where demand for IP rights is strong across all firm types). In those markets, strong IP protection is likely to be an important tool for enabling entry by entrepreneurial firms—that is, younger, smaller, and weakly integrated firms—that might otherwise have difficulty shielding their innovations from being expropriated by incumbents that enjoy the competitive advantages of scale and scope inherent to an established production, financing, marketing, and distribution infrastructure.[27] While this proposition has a firm grounding in relevant empirical evidence, there are two important objections to address before it can be adopted with confidence. Responding to these objections identifies with greater precision the circumstances in which IP rights are likely to be a necessary instrument for preserving entry opportunities for R&D-specialist, smaller, and less integrated firms that are often key sources of innovation in knowledge-intensive economies.

2.3 Commercialization by Contract

Even in a weak-IP environment, it could be argued that an entrepreneurial firm could mimic the scale economies, reputational capital, and internal know-how of a vertically integrated firm by contracting with external suppliers that can provide the required set of commercialization assets. Anchored in the seminal works of Ronald Coase and Oliver Williamson on the "theory of the firm,"[28] the institutional economics literature has analyzed the "make or buy" decisions that a firm makes with respect to the necessary inputs required to deliver a product to market, which in turn defines the scope of the firm. Whenever a firm elects "buy," its scope shrinks; whenever a firm elects "make," its scope expands. Using this terminology, the entrepreneurial firm could choose to substitute "buy" for "make": that is, it could shrink firm scope and contract externally for each commercialization function, rather than executing it internally. Consider Figure 2.1. The hierarchical firm has undertaken every innovation and commercialization function internally along the timeline running from conception to market release. Due to limitations of capital or expertise, the entrepreneurial firm can only independently execute the early-stage functions relating to innovation at an economically viable cost. But it could at least potentially enter into a series of contracts $(k_1 \dots k_5)$ with third-party suppliers for every other input and function required to achieve market release. By doing so, it could replicate through contract the financing, production, and distribution capacities of a hierarchical firm.

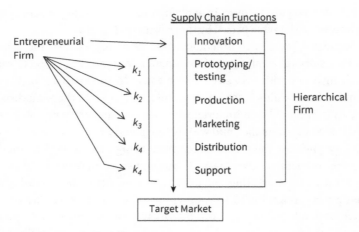

Figure 2.1 Paths to market by firm type

Given the possibility of contracting with external suppliers to mimic the integrated structure of a hierarchical firm, it might therefore appear that even entrepreneurial firms would be indifferent to significant reductions or even eliminations of IP rights. If that were true, the inverted case identified previously in Chapter 1, section 1.2.2—in which reducing IP rights erects an entry barrier that protects large-firm incumbents—would not arise, since the absence of IP would not deliver any competitive advantage to hierarchical firms. But this argument ignores the transactional hazards associated with the commercialization of innovation assets. The institutional economics literature on the "make or buy" decision anticipates that firms will execute a task internally when the costs of contracting in the market to execute that task are sufficiently high. Applying this logic to informational assets, we can identify two types of transactional hazards that innovators may encounter when contracting with third-party suppliers of the commercialization inputs that are required to reach market release.

(1) *Initial-stage expropriation risk.* The innovator is exposed to the risk that a sufficiently sophisticated counterparty can expropriate an informational asset that is disclosed in the course of negotiating the terms of a potential business relationship with a commercialization partner. This scenario corresponds to what Kenneth Arrow called the information paradox:[29] a counterparty will not consider purchasing a business or technical concept without disclosure, but after disclosure, its willingness to pay falls to zero.
(2) *Mid-stage expropriation risk.* After entering into a business relationship with a commercialization partner, the innovator is exposed to the risk that the partner may expropriate an informational asset that is disclosed to it in the course of this relationship.

Absent secure IP protection, these transactional hazards may compel the innovator firm to execute the relevant transaction in-house even if doing so would otherwise not be the most efficient choice. In the extreme (but not atypical) case, the costs of executing the transaction internally will be sufficiently high such that the innovator elects to abandon the project entirely. I will discuss several non-IP mechanisms that can partially, but not entirely, mitigate these transactional obstacles to mutually profitable interfirm relationships involving valuable informational assets.

2.3.1 Nondisclosure Agreements

It is sometimes suggested that a nondisclosure agreement (NDA) resolves the information paradox. However, NDAs suffer from three important limitations that at best provide a partial solution. First, in certain real-world information markets, such as pitches to VC firms in Silicon Valley, idea recipients that are critical gateways to target markets reportedly refuse to sign NDAs.[30] This most likely reflects either unwillingness to incur the transaction costs associated with negotiating an NDA or concern that an idea submitter may later opportunistically sue the recipient for breach of the NDA on factually dubious grounds. For this reason, Hollywood studios and other production companies sometimes, if not typically, require that idea submitters pre-emptively waive or substantially limit any legal claims they may otherwise be able to assert against the idea recipient under federal copyright or California state law (specifically, so-called *Desny* claims that permit suits for "idea theft")[31] in the event the recipient allegedly makes use of the idea without compensation. Second, even if an idea recipient agrees to sign an NDA, the idea submitter is likely to find that it is difficult to enforce. It is not a straightforward task to detect and demonstrate breach of an NDA by the counterparty or one of the counterparty's employees (who may have moved to another firm), especially if the counterparty can plausibly argue that it independently developed the relevant innovation. Third, NDAs typically do not protect the innovator against *use* by the recipient party. The idea recipient is unlikely to be willing to make that commitment, since it may already be developing or using the same or a related idea or technology (or, in the case of a VC firm, one of its portfolio firms may be doing so).[32]

2.3.2 Reputational Discipline and Graduated Disclosure

Reputational effects can mitigate expropriation risk in the context of raising capital for a nascent enterprise that has developed a potentially valuable innovation. A large VC firm that repeatedly partners with start-ups may rationally forgo a one-time expropriation gain in order to preserve a track record for fair dealing that attracts a stream of high-value start-ups in the future. Presumably it is on this basis that innovator-entrepreneurs commonly submit "idea pitches" to potential VC investors, even though, as noted, the idea recipient is usually unwilling to sign an NDA, or to Hollywood studios that, also as noted, typically require that the idea recipient partially or entirely forfeit all legal protections against expropriation. Consistent with this argument, empirical researchers have found that patenting is less common in informal or cooperative relationships involving innovation assets, while more common when an innovation is transferred through a formal license or acquisition.[33] In other circumstances, the innovator can mitigate expropriation risk by holding back part of the know-how required to implement the innovation, providing the prospective financing source with some but not all of the information relating to the innovator's technology.[34] This partial-disclosure strategy could be especially effective if the individual innovator is a "star scientist" or "star entrepreneur" who possesses unique human capital without which the technology cannot be developed at the same cost, quality, and time to completion.

2.3.3 Degrees of Expropriation Risk

Given the availability in some cases of contractual and reputational mechanisms to mitigate expropriation risk, the severity of this risk will be expected to vary across the universe of information-exchange transactions, as a function of certain key factors. These factors include:

(1) *Commercial value.* As an innovation increases in value, expropriation risk increases since the gains from opportunistic behavior increase.
(2) *"Lumpiness."* When informational assets are not easily divisible ("lumpy"), expropriation risk increases since it is not feasible to communicate only part of the innovation's value through a partial-disclosure strategy.
(3) *Reputational capital.* As the idea recipient's reputational capital increases, expropriation risk decreases since the counterparty expects increased long-term gains from non-opportunistic behavior.
(4) *Copying costs.* As copying costs increase, expropriation risk decreases since the counterparty has a limited ability to imitate without the cooperation of the innovator.

Figure 2.2 contemplates that these factors interact to generate different levels of expropriation risk in any particular transaction involving the exchange of informational assets. In the "high-risk" zone, expropriation risk is high under every parameter: the innovation has high value, the innovation is easy to imitate, the innovation is lumpy, and the counterparty is subject to weak reputation effects. In the "friendly" zone, expropriation risk is low under every parameter: the innovation has low value, the innovation is hard to imitate, the innovation is not lumpy, and the counterparty is subject to strong reputation effects. These relationships follow common sense: transferring small segments of low-value information to a trusted academic colleague may be a particularly safe transaction; transferring a "lump sum" of high-value and easily

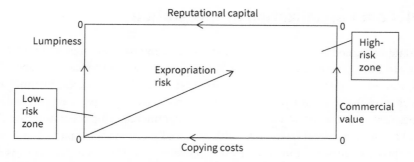

Figure 2.2 Expropriation risk in knowledge-exchange transactions
Source: Adapted from Barnett (2016, 12).

replicable information to a market competitor is particularly unsafe; all other scenarios imply some expropriation risk at different degrees of severity.

The high-risk zone identifies a transactional environment in which IP rights are a precondition for the interfirm bargaining that must take place for an entrepreneurial innovator to obtain the funding and commercialization capacities required to reach market and earn a positive return. Outside the high-risk zone, an IP right may no longer be a strict precondition for negotiating over or exchanging informational assets with third parties but will sometimes still reduce materially the early-stage and midstream expropriation hazards associated with those interactions. That function can be significant insofar as a robust IP right expands the universe of potential counterparties with which (and the transactional structures through which) (i) the innovator can comfortably negotiate a potential business relationship (early-stage expropriation risk) and (ii) even after entering into a transaction, the innovator can comfortably continue to share information in the course of a joint venture or similar business relationship (mid-stage expropriation risk). For example, even if the innovator could safely enter into negotiation over an informational asset with certain counterparties that have observable reputational capital, having a secure IP right enables the innovator to negotiate with (and, in the context of a joint venture, continuously share information with) a substantially larger population of potential business partners, including those that have little observable reputational capital to pledge against opportunistic behavior. Additionally, even if the innovator could safely enter into negotiation over a highly divisible informational asset using a graduated-disclosure mechanism that holds back part of the innovator's technological portfolio, having a patent enables the innovator to more fully disclose information concerning its innovation to potential investors and other business partners, most likely resulting in a higher and more accurate valuation of the relevant technology. It may sometimes be *feasible* to mitigate Arrow's information paradox through graduated-disclosure mechanisms involving reputation-rich counterparties; however, that hardly shows that it is feasible in the case of all types of parties, transactions, and informational assets, or even that it is ever *optimal* to do so.

2.4 Commercialization by Integration

It could be argued that, even in a reputation-poor environment that falls inside the "hostile zone," the entrant could avoid initial-stage and mid-stage expropriation risk without recourse to IP rights. The solution is simple avoidance. The innovator could raise funds to independently construct a vertically integrated production, marketing, and distribution infrastructure for commercializing the innovation that would require minimal interaction with potentially adverse third parties that pose expropriation threats.[35] But "keeping it in the family" does not substantially resolve the issue. There are two reasons. First, as noted, the information paradox can emerge in the case of any capital-raising transaction with an external investor, which is a necessary step to securing the funding necessary to construct an integrated structure that would mitigate the expropriation risk involved in interacting with all other commercialization partners. Second, even if a potential investor holds substantial reputational capital that might mitigate expropriation risk, the innovator firm still faces the cost-of-capital disadvantage typically borne by firms that must source R&D funding externally. External capital markets for funding innovation suffer from widely observed imperfections that derive from the forecasting costs, long lag times, and informational asymmetries inherent to R&D projects.[36] This predicament is exacerbated in the case of a smaller or younger firm, which likely lacks collateralizable assets (in the absence of IP rights), a past record of commercial success, or reputational capital to bolster its claims with respect to the value of its technology. Hence the innovator must offer a discount to attract investors to lend unsecured funds to, or invest equity in, a project with undemonstrated commercial value. This discount may be especially high in the case of the most innovative technologies, for which there may be no existing objective metric by which to measure technical feasibility or commercial value. As a result, the innovator either will be unable to raise sufficient capital at a feasible cost, resulting in exit from (or failure to enter) the market, or will do so at a premium that inflates commercialization costs, reduces expected returns, and, by anticipation, reduces incentives to innovate through an independent entrepreneurial venture.

It may be objected that this argument is sensitive to empirical assumptions concerning the relative efficiency of external capital markets in assessing the commercial value of an untested technology or other innovation. To explore the strength of this objection, I will assume an especially low-risk environment in which (i) the innovator interacts with a reputation-rich source of external financing (which can therefore credibly commit against expropriation), and (ii) the innovator firm is able to credibly communicate the value of its technology, so that capital can be obtained at a reasonable cost. With capital in hand, the innovator could recruit the necessary personnel and procure the necessary assets to set up a fully integrated commercialization infrastructure, thereby avoiding the expropriation risk attendant to information-intensive interactions with third parties. To "rig" the assumptions even more strongly against any efficiency case for IP rights, we can further observe that in some of these scenarios, innovators may be able to acquire rapidly, and at a relatively low cost, non-IP assets that are difficult for others to immediately replicate (for example, a large user base for a software application that generates network effects, so long as users bear sufficiently high switching costs). In this case, the innovator would apparently be able to feasibly avoid or mitigate expropriation risk through an internal commercialization infrastructure and, as a result, mimic the size and scope advantages of a hierarchical firm. (This hypothetical self-financing start-up is an intentionally unrealistic assumption made for the sake of argument; in reality, there are few start-ups that do not rely on outside capital as the largest source of funding, in which case the innovator's organizational calculus is inherently impacted to some extent by expropriation risk.) Excluding markets in which even non-IP alternatives cannot adequately protect the largest and most integrated firms against lower-cost imitation upon market release (for example, the pharmaceutical market), it may therefore seem that an innovator firm funded by high-reputation sources of outside capital could feasibly monetize its R&D investment without recourse to IP rights.

This line of argument again confuses adequacy for optimality. Even if it is feasible for the innovator to reach market through an integrated commercialization structure that mitigates expropriation risk and to do so at a reasonable cost of capital, there is no reason to assume that this is the optimal structure for funding and executing the commercialization process. Put differently, so long as the innovator does not have complete freedom to choose among the total feasible universe of transactional options, the outside observer cannot confidently conclude that a highly integrated technology supply chain represents a first-best efficient commercialization structure, rather than merely being a second-best adaptation to an insecure property-rights environment. To illustrate this point, consider Figure 2.3: it depicts a simplified range of transactional choices available to an innovator firm as it moves down the supply chain toward market release. With respect to each commercialization function, the innovator can execute it internally ("make") or procure it externally by contract ("buy"). Efficiency demands that the innovator construct the least-cost combination of "make or buy" choices at every point on the supply chain, thereby minimizing total innovation and commercialization costs. Without IP rights, the feasible set of transactional choices is truncated, compelling the innovator to select only the highest level of

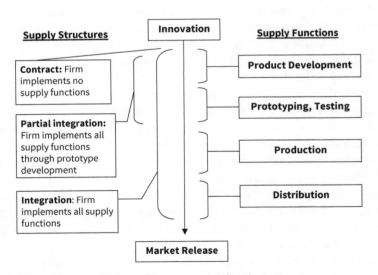

Figure 2.3 Possible organization of the commercialization process
Source: Adapted from Barnett (2011b, 797).

vertical integration—that is, the innovator is sometimes compelled to choose "make" when "buy" would otherwise be the most efficient choice. The potential result: even if the innovator can access reputationally validated sources of capital, substantially communicate the value of its innovation to outside investors, and acquire sufficient internal technical expertise to reach market independently, it may bear increased commercialization costs by forgoing transactions with third parties that can more efficiently supply some of the inputs required to reach market. This is not only a private loss but a social loss, since it means that the total costs of innovation and commercialization are inflated, resulting in a net social surplus that is smaller than would otherwise have been the case. Everything else being equal, restoring or increasing IP rights reverses those effects.

2.5 The Entrepreneurial Function of Intellectual Property

We are now in a position to identify two key functions of IP rights in supporting entrepreneurial innovation—that is, innovation that takes place outside the confines of a hierarchical entity. Both functions show how IP rights can reduce the costs of transacting over informational assets, lower the cost of financing and executing the commercialization of those assets, and, as a consequence, lower barriers for entry into markets dominated by integrated incumbents that have a rich suite of non-IP complementary assets.

2.5.1 Transaction Costs

IP rights reduce transaction costs that may otherwise preclude or frustrate arm's-length bargaining over commercialization inputs among unrelated parties. This effect is most pronounced in the most hostile transactional environments where economic stakes are high, reputation effects are weak, graduated disclosure is not feasible, and commercialization costs are high. The effect persists even in more friendly transactional environments insofar as secure IP rights expand the number of eligible contracting parties (by encompassing business partners that lack large stocks of reputational capital) and the menu of transactional structures and innovation projects (by encompassing idea-bargaining strategies that do not rely on, or "lumpy" innovation projects that do not accommodate, graduated disclosure). IP rights facilitate transactions between the largest possible pool of knowledge-input suppliers and commercialization-input suppliers by mitigating the expropriation risk that may otherwise impede profitable exchanges of informational assets. The supplier of a given commercialization function could be a specialist firm that has unique expertise in a discrete portion of the technology supply chain or a large distributor firm that seeks to source R&D inputs that it cannot generate internally at comparable cost, quality, and speed. These "win-win" transactions occur every day in technology markets, which are often populated by a concentrated hub of large integrated firms that source innovations from a dispersed periphery of smaller innovator firms and then embed those innovations in marketable products and services through a production and distribution infrastructure. This does *not* mean that interfirm knowledge transactions are always infeasible without IP rights. It simply means that those transactions are often less costly to execute as compared to an environment in which IP rights are insecure or absent. As will be discussed and illustrated further, this transactional function of IP rights is sometimes especially critical for smaller R&D-intensive firms that have strong innovative capacities but meager capital resources and weak commercialization capacities and therefore are most reliant on being able to securely negotiate and otherwise interact with potentially adverse third parties in order to reach the target intermediate or end-user market.

2.5.2 Financing Costs

Even assuming a friendly transactional environment characterized by weak expropriation risk (which would generally arise in reputation-rich environments populated by repeat-play entities), IP rights can reduce the financing costs incurred by an entrepreneurial firm that wishes to integrate forward into some or all commercialization functions without relying on the infrastructure, reputational capital, and scale economies of an existing dominant firm. There may be a number of reasons for doing so: to develop long-term commercialization capacities that provide the firm with a strategic advantage against actual or potential competitors, to capture a greater portion of the positive spillovers generated by the innovation, or to preserve a credible "outside option" when negotiating with suppliers. But forward integration into the downstream segments of the supply chain usually requires substantial capital. Patents and other forms of IP rights reduce the cost of capital in three ways. First, as has been both theorized and shown empirically, patents can sometimes provide a signal (albeit with considerable noise) of innovation quality, which in turn can result in improved valuations of a firm's equity[37] or increase the likelihood that a start-up secures outside financing.[38] Second, and relatedly, a patent offers creditors an asset that can be seized and liquidated in the event of default, thereby limiting the creditor's downside risk. This may be especially critical in the case of a young technology-intensive firm that has no other collateralizable assets and for which the likelihood of failure is high.[39] Third, a robust patent portfolio can allay investors' concerns about imitation by competitors following release of the relevant product into the target end-user market, thereby increasing the expected returns from investing in the development and commercialization of the relevant technology.

2.5.3 Illustration: How IP Rights Unlocked Value for Marvel

In Chapter 6, I provide detailed evidence of the transactional and financing advantages attributable to secure IP rights, drawn primarily from the biotechnology and semiconductor markets. For purposes of this discussion, I will illustrate IP rights' entrepreneurial function with an example from a content market.[40] Figure 2.4 provides a visual reference for the discussion that follows.

In 1998, Marvel, the famous but then-distressed comic-book franchise that had exited bankruptcy in 1996, sought to extract additional revenues from its portfolio of classic superheroes by entering into licensing transactions with multiple studios. After some success doing so, Marvel then sought to vertically integrate forward by independently producing films based on its copyright-protected characters and then entering into contractual relationships with major studios for distribution into the feature-film theatrical market. IP rights provided the legal foundation for these transactions. To secure the necessary financing, Marvel entered into a $525 million financing arrangement with Merrill Lynch in 2005. Simultaneously, Ambac, a third-party insurer, provided a guarantee to Merrill Lynch's credit facility. The guarantee's terms provided that in the event the movies did not reach a certain performance target, Ambac would cover Marvel's outstanding interest payment and would then be entitled to seize the supporting collateral—namely, the film rights to the characters in the financed productions. Anchored in Marvel's underlying copyright portfolio, this insured financing transaction supported the explosive growth of the Marvel franchise through two big-budget productions resulting in hit releases (*Iron Man* and *The*

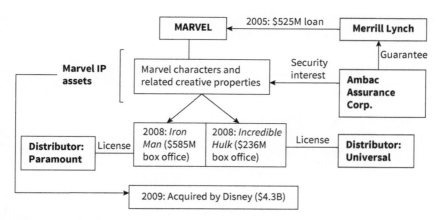

Figure 2.4 The rescue of Marvel

Sources: Leonard (2007); Marvel Enterprises Inc. (2005, item 1.01); Waxman (2007).

Incredible Hulk in 2008), which then led to Marvel's reincarnation as a motion-picture studio and subsequent acquisition by Disney for $4.3 billion in 2009.

The remarkable turnaround of Marvel vividly illustrates the value created by the transactional and financing functions of IP rights and, more generally, the manner in which IP rights can generate value by enabling transactions that would otherwise be inconsistent with economic rationality. Following the conventional approach adopted by much of IP scholarship, Marvel's copyright portfolio might be described in exclusionary terms as a tool by which to block access, entrench the Marvel franchise, and discourage subsequent improvements and adaptations. Viewed in enabling terms, however, those same rights are simply tools that facilitated the rise of a major new entrant in the motion picture market by structuring cooperative relationships between Marvel and a string of entities with specialized financing, production, and distribution capacities. Without secure IP rights to protect the value embedded in its less than fully exploited portfolio of creative assets, Marvel would have been unable to attract the risk capital required to support the cultivation of those assets in big-budget motion-picture projects. Those relationships supported hundreds of millions of dollars in investments in content production, marketing, and distribution activities, which in turn realized returns on the order of several billions of dollars for Marvel shareholders and entertained consumers around the world. Far from taxing consumption and impeding innovation, secure IP rights enabled a sequence of inter-firm transactions that unlocked the economic value and creative potential of Marvel's content assets.

3
Organizational Effects of Intellectual Property (Macro Level)

So far, I have analyzed the micro-level effects of IP rights on firms' costs of regulating access to intellectual assets and, as a result, those firms' innovation choices, *given* those firms' existing organizational structure and associated costs of adopting non-IP alternatives. But there is a second step required to complete the dynamic analysis of IP rights. Absent legal or technological constraints, organizational forms are not fixed but rather are subject to the discretion of the innovator and its cohort of commercialization partners. Given a certain level of IP protection, innovators will select the combination of organizational forms—ranging from the most hierarchical to the most entrepreneurial—to conduct each stage of the innovation and commercialization process at the lowest possible cost, thereby maximizing expected returns on investment in R&D and other innovation activities. Hence the proposed link between changes in IP rights on the one hand and changes in organizational form and ultimately market structure on the other hand. If changes in IP strength alter innovators' costs of capturing returns on innovation as a function of organizational form, then innovators will respond to changes in IP strength by adjusting their choices of organizational form so as to minimize those costs and maximize expected returns. To use an evolutionary analogy, market forces will "select for" firms that adopt the least-cost mix of organizational structures and "select against" firms that do not make equally efficient choices, *given* the existing level of IP protection supplied by the state. In the aggregate, individual firms' organizational adaptations in response to the surrounding IP environment generate the architecture of an innovation market.

3.1 Intellectual Property and Innovation Architectures

At each step on the pathway leading from idea conception through product development through market release, each innovator (or holder of an innovation asset) must elect the organizational form used to complete that step. To illustrate, suppose a physician-scientist is selecting the organizational entity or transactional form in which she will innovate and commercialize her medical-device innovation. Some possibilities include an academic position at a research university, a salaried position at a large integrated corporation, or a founder of an independent start-up. The innovator-physician's choice among those organizational options will be influenced

Innovators, Firms, and Markets. Jonathan M. Barnett, Oxford University Press (2021). © Oxford University Press.
DOI: 10.1093/oso/9780190908591.003.0004

by (among other things) the available level of IP protection. Weak IP elevates the cost of using stand-alone entrepreneurial forms that expose innovators to expropriation risk when interacting with outside providers of commercialization inputs and, as a result, compels innovators to secure the financing required to integrate forward independently. For the reasons discussed previously in Chapter 2 (section 2.5), financing can be difficult to secure at a reasonable cost without IP rights to mediate the exchange of information between the innovator and any prospective investor (or to provide a creditor with collateral to protect against default or an equity investor with a salvageable IP asset in the event of business failure). Absent sufficient capital, the innovation is not developed, or the physician must elect from the remaining two organizational options: she can develop the innovation as an employee of an integrated firm or an academic research entity. The former entity finances innovation through some combination of internal and external cash flow, while the latter entity finances innovation externally through tuition payments and governmental and philanthropic transfers.

Robust IP protection reduces the cost of using entrepreneurial forms to monetize R&D by mitigating the expropriation risk and informational asymmetries inherent to contracting with outside suppliers of commercialization and financing inputs. As a result, it enables innovators to select freely from the full range of organizational choices—ranging from the most hierarchical to the most entrepreneurial forms—throughout the innovation and commercialization process. Organizational choice results in private and social efficiency gains, since it enables innovators to freely select the combination of organizational forms that minimizes innovation and commercialization costs and maximizes expected net returns. This does not mean that innovators operating under a strong-IP regime will necessarily choose a low level of vertical integration; rather, it means that the innovator has the option to do so. By contrast, under a weak-IP regime, the innovator is confined to hierarchical organizational forms, which may suppress efficiencies that could have been achieved under less integrated organizational forms. Relatedly, coerced integration inflates, perhaps dramatically, the capital and technical requirements for achieving entry, which in turn impedes potential competitive threats to incumbents that enjoy an existing production and distribution infrastructure.

In the aggregate, innovators' organizational choices at each stage of the innovation and commercialization process—essentially, an iterated series of "make or buy" decisions—generate the innovation architecture in any given market. The interaction between IP and organizational form yields three core types of innovation architectures. Those architectures are distinguished by the extent to which innovation resources are allocated by external market forces rather than internal allocation by a firm or political allocation by the state. Three core types of innovation architectures can emerge under different IP regimes: (i) an *entrepreneurial* regime, (ii) a *hierarchical* regime, and (iii) a *bureaucratic* regime.[1] As IP protection declines in force, each regime is characterized by declining degrees of organizational freedom and a declining role for external market forces in the allocation of

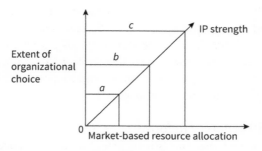

Figure 3.1 IP strength and innovation architectures

Note: a = bureaucratic innovation; b = hierarchical innovation; c = entrepreneurial innovation.

innovation resources (as distinguished from internal managerial forces within a firm or political forces within the state). An entrepreneurial regime emerges under the highest level of IP protection and allows innovators to select from the full range of organizational forms; a hierarchical regime emerges under zero to intermediate levels of IP protection and constrains the feasible set of organizational forms to large integrated entities; and a bureaucratic regime emerges under zero to weak levels of IP protection in environments where even large integrated entities do not have cost-feasible access to non-IP alternatives and innovation can only proceed with the support of governmental or philanthropic capital. In the last case, the market allocation of innovation resources is entirely displaced by cash transfers from the state or private patrons. These relationships can be represented as shown in Figure 3.1. In the discussion that follows, I describe the characteristics of each type of innovation architecture in greater detail.

3.1.1 Entrepreneurial Innovation

Increases in IP strength can be expected to trigger a three-step sequence of organizational innovation at the level of the firm and the market:

Stage 1. Growth in the number of small, upstream R&D-intensive firms that supply R&D inputs to large, integrated downstream enterprises.

Stage 2. The development of secondary markets that upstream R&D-intensive firms can use to realize the value of their innovations through assignments, licenses, or joint ventures with downstream firms or, subject to external financing, forward integration into production and distribution.

Stage 3. The development of tertiary markets that IP holders can use to transfer direct or indirect ownership of IP assets or other related interests through licenses, assignments, and other transactions with IP asset intermediaries, aggregators, and similar entities.

The connection between strong property rights and the development of robust trading, credit, and other secondary markets in the legally protected asset class would be a mundane observation in real- and tangible-goods markets. But the same principle is not widely recognized in the case of intangible-goods markets. A well-studied period in British patent history illustrates this relationship between IP protection and the formation of markets in intellectual assets.

Illustration: British Patent Reforms

Historians have argued that the British patent system supplied a cumbersome property-rights apparatus until reforms in the mid-nineteenth century.[2] The patent-examination process and related fees were burdensome, and patents were difficult to enforce (in part due to judicial hostility). Starting in the 1830s, English courts adopted a friendlier attitude toward the patent system, as indicated in part by patentees' greater rate of success in court.[3] The shift in judicial attitudes was then complemented by reforms in 1852 and 1883 that streamlined the examination process and reduced application fees.[4] Together these developments increased the expected value of a patent as compared to other mechanisms for extracting returns on innovation.

Following the dynamic approach, this effective increase in IP strength would be expected to induce entry by innovators that preferred to operate under entrepreneurial forms and therefore would require secure property rights to transact with potential buyers or licensees of R&D inputs or with suppliers of the financial and commercialization inputs required to monetize their innovations. This expectation is consistent with the historical record. After the 1852 reform, use of the patent system increased substantially (as indicated by a sharp increase in the number of patents issued),[5] which coincided with the emergence of a class of professional inventors that operated together with a secondary market of patent agents, manufacturers, and other potential licensees and assignees.[6] This emergent market in intellectual assets relied on the formation of partnerships between inventors and investors for purposes of commercializing patented inventions and, when necessary, bringing litigation against unauthorized users.[7]

The British experience shows the close tie between patent security, individual inventors, and the suppliers of the financing and commercialization inputs required to reach market. Specifically, it shows the manner in which the ability to credibly threaten legal action against unauthorized users, the function with which the patent system is most closely associated, drives a function with which the patent system is less commonly associated. Namely, the formation of business relationships between innovators, investors, and other parties that are critical in delivering a viable product to the target market. An observation in 1851 by a British lawyer (and located by Sean Bottomley) nicely describes this relationship:

> [I]f any person who may be disposed to think that patents should be done away with, comes to examine the way in which particular manufacturers have been built up by reason of the large amount of capital which has been thrown into them, in reliance upon the return to be obtained by means of the protection to be given for a short time, he will be very much surprised.[8]

As will be discussed subsequently and in significantly greater detail, the role played by patents in Great Britain during portions of the eighteenth and nineteenth centuries has been mirrored in the United States during the late nineteenth and early twentieth centuries and the late twentieth and early twenty-first centuries, which were two periods in which the U.S. patent system has been robustly enforced and actively used by firms in technology-intensive markets. In all three periods, an entrepreneurial class of individual inventors and smaller R&D-intensive firms used patents to secure financing from outside investors and to extract returns on R&D through licenses, sales, and other business relationships with third parties. In all three periods, patents induced investment in technological activity not only by erecting legal obstacles to the end-stage expropriation risk posed by unauthorized imitators in the target market (the conventional focus of incentive-based rationales for IP protection) but also by mitigating the initial-stage and mid-stage forms of expropriation risk that are inherent to the information-intensive transactions that precede market release. As a result, innovators could choose to enter the market as independent entrepreneurs, rather than being confined to hierarchical or bureaucratic entities (or declining to enter the market altogether).

3.1.2 Hierarchical Innovation

If strong IP tends to pull innovation assets out of the firm and into the market (or, more precisely, provides innovators with the option to do so), then weak IP should have the opposite effect. Specifically, we should expect that the number of specialized technology-intensive firms would decline, secondary markets in trading and financing knowledge assets would shrink, and internal R&D operations within large integrated enterprises would expand. This organizational shift does not necessarily alter the total volume of innovative output; however, it impacts the range of organizational structures through which that output can be feasibly generated and then developed into technically and commercially viable products. Given that innovators no longer have access to the full range of transactional structures for conducting the innovation and commercialization process, there is an inherent risk that the market will adopt a less than maximally efficient mix of transactional structures at any particular point on the technology supply chain. In any such circumstance, the costs of the innovation and commercialization process may rise, or resources may be allocated to a distorted mix of innovation projects that reflects the constraints on organizational choice under a weak-IP regime.

Illustration: AT&T's Bell Labs
AT&T's Bell Labs illustrates how R&D investment can persist at relatively robust levels under a weak-IP regime but is undertaken through a skewed mix of organizational structures consisting principally of hierarchical and bureaucratic elements. Those organizational distortions can have adverse effects in the form of some combination of reduced innovative output, a distorted selection of innovation projects, and price and

quality distortions due to the lack of competitive discipline inherent to markets in which a small number of large integrated entities provide the most effective (and, in some cases, the only commercially feasible) structure for capturing returns on innovation.

Revisiting the Bell Labs "Success Story"

During much of its tenure as a national telephone monopoly, ending with its breakup in 1984, AT&T operated under a 1956 consent decree that required it to license its patent portfolio at a zero royalty or, for patents issued after 1956, a reasonable royalty, in each case together with technical know-how and subject to a reciprocal license from any licensee.[9] Contrary to the expectations of conventional IP analysis, AT&T did not cease R&D investment as a result of this substantial curtailment of its IP rights and the inability to assert legal exclusivity over the results of its innovation efforts (although mitigated by the fact that the reciprocity clause in the compulsory license enabled AT&T to access the technology held by licensees).[10] Rather, AT&T supported extensive R&D activities at its research division, Bell Labs, which is widely credited as a legendary source of technological advances such as (among others) the transistor (although invented prior to the consent decree), the Unix operating system, the "C" programming language, and the fundamental elements of cellular-telephone communications.[11] During this time, AT&T's research budget and staff grew, reaching approximately 23,600 personnel (including non-research personnel employed at Bell Labs) by 1975.[12] Similarly, AT&T's "R&D employment intensity" (defined as the number of R&D-related personnel as a percentage of total employees) remained at high and growing levels throughout this period: 9.74 percent in 1960, 14.59 percent in 1965, 12.42 percent in 1970.[13] As of 1982, it was reported that Bell Labs funded 13 percent of all private R&D in the United States.[14] Clearly, AT&T cannot be described as an innovation laggard, despite the inability to exert legal exclusivity over its R&D output.

The R&D achievements at Bell Labs under a weak-IP regime might appear to support the proposition that innovation can succeed without patents or other exclusionary barriers. More specifically, the Bell Labs success story would appear to provide evidence that the deadweight losses inherent to IP rights are unnecessary to support innovation incentives. This interpretation is not compelling. Bell Labs enjoyed two powerful *non*-patent barriers to entry that supported its innovation capacities but imposed deadweight losses and other social costs of a likely greater magnitude as compared to a patent-anchored monopoly position. First, AT&T operated under a government-sanctioned monopoly over national telephone equipment and service, in connection with which the Bell operating companies paid a license fee equal to a percentage of their gross revenue to the AT&T parent firm, which then used the fee as the primary source of funding for Bell Labs operations.[15] That is, in lieu of a circumscribed patent-based monopoly over a particular technology asset (or a portfolio of technology assets), AT&T's innovation activities relied for funding on a sweeping monopoly over national telephone service. Second, AT&T held a powerful suite of complementary assets, including a difficult-to-replicate production, distribution, and communications infrastructure that posed a natural barrier to entry even to firms with comparable technological capacities. This may explain why Frank Jewett, the head of Bell Labs, testified to a congressional commission in 1939 that, while patents had been vital at the inception of the telephone industry, patents were no longer of great importance to AT&T, as the company had grown to a large size and was "not subject to competition in the ordinary sense." He concluded: "Patents are a pure incident in the business."[16]

The dominant and protected position enjoyed by AT&T in the national market for telephone equipment and service provides a clear illustration of a workable hierarchical and semi-bureaucratic structure for sustaining robust levels of innovation activity. Yet there is considerable evidence that this organizational structure resulted in social costs in the form of inflated pricing, reduced output, a distorted selection of innovation projects, and reduced investment in commercializing innovations. In particular, a comparison of the telecommunications industry before and after the breakup of AT&T in 1984 suggests that the Bell Labs research enterprise is best interpreted as a second-best organizational adaptation to a weak-IP regime rather than a first-best maximally efficient model for sustaining innovation and commercialization activities in general.

Pricing and Output Distortions

AT&T's legal and economic monopoly over much of the national telephone equipment and service market appears to have resulted in significant pricing and output distortions to the detriment of the U.S. consumer. Consider the long-distance telephone service market. Following the breakup of AT&T in 1984 and through 1991, long-distance rates dropped by 45 percent, the number of competitors (including resellers) grew from 42 (in 1982) to 597, and, unsurprisingly, given the drop in prices and increase in competitors, the market (as measured by number of minutes used) grew by 111 percent.[17] Subject to the effect of technological advancements, these dramatic improvements in the communications marketplace after the 1984 breakup suggest that the AT&T national telephone monopoly had inflated prices, constrained output, and (by definition) impeded entry for several decades relative to a more competitive environment. These are all social losses that must be taken into account in considering whether to interpret Bell Labs as a "successful" model of innovation under a weak-IP regime.

R&D Intensity: Mixed

Given Bell Labs' reputation as a leading research enterprise, it is surprising to learn that the "R&D intensity" of the AT&T parent entity—measured based on R&D expenditures as a percentage of operating revenues—was not especially high during the postwar period, at least in comparative historical terms. During 1962–1983, one study finds that the firm's annual research intensity was 2.6 percent on average.[18] By comparison, two current leading technology firms, Qualcomm and Google, had R&D intensities of 25 percent and 15.5 percent, respectively, as of 2018.[19] During 1984–1994, the ten-year period immediately after the 1984 breakup, AT&T's research expenditures grew both absolutely and on a relative basis, as measured by R&D intensity, which increased to an average of 7 percent.[20] This increase is even greater if one compares AT&T's R&D intensity prior to the breakup with the aggregate post-breakup R&D intensity of both AT&T and the regional "Bell" companies that were divested from the former AT&T parent.[21] AT&T certainly invested significantly in R&D under the postwar weak-IP regime; however, the "Bell system" (that is, the AT&T parent and the regional Bell subsidiaries) invested significantly more collectively under the strong-IP regime that prevailed after the 1984 breakup (in each case, as measured on a percentage basis by R&D intensity). While this increase in R&D intensity reflects in part other contributing factors, it nonetheless strongly suggests that the postwar hierarchical and semi-bureaucratic regime, which lacked secure IP rights and relied on a statutory monopoly to fund and support R&D, provided a workable, but not the maximally efficient, innovation environment, as compared to the post-breakup mixed hierarchical and entrepreneurial regime, which relied by contrast on IP rights and competitive discipline to fund and support R&D. It is hard to imagine that an efficiency-minded policymaker would choose to replace the post-breakup strong-IP regime, populated by a competitive market of multiple firms vigorously engaged in telecommunications R&D and exposed to market forces, with the pre-breakup weak-IP regime, populated by a statutory monopoly consisting of a single firm that was largely shielded by law from competitive threats.

Under-Commercialization

A robust innovation regime must channel adequate resources not only to innovation but to commercialization activities, without which new technologies cannot reach market. It appears that Bell Labs performed strongly in the former but performed weakly in the latter category. More specifically, some commentators observe that Bell Labs excelled in R&D in general but skewed its efforts toward long-term basic research,[22] resulting in a relatively meager flow of new communications equipment for businesses and consumers.[23] During much of the period in which AT&T enjoyed a statutory national monopoly over telephone service and equipment markets (subject to certain markets being opened to competition over time),[24] customers of AT&T's telephone service were required to lease telephone equipment from it.[25] As would be expected in the absence of competitive discipline, it appears that AT&T infrequently released improvements to telephone equipment[26] and offered little diversity in the products offered to customers.[27] For example, while AT&T engineers had developed electronic switches by 1959, the company did not integrate this innovation into its telephone system until 1976.[28] In the early 1980s, AT&T was still sufficiently behind state-of-the-art technology in this field that it was forced to purchase electronic switches from an outside firm.[29] In other cases, AT&T developed the building blocks of revolutionary technologies but then failed to move in a timely manner to convert them into commercially viable products, leaving others to reap those fruits. For example, AT&T pioneered cellular-phone technology starting in the late 1940s and continued to conduct research in this area through the 1970s,[30] but Motorola won the race to complete the first working prototype cellular telephone and base station in 1973 and thereafter released the first commercially available handheld cellular phone in 1983.[31] As the AT&T/Motorola comparison suggests, the pace of innovation-plus-commercialization in the communications market during the postwar period pales in comparison with the explosion of long-distance and digital communications products and services after the breakup of AT&T.[32] As a contemporary observer noted, this newly competitive environment appeared to have had a salutary effect on AT&T, which "began to regularly release new models with new features, a strategy responsive to the competitive sale market, but a major change from the Bell System."[33]

The Missing Inventor-Entrepreneur

The symptoms of potential under-innovation, "mis-innovation," and "under-commercialization" at Bell Labs suggest a broader point. The technological achievements with which Bell Labs is rightly associated may mask the suppression of "missing" technological contributions by smaller and less integrated innovator entities that could not achieve entry under the postwar period's weak-IP regime. Relatedly, we are unable to observe the potential suppression of efficient information-exchange relationships between a large entity such as AT&T and an external population of smaller innovator firms that may have been deterred from entry due to the transactional hazards inherent to a weak-IP environment.[34] Given elevated expropriation risk in the absence of robust IP rights, potential innovators would be reluctant to undertake (and few outside investors would be willing to bear) the risk of starting a stand-alone firm that would be exposed to loss of its intellectual capital during the commercialization process (early-stage and mid-stage expropriation risk) or following market release (end-stage expropriation risk). To be clear, this does not imply that innovation ceases; rather, the would-be innovator-entrepreneur may choose to work as a paid scientist at Bell Labs. However, this is not a mere relocation of innovation capital and labor; rather, it may give rise to adverse efficiency losses that would not exist under a stronger-IP regime. First, as illustrated by the pre-1984 telecommunications market, a weaker-IP regime may induce organizational choices that in the aggregate generate hierarchical market structures characterized by high capital and technical requirements to achieve entry, resulting in a decline in competitive vigor relative to the more entrepreneurial market structures that could feasibly arise under a stronger-IP regime. Second, the large-firm organizational bias of a weak-IP regime may distort the selection of innovation projects given larger firms' predilection toward incremental innovations that refine existing technologies (as discussed in section 3.2.1 of this chapter), which is exacerbated by the absence of competitive pressure from entrants that tend to undertake innovations that seek to displace existing technologies. With historical hindsight, the "glory days" of Bell Labs—the crown jewel of the postwar period's government-funded innovation oligopolies—may have reflected a skewed allocation of innovation and commercialization resources toward hierarchical entities, which may in turn have generated efficiency losses in the form of inflated innovation and commercialization costs, a distorted allocation of innovation resources, and a delay in converting innovations into new products and services for consumers.

3.1.3 Bureaucratic Innovation

In the most extreme (but not atypical) case, the absence of strong IP replaces market-financed innovation with two related alternatives: (i) altruistic transfer mechanisms administered by philanthropic entities and/or (ii) tax-based transfer mechanisms administered by the state. The second alternative includes government procurement arrangements in which the state funds innovation projects by private firms. In these settings, the state can be viewed as simply the culmination of an increasing use of integrated structures as IP strength deteriorates and entrepreneurial forms become an economically endangered species in the innovation ecosystem.[35] We can therefore expect that bureaucratic innovation will be most prominent in environments where IP is absent or weak and either (i) vertical integration or some other non-IP instrument is not an adequate device for capturing returns on innovation or (ii) legal constraints restrict firms' ability to grow internally or through acquisitions (which then precludes those firms from maximizing the economies of scale and scope that can substitute for missing IP rights).

Consistent with those expectations, as I will show (see Chapter 4, section 4.2.2), the reduction in patent strength and expansion in antitrust enforcement starting in the late New Deal and continuing throughout the postwar period were accompanied by dramatic increases in federal government funding of academic and industry R&D. The federal government, which had not previously been a principal R&D funding source, flooded the research market with billions of dollars in grants and procurement contracts. Those policies effectively pushed large swaths of R&D output outside the reach of the patent system, because either federal funding displaced private funding (which represented a minority of all R&D funding as early as 1943)[36] or recipients of federal funding were subject to contractual restrictions on patenting (or otherwise establishing legal exclusivity to) inventions developed as a result of those funds. The steady stream of federal R&D funding effectively superimposed a legal regime that substantially displaced the patent system—and, more generally, a market-driven system for allocating R&D resources—through the contractual "strings" attached to that funding. Reflecting this development, a 1968 government-commissioned report observed that "firms are so completely in the government market that they attach little or no importance to patent rights for commercial purposes."[37] More generally, postwar commentators observed that R&D had become "socialized"—that is, tax-supported state transfers had superseded the market as the principal source of financing innovation.[38] In 1962, a leading economist observed:

> [P]olitical feasibility and what the government considers to be the public need have become the principal instruments of control, replacing private profit

incentives and the traditional legal instruments of antitrust laws and the patent system.[39]

In Chapter 4, I provide a substantially more detailed analysis of the drastic change in R&D funding during the postwar period and the consequences for the organization of the innovation and commercialization process. At this stage, however, it is sufficient to observe that the historical shift away from entrepreneurial and toward hierarchical and bureaucratic innovation structures is consistent with a general principle. When IP rights are weak, innovation and commercialization costs are sufficiently high, third parties' reverse-engineering and commercialization costs are sufficiently low, and there are no adequate non-IP alternatives available at a reasonable cost, neither an entrepreneurial regime populated by unintegrated firms nor a hierarchical regime populated by integrated firms is feasible. Rather, innovation can only be preserved under a bureaucratic regime that is governed by administrative fiat and is inherently exposed to political rent-seeking.

3.2 Why Structural Effects Matter

So far, I have presented a theoretical case that a weak-IP regime is likely to induce hierarchical and bureaucratic market architectures (or some combination of those architectures), while a strong-IP regime is likely to reverse that effect—or, more precisely, will provide the market with the opportunity to use entrepreneurial structures when doing so is the most efficient innovation and commercialization pathway to market. This is a descriptive prediction of changes in the feasible range of organizational forms and market structures as a function of changes in IP strength. As a normative matter, these organizational effects might be viewed as merely aesthetic, in which case IP strength in any given market would be a matter of indifference. That is, different levels of IP strength support different types of innovation architectures—Edison's Menlo Park "idea factory" (entrepreneurial) versus Bell Labs (hierarchical) versus National Institutes of Health (bureaucratic)—but the resulting effects on total innovative output may be relatively insignificant, even if the effects on the innovative output of particular types of firms would be significant. If that were the case, then, as a matter of efficiency, there may plausibly be little social interest in preserving an entrepreneurial environment in which innovation takes place in smaller and vertically disintegrated entities, rather than a hierarchical environment in which engineers typically work as paid employees of a large corporate enterprise, or a bureaucratic environment in which scientists typically work as civil servants within a government bureaucracy or as paid employees of a tax-funded research institute. At least from an economic point of view (meaning ignoring any distributive considerations that might independently favor advantaging small firms and individual inventors), that conclusion would erode the case for a robust IP regime, which could be potentially dismissed as an unnecessary "tax" given the availability of non-IP-dependent structures for supporting the innovation and commercialization process.

This is an old argument made by skeptics of IP rights. In a well-known article, Supreme Court Justice Stephen Breyer (then a Harvard Law School professor) suggested that the case for copyright was "uneasy," because in the late nineteenth century, U.S. publishers had exploited delays in copying and used below-cost pricing strategies to extract profits from publishing works by British authors even though U.S. copyright protections did not at the time extend to foreign authors.[40] The underlying logic suffers from a basic defect, because it does not assess the social costs of compelling innovators, and, in Breyer's example, the entities that commercialize innovations, to rely on non-IP alternatives to extract returns from legally unprotected knowledge assets.[41] Given that omission, this type of argument implicitly assumes that business models that rely on non-IP alternatives—scale economies, secrecy precautions and reverse-engineering barriers, internal financing, reputational capital, and so on— always impose fewer social costs as compared to business models that rely on formal IP rights to extract returns from innovation. But there is no reason to make that assumption without further inquiry in any particular case. Breyer's own example shows why. As demonstrated by Zorina Khan and Stan Liebowitz, large U.S. publishers were able to capture returns on otherwise unprotected creative works by foreign authors by entering into an informal arrangement among participating publishers that allocated exclusivity rights to each author's works to a specific publisher.[42] Assuming compliance with this informal arrangement,[43] these "synthetic" copyrights were more powerful on at least one parameter than the copyrights that applied to U.S. authors, since they applied to an author on a lifetime basis, rather than to only a single work.[44] Put differently, it appears that the publishing market was only able to operate without formal IP rights because it had engineered a cartel-like mechanism that could allocate and enforce informal equivalents that potentially *increased* access costs relative to a formal IP regime.

The story of the publishers' cartel supports a broader principle. Contrary to the presumption behind Breyer's argument (and much of IP scholarship that makes similar arguments), a reduction in the strength of IP rights does not necessarily create a public domain in which access costs fall to zero. Rather, following the dynamic approach elaborated in Chapter 1, the real effect of any such reduction must be assessed by anticipating that firms will respond by adopting the next least-cost mechanism for extracting returns on innovation investment. That non-IP alternative mechanism may result in a net welfare loss, even assuming no decline in innovation investment. That is because the absence of IP rights may induce firms to adopt alternative mechanisms that impose greater social costs relative to a market in which IP rights are made available and securely enforced. In Breyer's example, a market that is free from copyright but operates subject to a publishers' cartel would seem to be almost certainly less preferred than a competitive market in which authors can securely negotiate with publishers under the protection provided by a robust copyright regime. Relatedly, the synthetic IP rights that emerged in response to weak formal IP rights lacked the tradability features that enable the formation of secondary markets in exchanging, licensing, and financing IP assets.

The cartel mechanism adopted in the nineteenth-century U.S. publishing market is just one of many alternative mechanisms that firms can adopt in order to compensate for missing appropriation capacities under a weak- or zero-IP regime. As I have discussed, the most common and often most effective alternative is the internal information and capital market supplied by the vertically integrated firm. That is, firms that adapt most successfully to weak-IP regimes are firms that employ non-IP mechanisms in order to capture dominant market positions that are often more securely protected than the nominal monopoly positions commonly attributed to holders of IP rights. Just as the cartel mechanism gives rise to social costs that would not arise under a stronger-IP regime (and just as the pre-breakup, weak-IP telecommunications market gave rise to social costs that did not arise under the post-breakup, strong-IP telecommunications market), so, too, the organizational bias under weak-IP regimes can give rise to social costs by endangering the viability of external capital and information markets for supporting innovation and commercialization activities. In the following discussion, I describe in greater detail three particular types of efficiency gains that rely on a secure IP regime and are likely forfeited or diminished once that legal input is withdrawn.

3.2.1 Division of Innovative Labor

At least since Adam Smith's famous example of the pin factory, it has been widely recognized that specialization yields efficiencies by allocating each step in a supply chain to the firm or firms that can execute that step most efficiently. It has been less widely recognized that in technology-intensive markets, secure IP rights facilitate the efficient disaggregation of technology supply chains among firms that tend to excel in upstream innovation and product-development functions and firms that tend to excel in the downstream production and distribution functions required to reach market. In general, it is expected (and, as will be discussed in greater detail in Chapter 6, observed) that smaller R&D-specialist firms tend to undertake the former category of tasks, while larger integrated firms tend to undertake the latter category of tasks. Relatedly, specialization efficiencies arise to the extent that larger firms tend to excel in incremental and process-related innovation that improves upon existing technologies, while smaller R&D-specialist firms tend to excel in product innovation that can challenge and displace existing technologies. This divergence in innovation and commercialization capacities can give rise to a symbiotic environment in which start-ups "feed" R&D inputs to large firms, which then efficiently embed those inputs into commercially viable products and services through an existing production and distribution infrastructure. As I will discuss, both the biopharmaceutical market and certain segments of the semiconductor market have developed highly granular and substantially disaggregated structures that conform closely to the proposed relationship between secure IP rights, transactional innovation, and specialization of labor in technology supply chains.

Theory: Radical Entrants, Conservative Incumbents

In 1962, Kenneth Arrow identified a rational basis for the expected divergence in the innovation preferences of larger and smaller firms. He argued that a dominant incumbent inherently has a weaker incentive to invest in innovations that displace existing technologies, since it must offset anticipated profits from the innovation against existing profits from its existing technology. By contrast, entrants have no existing profits to forfeit and hence have a stronger incentive to invest in "radical" innovations that seek to displace existing technologies.[45] Following in the wake of Arrow's contribution, other commentators have identified complementary factors that push incumbents to favor lower-risk, incremental innovations over higher-risk, groundbreaking innovations. These include (i) "low-powered" incentives in large bureaucratic entities that cannot provide sufficiently performance-contingent compensation packages to personnel willing to undertake the highest-risk projects, (ii) agency costs in large-firm organizations that lead management to favor lower-risk projects that limit reputational penalties in the event of failure, and (iii) large-number conditions and associated communication and monitoring costs that generate diseconomies of scale in R&D and product development in large organizations.[46] In small firms in which there is little to no separation between ownership and management, low-powered incentives are replaced by high-powered incentives, agency costs are reduced, and large-number conditions do not apply, all of which suggest a bias toward higher-risk, higher-return forms of innovation.

Empirical Evidence

While the results are not uniform, empirical inquiry has provided substantial support for these theoretical expectations concerning the innovation tendencies of larger and smaller firms. A 2010 review of fifty years of empirical studies identifies several fairly well-established patterns:

(1) R&D expenditures tend to increase proportionately with firm size.
(2) R&D productivity tends to decline as firm size increases.
(3) Larger firms tend to allocate R&D resources to incremental and process innovation, rather than "radical" and product innovation.[47]

More specifically, empirical studies on the relationship between firm size and innovation activity generally find that smaller and younger firms have higher levels of R&D productivity and are disproportionately responsible for more dramatic forms of technological innovation,[48] as indicated imperfectly by various indirect measures of innovative output, including number of patents relative to firm size,[49] number of patents and innovations per employee, and number of citations to patents per R&D expenditures.[50] By contrast, with some exceptions, large firms tend to be less efficient sources of product R&D, focus on incremental improvements to existing process and product technologies, and excel in the testing, production, and distribution of products that embody those technologies.[51] Consistent with these tendencies, an empirical study commissioned by the Small Business Administration (SBA) shows that for the period 1984–1997, the mix of larger and smaller high-growth firms changed as a function of a market's focus on upstream R&D or downstream production functions. As industries became more oriented toward R&D and technical functions (as indicated by increased employment of scientists and engineers), the distribution of small, new, and private firms and large, established, and public firms shifted in favor of the former population; as industries became more oriented toward production functions, that same distribution shifted in favor of the latter population.[52] A 2013 study (again commissioned by the SBA) examines innovation activity in a large sample of public and private firms, evaluated as of 2002 and 2007, and finds that smaller and younger firms outperform larger and older firms on various measures of innovative performance. R&D productivity in general declines as a firm ages and grows in size, as measured by the number of product innovations per employee or per sales dollar and the number of patent citations per R&D dollar, per employee, and per sales dollar.[53]

Historical Evidence

The body of empirical evidence concerning certain persistent differences in large-firm and small-firm innovation tendencies is consistent with historical evidence that tends to show a similar pattern. While there are important exceptions (often in the case of large firms that seek to diversify and act as entrants into a new industry),[54] historical studies support the view that large firms typically focus on commercializing inventions through their existing production and distribution infrastructure or refining inventions through incremental R&D. By contrast, smaller firms and individual inventors have often been the source of key innovations that have challenged existing technological designs.

In an exhaustive study of innovation in the petroleum industry during 1909–1943, John Enos found that, with one exception, all major process innovations in the industry had been developed by individual inventors operating outside the laboratories of the major firms.[55] In a historical study of invention principally covering the late nineteenth through mid-twentieth centuries, James Jewkes, David Sawers, and Richard Stillerman identified a large group of inventions that were developed, either fully or partially, by smaller firms or individuals operating outside a corporate entity or research institution (or, if employed by the latter, enjoying autonomy with respect to their research program). Those small firms or individuals then sometimes partnered with a large firm to execute the commercialization process. These inventions cover an impressively wide range of transformative technologies, including the automatic transmission, the ballpoint pen, cellophane, continuous casting of steel, extraction of insulin, the jet engine, the color photograph development process, power steering, magnetic recording, the instant camera, penicillin, various radio transmission technologies (as discussed further in Chapter 5, section 5.1.1), the safety razor, the zipper, and xerography (as discussed further in Chapter 6, section 6.3.1).[56]

In a study published several decades later covering a broader range of industries during 2007–2009, Ashish Arora, Wesley Cohen, and John Walsh reached remarkably similar findings. In a large sample of more than six thousand U.S. manufacturing and service-sector firms, the authors found that small firms represented a source of invention for 13 percent of the sampled firms, even though small firms constituted only 2.5 percent of the total sample. Additionally, among all firms that introduced a new or significantly improved product, 49 percent stated that their most significant innovations had originated from "technology specialists" (a category encompassing universities, consulting firms, and independent inventors). Among these outside sources of invention, technology specialists were in turn responsible for the most commercially valuable inventions and, compared to other sources of invention, were substantially more likely to have patented their invention and transmitted it through licensing or other formal contractual channels.[57] These findings track both theoretical expectations and empirical observations in other contexts that patents facilitate trade in informational assets, which in turn promotes entry by smaller R&D-intensive entities and facilitates the specialization of labor among innovation and commercialization entities along the technology supply chain.

3.2.2 Organizational Flexibility

The organizational case for IP rights would be compelling from a social point of view even if it were construed as a special case for supporting innovation by small firms, individual inventors, and other weakly integrated and R&D-intensive entities that have often been particularly critical in the upstream stages of the innovation process and the most radical types of product innovation. But it is important to recognize that the organizational case for IP has a broader scope of application that covers all types of entities and yields social gains for the innovation ecosystem as a whole, including in many cases large incumbent firms. Under weak- or zero-IP regimes, innovation may continue at robust levels but necessarily retreats to hierarchical entities that can deploy non-IP assets and capacities for "missing" IP rights. Even a successfully adaptive response to a weak-IP environment can give rise to two potential social losses. First, in the most challenging innovation environments in which organizational integration cannot sufficiently substitute for IP rights (as in the pharmaceutical markets or other environments that exhibit both extreme capital requirements and extreme cost differentials between inventors and imitators),[58] the private sector would be compelled to substantially withdraw in favor of some combination of state-based and philanthropic funding structures. Second, and more commonly, even in markets in which there are "adequate" non-IP alternatives, efficiency losses will necessarily arise to the extent that there is no longer any assurance that, at any given point in time, the market has selected the maximally efficient mix of organizational structures for conducting innovation and commercialization activities.

To be clear, the efficiency loss under a weak-IP regime does not derive from the fact that entrepreneurial market structures are universally more conducive to innovation than hierarchical and bureaucratic environments. Rather, the efficiency loss derives from the fact that a weak-IP regime distorts the market's capacity to select among entrepreneurial and hierarchical organizational forms (or, more realistically, some hybrid mix of those forms) and adjust that selection on a continuous basis in response to changes in market conditions. As a result, there remains uncertainty about whether observed levels of integration at any stage of the innovation and commercialization process are the most efficient levels of integration for that particular supply-chain function at that particular time. Under a weak-IP regime, which inherently truncates the available set of transactional options, the outside observer can no longer infer that the market selection of organizational choices reflects the value-maximizing set of institutional arrangements for innovation and commercialization activities.

In particular, weak-IP environments are inherently exposed to the risk of over-integration, which implies that the innovation and commercialization process is being organized at a higher cost than is technologically feasible. Over-integration as an adaptive response to weak-IP regimes can punish all firms, regardless of size or scale, by forcibly substituting internal markets for external markets for technology financing, transfer, and commercialization activities, even in cases where the latter is more efficient than the former. More specifically, compelled integration gives rise to social costs by raising entry costs for smaller and less integrated firms and erecting obstacles to information-exchange transactions from which larger firms could benefit. At congressional hearings held in 1938, the then-president of Bell Labs effectively recognized this possibility, observing that, while AT&T (its parent) placed little value on patents for its own purposes, it still valued patents being issued to smaller firms that could provide new ideas and technologies for acquisition by AT&T.[59] Similar sentiments were expressed at those hearings by Ford's patent counsel, who, while noting that Ford offered nonexclusive, royalty-free patent licenses to all interested parties (suggesting that Ford placed little value on patents), recognized that "the absence of a patent system for the small company and the small inventor would be quite a detriment."[60] He further stated that "there are a larger number of cases where the small company had perfected a very good device" but may be precluded from selling its invention without "some sort of patent protection."[61] Following the same rationale, suppliers of automotive parts and accessories (as distinguished from the automotive manufacturers) testified at those same hearings in support of strong patent protection.[62] These observations closely track the dynamic approach to IP rights, which anticipates that R&D-intensive, upstream suppliers require robust patent protection in order to mitigate the expropriation risk inherent to informational exchanges with larger, sophisticated, and well-resourced downstream producers and distributors.

Illustration: Technology-Intensive Foreign Investments

Even a large integrated firm will incur losses under a weak-IP regime to the extent that it would have selected a lower level of integration at any point on the supply chain to minimize its innovation and commercialization costs. This proposition is illustrated by systematic patterns in the organizational structures used by technology firms that establish R&D, production, distribution, or other operations in foreign countries. When making these investments in a foreign jurisdiction, a firm that holds valuable intellectual capital faces the equivalent of the "make or buy" choice contemplated by the institutional economics literature. In this context, "buy" refers to entering into an arm's-length contractual relationship with a local partner, and "make" refers to establishing a wholly owned local subsidiary for the same purpose. In general, the "buy" choice, which inherently requires some level of information disclosure to a potentially adverse third party, involves a higher level of expropriation risk.

Empirical studies generally find that investing firms tend to operate through the local division of the corporate parent (the "make" option) when transferring technology to jurisdictions with weak IP protections but tend to enter into joint ventures with local third parties (the "buy" option) in jurisdictions with strong IP protections.[63] Everything else being equal, this suggests that firms in weak-IP jurisdictions are operating under less than maximally efficient organizational arrangements that reflect the deficient level of available property-rights protections. This interpretation is supported by the fact that other studies find that firms shift from foreign direct investment to licensing arrangements once a target jurisdiction moves from a weak- to a strong-IP regime.[64] Tellingly, these relationships between IP strength and transactional structure are even clearer in the case of jurisdictions that have strong technical capacities to imitate foreign-supplied technology and therefore pose a higher expropriation risk to the IP owner.[65] Other studies find that firms tend to export to, or manufacture but decline to conduct R&D in, jurisdictions with weak IP rights.[66] Exhibiting a remarkable sensitivity to the applicable level of IP protection, semiconductor and computing firms appear to allocate different functions of the supply chain across jurisdictions as a function of the expropriation risk attendant to each function, reflecting the strength of IP protections in each jurisdiction. In particular, firms typically avoid allocating R&D and design tasks (when informational assets have not yet been embodied in a tangible product and are therefore most vulnerable to expropriation) to jurisdictions with weaker-IP regimes.[67]

These remarkably consistent organizational patterns confirm theoretical expectations that secure IP rights multiply organizational options by enabling information-exchange transactions that would otherwise be inconsistent with business rationality. In weak-IP jurisdictions, investing firms do not allow costly informational assets to escape into the hands of a local business partner; rather, those firms regulate access through vertical integration into the target jurisdiction or, in some cases, withhold the highest-value IP assets altogether. In strong-IP jurisdictions, those same IP owners have the required legal security to engage in transactions with unrelated third parties, expanding the population of firms with which, and the structures through which, the firm can safely transact. Note that a weak-IP regime in this context does not expand the public domain following conventional expectations; rather, access costs to the relevant set of technology inputs counterintuitively *increase* as IP-rich firms are compelled to construct internal capital and informational markets in order to adequately mitigate expropriation risk. A weak-IP regime also limits entry opportunities for local firms, which cannot credibly commit against expropriating the informational assets of the investing firm. While investing firms can at least sometimes use vertical integration as an adequate workaround to enter markets that operate under weak-IP regimes, the limited menu of transactional options raises the prospect that those firms are operating under an adequate, rather than optimal, mix of organizational structures.

3.2.3 Markets for Ideas

Scholarly, judicial, and popular writing often emphasizes the manner in which IP rights inhibit the flow of knowledge, thereby impeding access by end users and innovation by intermediate users. Any such unqualified assertion ignores the counterfactual that absent secure IP rights, the holders of informational goods may no longer find it economically rational to exchange information with third parties (or, at least, third parties that lack a sufficient stock of observable reputational capital) and must therefore rely on integrated organizational structures to execute the commercialization pathway to market release. If that is the case, then restoring IP protection would enhance, rather than depress, informational exchange by enabling firms to execute at least part of the commercialization process through the market, rather than the firm. Specifically, patents and other formal IP rights can act as "property envelopes" that *reduce* the transaction costs of informational exchange, promote the flow of intellectual assets, and mitigate knowledge-related entry barriers, relative to a state of affairs in which patents or other formal IP rights are absent or weaker.

To appreciate this somewhat counterintuitive point, compare the dissemination incentives of a stand-alone R&D-intensive entity that interacts with intermediate users and those of an operational entity that is vertically integrated through the point of sale in the retail market. The upstream entity is an innovation specialist that may maximize revenues by licensing its technology at a reasonable rate to a large population of licensees, thereby maximizing the pool of users from which it can extract a license fee. But this broad licensing strategy may not be the preferred option for an operational entity, which may have strategic incentives to deny access to a patented technology even in the case of a third party that is willing to pay the short-term profit-maximizing license fee. While denial of access results in an immediate loss of licensing revenue in the intermediate-user market, it may nonetheless be a long-term profit-maximizing strategy for an integrated firm to the extent that it limits competitors' entry opportunities and therefore bolsters the firm's pricing power in the end-user market. This contingency is especially likely if the firm has a robust package of complementary assets, in which case it can monetize its R&D investment through sales of products embodying its technology, rather than extracting value from "disembodied" licenses of the underlying technology. Consistent with these expectations, empirical analysis has shown that the availability of patent protection has substantial positive effects on licensing activity only in the case of small firms and entities in which R&D activities are not substantially integrated with downstream commercialization functions.[68]

Illustration: The Sewing-Machine Patent Pool

The divergence in dissemination incentives between stand-alone R&D-intensive entities and vertically integrated firms can be illustrated by the first patent pool, a cross-licensing arrangement established in the nineteenth century to resolve a patent-infringement dispute involving sewing machines.[69] In October 1856, the three leading sewing-machine manufacturers and Elias Howe, the pioneer patentee, resolved the dispute by forming the Sewing Machine Combination, which held nine patents required to manufacture a sewing machine and is widely considered to be the first patent pool. The Combination collected a fee of five dollars per machine from members and fifteen dollars per machine from nonmembers (later reduced to one dollar and seven dollars, respectively, and subsequently, to zero and five dollars)—a material percentage of the average price of sixty-five dollars for a sewing machine.[70] What is interesting for our purposes is that Howe, the individual patent holder, insisted that the pool commit to licensing at least twenty-four firms.[71] Whereas the manufacturers solely sought to enter into a cross-licensing arrangement in order to eliminate litigation risk among themselves, Howe also sought to maximize the licensing revenue that could be earned from the downstream market. Not being an integrated manufacturer, he wished to maximize access to the sewing-machine technology covered by the pool and in that manner cultivate a broad licensee base from which to extract royalty income. By contrast, the manufacturers captured revenues through downstream production and distribution activities and therefore had an interest in limiting access to the underlying technology in order to deter entry by potential competitors.

The sewing-machine patent pool suggests a broader proposition. Rather than stifling the flow of knowledge into the broader market, patents can enable the formation of R&D-specialist entities that earn revenues by disseminating their knowledge assets as widely as possible, subject to payment of a royalty and other valuable consideration. Conversely, the reduction or withdrawal of patent protection favors entities that earn revenues on R&D investment through integrated organizational structures and therefore have few, if any, incentives to disseminate knowledge assets outside the firm's boundaries. In a world without patents, the stand-alone licensing entity (in this case, Howe as the individual inventor) would not be viable, and knowledge assets would be held primarily or entirely by integrated entities (in this case, the sewing-machine manufacturers) that can monetize R&D through non-patent mechanisms. (For example, business historians observe that the Singer Company achieved dominance in the sewing-machine market not due to any patent-protected technological advantage but rather due to the fact that it pioneered the development of installment purchase plans that were attractive to lower-income buyers.)[72] This provides another illustration of the manner in which reducing IP protections can counterintuitively increase access costs (as anticipated theoretically in the "inverted" scenario contemplated in Chapter 1, section 1.2.2). The absence of secure IP rights endangers the viability of R&D-specialist firms that rely on licensing and other contractual relationships to achieve commercialization and implicitly favors firms that adopt vertically integrated structures, thereby limiting access to the upstream pool of technology inputs and increasing entry costs as compared to a more complete property-rights environment.

PART II

HISTORY

Intellectual Property and Organizational Forms

4

Constructing an Objective History of the U.S. Patent System

So far, I have asserted a theoretical relationship between IP strength and organizational choice, as illustrated by selected historical and contemporary examples. In this part (which comprises Chapters 4, 5, and 6), I will assess the explanatory force of this proposition by examining both changes in patent protections (including changes in antitrust law that affect patents) and organizational structures for conducting innovation and commercialization during the period from 1890 (the year in which the Sherman Act was enacted) through 2006. (The period after 2006 through the present will be most directly discussed in Chapter 8.) To determine the extent to which there exists a relationship between IP strength and organizational structure, it is necessary as a first step to identify changes in IP strength over time. Any systematic effort to do so confronts an abundance of potentially relevant features and therefore must settle for reasons of expediency on a limited number of those features. For purposes of the analysis that follows, I define IP strength principally as a function of two broadly defined factors: (i) patentees' expectations of being able to enforce a patent and secure injunctive relief and (ii) patentees' expectations concerning the likelihood that the antitrust laws could be applied to limit licensing freedom (up to and including compulsory licensing).

If IP strength is conceived as a dual function of patent and antitrust law, then, as shown in Figure 4.1, we can identify four potential IP regimes. Regimes I and IV are diametrical opposites: the former sets IP strength at its highest possible level (strong patent, weak antitrust), while the latter sets IP strength at its lowest possible level (weak patent, strong antitrust). Regimes II and III set IP strength at intermediate levels.

Subject to certain qualifications to be discussed, U.S. patent history since 1890 and through 2006 can be divided approximately into three broadly defined periods that alternate between Regimes I and IV, as indicated in Figure 4.1. In summary form, these periods can be described as follows:

(1) *Strong-Patent Period I (1890–mid-1930s).* A strong-patent regime characterized most of the period, although patents were viewed more skeptically by courts during the 1930s.
(2) *Weak-Patent Period (late 1930s–1970s).* A weak-patent regime characterized most of the period. Patent protection was especially weak from the late 1930s through the early 1950s.
(3) *Strong-Patent Period II (1980s–2006).* A strong-patent regime characterized this period. Patent protection was especially strong during 1982–1990.

Innovators, Firms, and Markets. Jonathan M. Barnett, Oxford University Press (2021). © Oxford University Press.
DOI: 10.1093/oso/9780190908591.003.0005

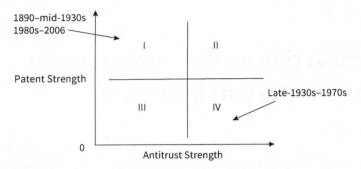

Figure 4.1 Basic typology of U.S. patent regimes (1890–2006)

This tripartite division of U.S. patent history is largely consistent with two existing divisions of U.S. patent history set forth in the leading "Chisum" patent treatise[1] and identified empirically in a comprehensive study by Matthew Henry and John Turner of court decisions in patent-infringement litigation. Each of these broadly defined periods comprises sub-periods that vary in strength with respect to particular elements of patent law—for example, the period since the establishment of the Court of Appeals for the Federal Circuit (the "Federal Circuit") in 1982 subdivides into an especially strong period during 1982–1990 and thereafter a moderately strong period through 2006. As I will discuss in Chapter 8, judicial and legislative changes to patent law since 2006 suggest that we are currently taking steps toward newfound territory—namely, Region III, which combines weak patent law with weak (although, as of this writing, possibly mildly strengthening) antitrust law.

The discussion is structured as follows. First, I will discuss broad historical changes in patent strength—that is, changes in innovators' expectations of being able to enforce a patent and secure injunctive relief against infringing users. Second, I will discuss broad historical changes in patent-related elements of antitrust law, which impact patentees' expected scope of licensing freedom. Together, these two analyses support the proposed tripartite division of U.S. patent history.

4.1 Trends in Patent Strength

It remains to define more precisely what is understood by patent strength. This rubric can encompass a large number of relevant factors, including (among others) validity standards, claim-construction standards, infringement standards, application and maintenance fees, duration, injunctive relief, and monetary damages. As a matter of analytical manageability, it is necessary to select a limited number of factors that are deemed to be most impactful or for which data is most readily available. I focus on three principal factors that correspond to three critical points in a patent-infringement litigation. In particular, I discuss information relevant to actual and prospective patentees' expectations concerning the likelihood of defending patent validity, prevailing on infringement liability, and, in the event those objectives are achieved, securing injunctive relief. With respect to each element, I discuss both qualitative changes in legal doctrine (and related institutional elements) and, where available, quantitative data on legal outcomes. (Concerning data on legal outcomes, I will discuss where applicable the extent to which "selection effects" may limit making inferences about changes in legal standards from litigation outcomes, but taking into account that both theoretical analysis and empirical evidence support the nuanced view that selection effects do not always apply or may sometimes only apply partially.)[2] Expectations concerning each of these key elements of patent-infringement litigation necessarily influence whether a firm that holds a patent can credibly threaten litigation against unauthorized users, which in turn influences whether patents (and patent-enabled transactions) offer an economically attractive strategy for extracting value from innovation, as compared to non-IP-dependent strategies.

4.1.1 The Patent Heyday: 1890 to Mid-1930s

The late nineteenth and early twentieth centuries are generally viewed as a period in which U.S. courts accorded patents a historically strong level of protection. As Zorina Khan and Adam Mossoff have emphasized, this reflected a long-standing approach in U.S. patent law that had generally treated patents as property rights, rather than (as had sometimes been characteristic of the British and other European patent systems) privileges or charters specially granted by the state.[3] In a decision identified by Mossoff as making the first use of the phrase "intellectual property," Justice Levi Woodbury of the Supreme Court wrote in 1845:

> [A] liberal construction is to be given to a patent . . . only in this way can we protect intellectual property, the labors of the mind, [which are] production and interests as much as a man's own, and as much as the fruit of his honest industry, as the wheat he cultivates, or the flocks he rears.[4]

In the historical period that is relevant to this discussion (meaning the period starting with the enactment of the Sherman Act in 1890), this rhetoric continued to translate into robust legal protection for patent owners. The dominant direction of the Court's patent decisions, trends in patent validity rates (that is, the rate at which patents survived challenges to validity in litigation), and the standards used by courts to grant injunctive relief are generally consistent with the customary characterization of this period as a strong-patent regime. However, there were shifts toward weaker protection starting in the 1930s, which anticipates the significant and lasting dilution of patent protection during World War II and several decades thereafter.

Validity Rates

Validity rates during this period are for the most part consistent with a strong-patent regime, with indications of a movement toward patent hostility in the early 1930s. An older study by H. R. Mayers, which covers the years 1891–1957, determined the rate at which the Supreme Court and federal appellate courts upheld or rejected the validity of a patent in infringement litigation.[5] The study suffers from certain limitations insofar as it does not cover the years 1915–1924 and, with respect to appellate court decisions, relies on secondary case reporters (rather than direct examination of court decisions) for the years 1915–1950.[6] With respect to Supreme Court patent litigation, which, as expected, involves a relatively limited number of decisions, the Mayers data shows that during 1892–1899, patentees had a fairly low validity rate (24 percent); however, during 1900–1919, patentees enjoyed fairly high chances of surviving a validity challenge, prevailing 53 percent of the time during 1900–1909 and 62.5 percent of the time during 1910–1919.[7] Thereafter, the validity rate sharply declined: 31.8 percent during 1920–1929 and 15.4 percent during 1930–1939.[8] Aside from important signaling effects, the small number of Supreme Court decisions in each period may not provide a reliable indicator of patent strength. However, appellate litigation, which involved a substantially larger number of decisions, exhibits a similar pattern in validity rates, with the principal difference being a substantially higher rate during the last decade of the nineteenth century. For each five-year period starting in 1891 and ending in 1930 (with the exception of 1915–1924, for which no data is presented), the validity rate fell within a range of 45 to 50.4 percent. The validity rate then declined to 43.9 percent during 1929–1934.[9] Even allowing for some degree of measurement error due to the methodological limitations as noted, the period from 1890 through the 1920s appears to be a time when patentees generally enjoyed a comparatively strong expectation that a patent's validity would be upheld if contested in court and then experienced a downward shift starting in the 1930s. As will be discussed, this decline presaged the weak-IP regime that would prevail during World War II and several decades thereafter.

Injunctive Relief

Defending the presumption of patent validity is only a stepping stone for a patent owner to reach the ultimate goal of injunctive relief. Patent case law in the late nineteenth century generally supported patent owners' expectations that courts would grant this relief as a matter of course so long as a patentee successfully defended validity and demonstrated infringement.[10] Even for purposes of preliminary injunctive relief (at which stage neither validity nor infringement has been established), courts tended to employ standards that were relatively generous toward patent owners. In particular, some courts operated under the presumption that the irreparable injury requirement (a prerequisite for awarding preliminary injunctive relief) was met so long as the plaintiff had merely shown "reasonable cause to believe" that the defendant had infringed upon its patent.[11] While there were limited cases in which a court declined to issue a permanent injunction due to excessive hardship to the defendant or harm to the public interest,[12] these were exceptions that proved the rule. The strength of the presumption favoring injunctions as a remedy for patent infringement can be illustrated by the Court's 1908 decision, *Continental Paper Bag Co. v. Eastern Paper Bag Co.*[13] In that case, the defendant had argued that an injunction should not issue, because the plaintiff was not making use of the patented technology and therefore money damages would be sufficient. The Court rejected this argument, which would have effectively implemented a modified version of a working requirement through remedies principles. (As we will see in Chapter 8, section 8.1.1, courts since 2006 have effectively done just that.) The decision is consistent with the view that courts in the nineteenth and early twentieth centuries tended to view patents as akin to property rights and, as such, contemplated few exceptions to the patentee's right to exclude unauthorized users.

4.1.2 The Patent Winter: Late 1930s to 1970s

The decade of the 1930s marks a transition period from a strong-patent to a weak-patent system, which then persisted through the 1970s. We can gather more precise insight into the extent to which the strength of patent protection declined during this period by assessing evidence concerning patentees' expectations that a court would find a patent valid and infringed and in such a case award injunctive relief. As will be discussed, patent owners had substantially reduced expectations that a court would find a patent valid and infringed, although if a patent owner succeeded in achieving this outcome, it appears that courts still viewed themselves as being bound to award injunctive relief.

Validity Rates

Starting in the 1930s, the Supreme Court bolstered the standards that courts should apply in reviewing the validity of an issued patent. As noted, the Mayers data finds a sharp downward trend in validity rates at the Supreme Court starting in 1920–1929 (31.8 percent being upheld, as compared to 53 percent during 1910–1919), which then persisted during 1930–1939, when only 15.4 percent of contested patents were upheld as valid.[14] The highest court's tendencies toward finding invalidity influenced the lower courts. In a 1935 decision, Judge Learned Hand of the Second Circuit made the following observation concerning the validity of a litigated patent: "We should indeed have no question as to [patent] validity, were it not for the high standard demanded for invention by the decisions of the Supreme Court."[15] As shown in Figure 4.2, this observation is confirmed by the Mayers data on validity determinations in appellate court (excluding Supreme Court) decisions. During 1935–1941 and 1940–1944, a patent's average validity rate in appellate court litigation (32.6 percent and

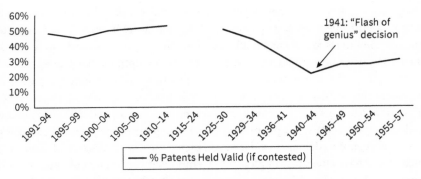

Figure 4.2 Patent validity rates in appellate litigation (1891–1957)
Note: Data missing for 1915–1924.
Source: Reflects average values over four-year periods as reported in Mayers (1959, 35, 52).

21.6 percent, respectively) declined substantially relative to the average validity rate of 48.6 percent during 1891–1934 (again excluding 1915–1924, for which the Mayers study provides no data). This decline in validity rates signaled the onset of the weak-patent regime that would largely persist in the postwar period.

These patent-skeptical decisions culminated in the Supreme Court's 1941 decision in *Cuno Engineering v. Automatic Devices*, which appeared to raise the threshold for patent validity by declaring that patents were limited to inventions that represented a "flash of creative genius, not merely the skill of the calling."[16] There is some doubt about whether the Court intended to adopt a higher validity standard in *Cuno Engineering* or was merely reiterating an 1851 precedent targeted more narrowly at "obviousness" challenges to the patentability of inventions involving combinations of existing elements.[17] As a practical matter, however, the "flash of genius" language was interpreted as the culminating point of recent tendencies in the Court's jurisprudence to raise the standards for adjudicating patent validity. In 1942, a federal judge stated: "We cannot ... ignore the fact that the Supreme Court ... has for a decade or more shown an increasing disposition to raise the standard of originality necessary for a patent."[18] In 1948, the Court itself confirmed this impression, stating: "[S]killful experiments in a laboratory, in cases where the principles of the investigations are well known, and the achievement of the desired end requires routine work rather than imagination, do not involve invention."[19] Those types of decisions motivated Justice Robert Jackson to observe in 1949 that "the only patent that is valid is one which this Court has not been able to get its hands on."[20]

It is sometimes stated that the Patent Act of 1952 rejected the "flash of genius" test and the Court's associated case law that had erected obstacles to defending patent validity. Considerable legislative history supports this view.[21] However, this legislative change did not have the apparently desired effect. Empirical data indicates that the high bar for patent validity largely persisted through the 1970s. While the Mayers data ends in 1957, Henry and Turner have collected more comprehensive data on judicial decisions concerning patent validity in district and appellate courts during 1929–2006.[22] Like the Mayers data, the Henry and Turner data identifies a downturn in validity rates around 1940, and then shows that this downturn persisted for several decades thereafter. Specifically, Henry and Turner find that average validity rates in district courts moved from 64.5 percent during 1929–1938 to 45.8 percent during 1939–1983.[23] Appellate courts reinforced patent skepticism at the district court level, as indicated by the fact that in 1940, the rate at which appeals courts affirmed district court findings of patent invalidity increased from approximately 77 percent to 86 percent.[24] Certain appellate courts took a particularly inhospitable position on patent validity. Another researcher found that validity rates in the Second Circuit fell from 57 percent during 1921–1930, to 36 percent during 1931–1940, to 15 percent during 1941–1950, and then (even after passage of the 1952 Act and apparent rejection of the "flash of genius" test) remained at 18 percent through 1973.[25] By the early 1970s, a former Supreme Court justice appropriately remarked that "judicial nullification of patents and denial of their enforcement are the order of the day."[26]

Win Rates

To prevail in a patent-infringement litigation, a patentee must defend the presumption of validity and show infringement (and, where applicable, defeat equitable defenses that can be raised by infringers). The interaction between validity and infringement findings is reflected in data presented by Henry and Turner on trends in patentees' win rates (meaning a positive finding of validity and infringement) in district and appellate court litigation during this period (but ignoring district court decisions if reversed on appeal). The relationship is somewhat complex. Reflecting the impact of late–New Deal patent and antitrust policy, average win rates declined substantially starting in the late 1930s, falling from 31.1 percent during 1929–1938 to 18.4 percent during 1939–1950; however, the win rate substantially recovered to 28.3 percent during 1950–1983.[27] That is, even though validity rates remained at historically low levels throughout the postwar period, patentees who succeeded in defending validity (typically a threshold issue in patent litigation) became more successful in showing infringement (which may have at least initially reflected the impact of the reaffirmed doctrine of equivalents in the Supreme Court's 1950 decision *Graver Tank & Manufacturing Co. v. Linde Air Products Co.*).[28] The substantial restoration of win rates to pre–New Deal levels during the post-1950 period may reflect selection effects insofar as litigants made filing and settlement decisions in response to the elevated threshold for defending validity (offset to some extent by the somewhat relaxed threshold for showing infringement).[29] The initial prolonged drop in win rates may reflect the fact that litigants did not adapt quickly to the changed infringer-friendly legal standard, either because it was not immediately recognized or because litigants were unsure whether the change would be moderated by some courts. Once this "legal fact" was more fully established and internalized, parties adjusted their litigation and settlement decisions accordingly, restoring the average win rate to the historical range of 28 to 31 percent that prevailed during 1929–1983 (with the exception of the sharp drop during 1939–1950). However, there is some doubt on this point, given the relatively extended drop in win rates from the late New Deal through 1950 (a period of almost fifteen years), in which case there may be other factors that explain why selection effects did not cause win rates to reset within a short period to the approximate historical average.[30]

Injunctive Relief

A key component in assessing the postwar patent regime is the likelihood that patentees could secure injunctive relief following a finding of validity and infringement. On this point, the postwar period made it considerably more difficult to secure preliminary injunctions. Starting in the 1930s, courts adopted more demanding standards for preliminary injunctions, requiring that patentees show validity "beyond all question," rather than (as had previously been the case) merely showing "public acquiescence" to the patent's validity as evidenced by widespread licensing or failure to challenge its validity.[31] Additionally, courts typically declined to find irreparable injury (a prerequisite for a preliminary injunction) unless the patent owner could demonstrate "a permanent loss of market position or sales, that the infringer was insolvent or near insolvency, or that other infringers were likely to enter the market."[32] With respect to permanent injunctive relief, however, it appears that the legal status quo was maintained: as a commentator wrote in 1963, "permanent injunctions continued to be granted as a matter of course."[33] As a practical matter, however, the availability of injunctive relief may have exerted limited deterrent force, given the obstacles faced by patent owners to prevail in the liability stage of any infringement litigation.

4.1.3 The Federal Circuit Reigns: Early 1980s to Mid-2000s

The patent-skeptical environment that characterized the postwar decades was brought to a halt by two key events: (i) enactment of the Bayh-Dole Act in 1980, which enabled academic and other nonprofit recipients of federal funding to seek patents on inventions developed using that funding, and (ii) the establishment of the Federal Circuit in 1982 and the case-law changes the court adopted shortly thereafter. Table 4.1 lists the salient actions that reinvigorated patent protections and marked a clear exit from the postwar weak-patent regime.

Validity Rates

Only two years after being established, the Federal Circuit adopted a "clear and convincing" evidence standard for defeating the statutory presumption of patent validity, thereby rejecting the weaker "preponderance of the evidence" standard that had been adopted by some courts.[34] (In 2011, the Supreme Court affirmed the Federal Circuit's "clear and convincing" standard in *Microsoft Corp. v. i4i Ltd. Partnership*.)[35] The change announced by the Federal Circuit mattered. The Henry and Turner data

Table 4.1 How the patent system was restored (1980–1988)

Year	Event	Effect
1980	Bayh-Dole Act	Enabled small firms and nonprofit institutions that receive federal funding to patent inventions developed with that funding.
1981	*Diamond v. Diehr*	Extended patent protection to certain software applications.
1982	*Diamond v. Chakrabarty*	Extended patent protection to genetically engineered microorganisms.
1982	Federal Courts Improvement Act	Established Court of Appeals for the Federal Circuit as the exclusive appellate court for patent cases.
1983	*Smith Int'l v. Hughes Tool Co.*	Raised the standard for overcoming patent's presumption of validity.
1983	Presidential Memorandum	Extended Bayh-Dole Act to all government contractors.
1985	*Atlas Powder Co. v. Ireco Chemicals*	Relaxed standard for patentee to obtain preliminary injunction.
1986	*Polaroid Corp. v. Eastman Kodak*	Injunction in patent infringement litigation closed large Kodak facility. Largest patent damages award at the time ($901M).
1986	Federal Technology Transfer Act	Extended Bayh-Dole Act to private firms that are recipients of federal R&D funding.
1988	Process Patents Amendment Act	Finished goods made outside the U.S. using a patented process are infringing.

Judicial opinions: For full case citations, see References—Judicial Opinions and Administrative Rulings. *Statutes and other materials:* Patent and Trademark Law Amendments (Bayh-Dole) Act, Pub. L. No. 96-517, 94 Stat. 3015 (1980), codified by 35 U.S.C.S. §§ 200-212 (amended 1984, 2000); Federal Courts Improvement Act of 1982, Pub. L. No. 97-164, 96 Stat. 25 (1982); Presidential Memorandum on Government Patent Policy, 1983, 252 Weekly Compendium Pres. Doc. 19 (Feb. 21, 1983); Federal Technology Transfer Act of 1986, Pub. L. No. 99-502, 100 Stat. 1785 (1986); Process Patents Amendment Act (1988) (enacted as part of the Omnibus Trade and Competitiveness Act of 1988, Pub. L. No. 100-418, 102 Stat. 1107).

shows that the average validity rate in district court litigation jumped to 74.3 percent during 1984–2006, as compared to 45.8 percent during 1939–1983 and 64.5 percent during 1929–1938.[36] Moreover, not only were district courts less prone to find a patent invalid, but when they did so, appeals courts were less likely to uphold a finding of invalidity (56 percent as of 1983, as compared to 86 percent at the height of patent skepticism in 1940).[37] While appellate courts during the postwar period appear to have reinforced patent skepticism at the district court level, appellate courts during the post-1982 period reinforced patent-friendly tendencies at the district court level.

Win Rates

Data on patentees' win rates in district and appellate litigation (again, ignoring district court decisions if reversed on appeal) illustrates a shift toward more robust patent protection in the years immediately following establishment of the Federal Circuit. During 1983–1991, the patentee win rate increased to 48.4 percent, as compared to rates of 18.4 percent for 1939–1950 and 28.3 percent for 1950–1983.[38] After 1991 and through 2006, however, the Federal Circuit's pro-patentee shift as measured by win rates was substantially attenuated, dropping to 29.4 percent, which represents a reversion to the 28 percent rate that had prevailed during 1951–1982 and a substantial reversion to the 31.1 percent rate that had prevailed during 1929–1938.[39] Win rates during the post-1982 period follow a two-step pattern that is symmetrical to the pattern exhibited by win rates during the period starting in the late New Deal and World War II through the 1970s: a sharp adjustment in win rates (upward in the post-1982 period and downward in the late–New Deal and World War II period), followed by a reversion to historical win rates (approximately one-third). As discussed previously with respect to win rates in the postwar period (see section 4.1.2 of this chapter), this pattern is consistent with selection effects,[40] assuming the market takes significant time to recognize and adjust to a legal change, which then resets win rates to historical averages for patent litigation. At first, the market apparently exhibited a lagged response to the patentee-friendly increase in patent strength following establishment of the Federal Circuit, resulting in a significant increase in win rates for a limited but substantial period of time (reflecting the fact that the population of litigated cases had not yet adjusted to the new legal standard). Once the legal change is established and recognized, selection effects "reorder" the population of infringement disputes that are filed and not settled, pushing win rates back approximately to historical levels. As noted, however, there are multiple grounds for doubt concerning this interpretation.[41]

Injunctive Relief

The Federal Circuit moved swiftly to lower the burden of proof required to secure a preliminary injunction. In a 1983 case, it held that irreparable harm, one of the conditions for a preliminary injunction, is presumed once validity and infringement have been "clearly established."[42] As the court noted, this standard represented a departure from the standard adopted previously by many courts that preliminary injunctive relief requires that the plaintiff show that the patent is "beyond question valid and infringed,"[43] obviously a threshold that would be difficult for any plaintiff to meet at an early stage in an infringement litigation. This change represented a return to judicial tendencies, once prevalent in the late nineteenth and early twentieth centuries, to generally presume irreparable injury once validity and infringement had been established (as discussed in section 4.1.1 of this chapter). In a 1987 case, the Federal Circuit reaffirmed this principle and expressed a strong view in favor of preliminary injunctive relief, noting that, without at least a credible risk that a court would grant this remedy, an alleged infringer would have the upper hand in settlement negoti-ations, especially if the patentee's technology applied to a product with a high rate of commercial obsolescence. The court's exact language is worth reproducing to il-lustrate the strong property-rights approach to the patent system adopted by the Federal Circuit, which starkly contrasts with the views expressed by courts during the postwar period (and, as we will see in Chapter 8, contrasts with the views mostly expressed by courts today):

> In matters involving patent rights, irreparable harm has been presumed when a clear showing has been made of patent validity and infringement.... The opportu-nity to practice an invention during the notoriously lengthy course of patent litiga-tion may itself tempt infringers. The nature of the patent grant thus weighs against holding that monetary damages will always suffice to make the patentee whole, for the principal value of a patent is its statutory right to exclude.[44]

Breaking with New Deal Patent Policy

The patent-skeptical heritage of the late New Deal had cast a long shadow that came to an end with the establishment of the Federal Circuit. The newly established appel-late court's early jurisprudence signaled a sharp break from postwar patent policy and a return to the property-like approach that had driven judicial decisions in the late nineteenth and early twentieth centuries. Just as the Supreme Court's patent-skeptical decisions in the 1930s and 1940s had sent a strong signal to lower courts adjudicating patent-infringement litigation, so, too, the Federal Circuit's patent-friendly decisions in the 1980s sent a signal to federal district courts. Concurrently, the Supreme Court endorsed an expansive understanding of patentable subject matter, famously stating in a 1980 decision that the patent laws cover "all things under the sun made by man."[45] This generous definition of the ambit of the patent statute was a far cry from the "flash of ge-nius" test adopted by the Court in 1941, which had reflected precisely the opposite view. The signaling effect of these early judicial rulings is perhaps best illustrated by the land-mark patent litigation brought by Polaroid, the firm that pioneered the instant camera, against Kodak, which, in a classic "fast second" strategy (see Chapter 2, section 2.1.1), had released a competing instant-camera product.[46] In 1986, Polaroid prevailed in the litigation, and the district court issued a devastating remedy: a permanent injunction that shut down a business division with eight hundred employees. In the damages pro-ceedings, Polaroid was awarded $909 million in damages for past infringement, then representing the highest monetary award in patent-infringement litigation.[47] Kodak's loss in the litigation and the court's willingness to issue a "shutdown" injunction against a substantial business operation exerted a demonstration effect on the market, signaling a clear turn in both the Federal Circuit's and the lower courts' attitude toward the patent system. This was now a system in which patent holders had a considerably enhanced expectation of securing an injunction and substantial monetary damages against infringers. That in turn undoubtedly strengthened patent owners' hand in negotiating licensing terms with potential partners in the commercialization process.

4.2 Trends in Antitrust Strength

Antitrust law influences IP strength in both transactional and litigation settings. First, antitrust law places limits on the legally feasible menu of licensing and related transactions (and associated revenue streams) available to a patentee. As antitrust constraints on licensing increase in severity, the universe of legally feasible transactions shrinks, and, everything else being equal, the value of a patent declines. The opposite effect results as those constraints are relaxed. Second, antitrust law impacts a patentee's expected litigation costs and likelihood of success in an infringement claim. Any patentee who contemplates filing an infringement suit must contemplate that the defendant may be able to raise a defense, or file a counterclaim, on antitrust grounds. In a hospitable legal regime, the defendant can credibly threaten a sufficiently high prospect of antitrust liability such that patent enforcement would yield a net expected loss. The result: patentees cannot credibly threaten to sue for infringement and, by anticipation, innovator firms either do not incur the costs of filing for a patent or lack a credible litigation threat when negotiating license terms with third parties. As shown in the following discussion, antitrust constraints on licensing have tended to increase in severity as patent enforceability has tended to decline, thereby compounding the associated decrease in patent values, and vice versa.

4.2.1 Weak Antitrust (Late Nineteenth to Early Twentieth Centuries)

In the years following enactment of the Sherman Act in 1890, the Court made clear its view that antitrust law implies few limitations on licensing or other agreements involving patents or IP rights. In a 1902 case, *E. Bement & Sons v. National Harrow Co.*, the Court upheld a minimum resale price requirement in a patent license agreement, which had been challenged as a violation of the Sherman Act. In its opinion, the Court unambiguously stated its hands-off approach toward patent licensing: "[T]he general rule is absolute freedom in the use or sale of rights under the patent laws of the United States."[48] Going a step further, a prominent appellate court expressed the view that patents were not "articles of commerce" and therefore were entirely outside the scope of the Sherman Act.[49] This laissez-faire approach culminated in the Court's controversial (and closely divided) decision in 1912 in *Henry v. A. B. Dick Co.*[50] The Court upheld use of a tying clause in the lease of a patented mimeograph machine that obligated the user to purchase certain unpatented supplies from the manufacturer of the machine. This was not an "outlier" view. As the Court noted, "[t]he books abound in cases upholding the right of a patentee owner of a machine to license another to use it subject to any qualification in respect of time, place, manner of purpose of use.... This is so elementary we shall not stop to cite cases."[51] *A. B. Dick* effectively applied a rule of per se legality for the terms of any patent license, and as the Court indicated, so, too, had many other courts.[52]

Later in that same term, however, the Court showed preliminary signs that it would more readily scrutinize patent licenses that were challenged either under the antitrust laws or on related grounds of patent misuse (which bars use of a patent beyond the "scope" of the patent grant). In *Standard Sanitary Manufacturing Co. v. U.S.*, the Court rejected any blanket antitrust immunity for patent licenses (specifically distinguishing *Bement* and *A. B. Dick*)[53] and struck down a patent-pooling agreement under Section 1 of the Sherman Act on grounds that it facilitated collusion among competitors.[54] Only two years later, Congress enacted the Clayton Act, which specifically prohibits tying clauses that "substantially lessen competition or tend to create a monopoly."[55] In 1917, the Court ruled in the *Motion Pictures Patents* case[56] that Congress's specific prohibition of tying clauses in the Clayton Act had effectively overruled *A. B. Dick*. It then proceeded to invalidate a tying clause that conditioned the sale of patent-protected film projectors on an agreement to purchase film supplies exclusively from the manufacturer.[57]

The somewhat dramatic reversal of *A. B. Dick* ultimately signaled, however, a fairly modest adjustment of the case law. In *U.S. v. General Electric*, decided in 1926, the Court clarified that its decision in the *Motion Pictures Patents* case had not overruled the *Bement* precedent.[58] Specifically, the Court stated that a patentee may grant a license "upon any condition the performance of which is reasonably within the reward which the patentee by grant of the patent is entitled to secure."[59] Consistent with that moderate approach, some courts continued to uphold contractual restrictions on the use of patented and copyrighted articles under a "reasonableness" standard, so long as the restrictions were made known to subsequent purchasers.[60] The Court applied this deferential notice-based approach in a 1938 decision, *General Talking Pictures Corp. v. Western Electric Co.*,[61] in which it upheld an infringement finding against a firm that had purchased a patented product from a licensee and had knowingly made use of the product outside the authorized field of use in the governing license.

Table 4.2 provides an overview of selected Supreme Court decisions during the late nineteenth and early twentieth centuries that relate to patent licensing. With the exception of the *Standard Sanitary Manufacturing* and *Motion Picture Patents* cases, these decisions upheld the right of patentee-licensors to negotiate terms with prospective licensees subject to few restrictions.

4.2.2 Strong Antitrust: Late 1930s to 1970s

The appointment of Thurman Arnold in 1938 as head of the Antitrust Division launched the start of a vigorous campaign to bolster enforcement of the antitrust laws. From 1938 to 1941, the Antitrust Division's budget tripled, and the number of personnel increased from 111 to 325.[62] The division filed ninety-three lawsuits during Arnold's five-year tenure, slightly fewer than the number that had been filed in the

Table 4.2 Early-twentieth-century Supreme Court rulings on patent licensing (selected)

Year	Decision	Holding
1902	*Bement v. National Harrow Co.*	Upheld resale price maintenance clause in patent license.
1912	*Henry v. A. B. Dick Co.*	Upheld tying clause in patent license.
1912	*Standard Sanitary Manufacturing Co. v. U.S.*	Struck down patent-pooling agreement.
1917	*Motion Picture Patents Co. v. Universal Film Mfg. Co.*	Struck down tying clause in patent license. Overruled *A. B. Dick Co.*
1926	*U.S. v. General Electric*	Upheld resale price maintenance clause in patent license.
1931	*Standard Oil Co. v. U.S.*	Upheld patent-pooling agreement among holders of oil-refining patents.
1938	*General Talking Pictures Corp. v. Western Electric*	Upheld use limitation in a patent license against a third-party purchaser with knowledge.

Source: For full case citations, see References—Judicial Opinions and Administrative Rulings.

forty-eight preceding years since enactment of the Sherman Act.[63] Intensified public enforcement of the antitrust laws led to an increase in private enforcement that lasted throughout the postwar period. From 1945 to 1949, there were 399 private antitrust actions filed; from 1950 to 1954, there were 1,002; from 1965 to 1969, there were more than 3,000.[64] Throughout the postwar period, courts were reluctant to enforce patents, while the antitrust agencies and private plaintiffs were eager to enforce the antitrust laws. Antitrust enforcement sometimes targeted patent-licensing practices and indirectly reduced patent strength by producing precedents that limited the value of patents as a tool by which to extract returns from innovation through licensing and other IP-dependent contractual relationships.

Antitrust Constraints on Patent Licensing

Under Arnold's leadership, the Antitrust Division allocated significant enforcement resources to suits involving allegedly anticompetitive "misuses" of patents in licensing and other transactions. Between December 1939 and February 1945, the Antitrust Division filed fifty-six lawsuits involving antitrust or patent-misuse claims targeting various patent-licensing practices.[65] The courts were hospitable to these claims, and the result was a body of precedent that limited significantly patent owners' licensing freedom, either through the patent-misuse doctrine or the application of per se rules of antitrust liability to licensing practices. The first important win for the Antitrust Division was *Morton Salt Co. v. G. S. Suppiger Co*, [66] decided in 1942. The decision included three key holdings. First, the Court held that patent misuse provided a complete defense to a patent-infringement action. Second, the Court upheld a claim of patent misuse even though the contested licensing practice had not "substantially lessened competition." This holding effectively enabled plaintiffs to contest a patent license even in the absence of sufficient evidence of competitive harm to support a claim under antitrust law. Third, and relatedly, the Court effectively adopted a per se prohibition against use of a patent to enforce contractual ties requiring that the purchaser or lessee of a patented product purchase certain supplies from the patentee-manufacturer. In *U.S. v. Univis Lens Co.*, [67] also decided in 1942, the Court extended the application of per se illegality to resale price floors in patent licenses,[68] an effective reversal of the Court's decision four decades earlier in *Bement*, which had adopted something close to a rule of per se *legality* concerning the same type of clause. In the remainder of the postwar period, courts continued to apply something close to per se liability rules against tying,[69] resale price maintenance,[70] exclusive dealing,[71] and other terms in IP licenses, even absent evidence of market power or anticompetitive effects.[72] This licensor-unfriendly legal climate is often illustrated by a speech in 1972 by a Department of Justice official, in which he listed "Nine No Nos" corresponding to license terms deemed potentially or clearly illegal under the antitrust laws.[73] This interventionist regime bore little resemblance to the legal environment of secure property rights and largely unfettered contractual freedom in which patent licensors and licensees had operated in the late nineteenth and early twentieth centuries.

Patent Expropriation

Concurrently with the launch of Arnold's vigorous antitrust enforcement campaign at the Department of Justice, Congress established the Temporary National Economic Committee (TNEC) in 1938, for the purpose of conducting a comprehensive inquiry into economic concentration and, relatedly, the alleged anticompetitive harms of the patent system. In its final report, issued after extensive hearings during 1938–1941, the TNEC expressed deep skepticism toward the patent system: "In many important segments of our economy the privilege accorded by the patent monopoly has been shamefully abused.... It has been used as a device to control whole industries, to suppress competition, to restrict output, to enhance prices, to suppress inventions and to discourage inventiveness."[74] To address these alleged abuses, the TNEC adopted a proposal, originally put forward by the Roosevelt administration, to mandate licensing of all patents at a "reasonable rate."[75] A subsequent government commission rejected the TNEC's compulsory-licensing recommendation.[76] Aside from targeted compulsory-licensing provisions in the Atomic Energy Act of 1946,[77] the National Aeronautics and Space Act of 1958,[78] and a handful of agency-specific statutes,[79] Congress did not proceed with the proposed amendment to the patent statute. However, as I will describe in the following discussion,[80] the Roosevelt administration's compulsory-licensing proposal was effectively executed in partial but substantial form through a mix of legislative and administrative actions during the postwar period.

Implicit Compulsory Licensing

The first mechanism by which compulsory licensing was effectively carried out was through contractual restrictions attached to government funding of private R&D. Prior to World War II, the U.S. federal government had not invested substantially in funding R&D. During World War II, this historical norm was abandoned. By 1942, as shown in Figure 4.3, the federal government was the largest R&D funding source in the U.S. economy. After the war, the government continued to disburse substantial funds for R&D by private entities, which followed the policy vision famously set forth by Vannevar Bush in 1945 in *The Endless Frontier,* in which he had advocated a central role for the federal government in supporting basic research,[81] a mission that was accelerated with the start of the "Space Race" following the Soviet Union's launch of the Sputnik satellite in 1957. During the postwar period, government R&D funds to the private sector were disbursed in the form of grants and procurement contracts, principally through the Department of Defense (DOD),[82] the Atomic Energy Commission (AEC), and the National Aeronautics and Space Administration (NASA).[83] As shown in Figure 4.3, the government remained the largest source of U.S. R&D funding throughout the postwar period, reaching a peak level of approximately 67 percent in 1964 (as compared to only approximately 14 percent as of 1930).[84]

These gifts, however, came with strings attached that effectively contracted the practical scope of the patent system. Recipients of federal R&D funds were subject to

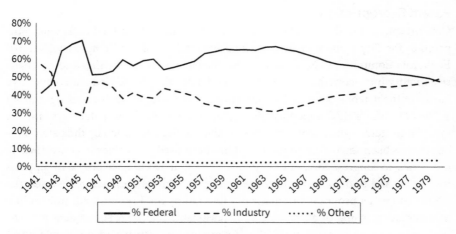

Figure 4.3 U.S. R&D funding sources (1941–1980)

Sources: Author's calculations, based on: for 1953–1980, National Science Foundation, National Center for Science and Engineering Statistics, National Patterns of R&D Resources (annual series); for 1941–1952, U.S. Department of Commerce (1953). Note that data collection and analysis may differ to some extent between these two sources. "Other" refers to non-federal governmental and nonprofit entities. This graph also appears in Barnett (2021).

constraints on patenting inventions developed using those funds, with the severity of those constraints varying across agencies. NASA had the most restrictive policy: it retained ownership of any patents arising out of research that it funded but granted an exclusive or nonexclusive license to the contractor. The AEC adopted a policy that provided for government ownership of patents that related solely to military purposes while, in all other cases, the government retained ownership but granted the contractor a royalty-free, nonexclusive license.[85] The DOD, which represented approximately 90 percent of government R&D funding during much of this period,[86] adopted a more contractor-friendly policy. R&D contractors could elect to patent inventions but were deemed to grant the government a royalty-free, nonexclusive license.[87] The apparent generosity of this approach is, however, misleading. First, the contractor never had exclusivity, given the automatic license to the government (which could then potentially sublicense the technology to, or otherwise share the technology with, suppliers or bidders on other projects). Second, the contractor was limited by law to seeking monetary damages (that is, it could not seek injunctive relief) against entities that infringed upon its patents in connection with a government contract.[88] Third, in some cases, the DOD required that the contractor license its "background" patents (that is, the contractor's already-existing patents relating to the contracted technology) to, or share related technical information with, the government.[89] Lastly, the DOD sometimes required that the contractor provide know-how to another supplier so it could act as a "second source" for the relevant technology.[90]

The logic behind these ownership restrictions was twofold. First, as a matter of principle, it reflected a widespread view that government-funded research should be accessible to all since it had been funded by taxpayer dollars. Second, it reflected the view that granting the government title or a royalty-free license to the relevant technology would enable the government to sublicense the technology to other firms, which would then promote entry into the relevant market. This theory did not match market realities. Licensing activity under postwar statutory mechanisms that provided for compulsory licenses of patents arising out of government-sponsored R&D was low, despite marketing efforts by federal agencies such as NASA and the AEC.[91] Contractors showed little interest in commercializing the results of federally funded R&D, especially in cases where the contractor did not retain title, the contractor was small, or the relevant technology required significant additional investment to achieve commercialization.[92] As of 1980 (just prior to enactment of the Bayh-Dole Act, which enabled federal R&D funding recipients to apply for patents), it is estimated that only 5 percent of federally owned patents were being used.[93] Apparently, the market required a clearer commitment to IP rights in order to divert risk capital to the costly commercialization tasks required to deliver a viable product to market.

Explicit Compulsory Licensing

In 1942, Arnold, as head of the Antitrust Division, had proposed an amendment to the Sherman Act that would have made illegal the use of a patent "which has the effect of unreasonably limiting the supply of any article in interstate commerce" and, as a remedy, would empower the government to cancel a patent that had been used in this manner.[94] While Arnold's proposal (an attenuated version of President Roosevelt's 1938 proposal[95] and TNEC's 1941 recommendation to subject all patents to compulsory licensing)[96] was never adopted by Congress, the antitrust agencies, both during Arnold's tenure as head of the Antitrust Division and in the ensuing postwar decades, partially implemented it through more than one hundred antitrust enforcement actions that subjected large portions of the U.S. patenting landscape to compulsory licensing or forfeiture remedies.[97] The agencies, wielding the threat of treble damages or a dissolution order against litigation targets, typically entered into consent decrees requiring that patentees provide "reasonable" or zero-fee licensing to all interested parties or, in some cases, ordered "dedication" of the patent to the public domain (effectively nullification of the patent). The Supreme Court tentatively and then less reservedly endorsed the practice in 1945 and 1947.[98]

Thereafter, the agencies used the remedy regularly. During 1941–1975, the agencies secured a total of 133 compulsory patent-licensing orders through antitrust enforcement actions, plus one compulsory license in connection with the settlement of an antitrust suit against Alcoa in 1948.[99] According to a report commissioned by a Senate subcommittee, compulsory-licensing orders issued during 1941–1959, the most intensive period of compulsory licensing, affected an estimated forty thousand to fifty thousand patents, representing an estimated 8 percent of all unexpired patents at that time.[100] After 1959, as shown in Figure 4.4, the use of the remedy abated, but consent decrees periodically resulted in significant compulsory-licensing orders (most notably, the compulsory licensing of Xerox's patent portfolio in a 1975 enforcement action).[101]

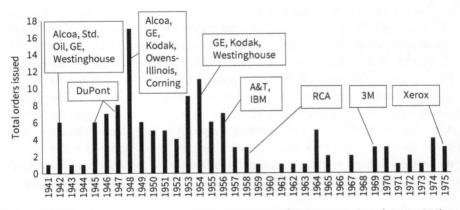

Figure 4.4 Compulsory licensing orders in antitrust enforcement actions (1941–1975)

Source: All information based on review of compulsory licensing orders, available through the Cheetah (formerly IntelliConnect) Antitrust and Competition Law database. This figure also appears in Barnett (2021).

The practical effect of these antitrust remedies was a de facto compulsory-licensing regime that quasi-nationalized large portions of the patent portfolios of some of the country's leading industrial firms, including Alcoa, AT&T, DuPont, General Electric, IBM, RCA, and Westinghouse. Table 4.3 provides more detail on the compulsory-licensing orders issued as part of the agencies' antitrust enforcement actions during 1941–1975. These orders varied in severity, which depended on various characteristics of the license: (i) whether the license imposed a zero royalty (which exacerbates the impact of the license); (ii) whether the licensee was required to enter into a cross-licensing agreement with the licensor (which attenuates the impact of the license); (iii) whether the license covered future patents for a certain period (which exacerbates); and (iv) whether the licensor was required to deliver technical know-how to the licensee together with the patent (which exacerbates). As noted in Table 4.3, a substantial portion of the licenses included features that increased the severity of the order, such as a royalty-free requirement, application to future patents (for a certain period of time), and a requirement to provide technical know-how together with the license.

These confiscatory remedies were consistent with then-prevalent academic views that had motivated Arnold's antitrust enforcement strategy and similar policies during the postwar period.[102] Perhaps the most influential academic commentator on this topic, Joe Bain, characterized patents as an "absolute institutional blockade" that protected incumbents from firms that lacked the resources to match incumbents' R&D efforts.[103] Given that view of patents as a potent exclusionary device that perfectly shields incumbents from competitive entry, it then followed that opening up dominant firms' patent portfolios would reduce entry costs, decrease market concentration, and enhance competitive intensity. As we will see, the postwar market declined to conform to these theoretical expectations.

Table 4.3 Characteristics of compulsory-licensing orders (1941–1975)

Characteristics	Incidence (% Total Orders)
Reasonable royalty license	82
Royalty-free license	33.1
Patent dedication	15.8
Applies to future patents	41.4
Requires reciprocal license	10.5
Must provide technical know-how	41.4

Notes: Percentages for royalty-free license, reasonable royalty license, and patent dedication may add up to greater than 100 percent because some orders prescribed different types of licenses for different portions of the defendant's patent portfolio.

Source: All information based on review of compulsory licensing orders, available through the Cheetah (formerly IntelliConnect) Antitrust and Competition Law database. This table appears in modified form in Barnett (2021).

4.2.3 Weak Antitrust: Early 1980s to Present

The "Chicago revolution" in federal antitrust law starting in the late 1970s over-turned key elements of postwar antitrust jurisprudence and, most important for our purposes, rejected or extensively attenuated per se rules of illegality that the courts had applied to a wide range of IP-licensing practices. Commencing with the Court's landmark 1977 decision in *Continental T.V. v. GTE Sylvania*,[104] the federal judi-ciary progressively limited the number of practices to which per se liability could be applied. In *Sylvania*, the Court held that vertical restraints (that is, relationships involving entities at different levels of a supply chain) are subject to the "rule of reason" standard for antitrust liability, so long as those restraints involve non-price terms. This substantially increased the probative burden for antitrust plaintiffs that sought to contest the non-price term of a license between a supplier and a down-stream wholesaler, retailer, or other entity. Under a "rule of reason" analysis, plain-tiffs would be required to show that the licensor enjoyed market power and that the practice caused competitive harm and would also have to counter defendants' argu-ments that the practice generated procompetitive effects that resulted in a net gain for consumer welfare.

Decisions such as *Sylvania* were motivated in part by the argument that courts addressing vertical restraints faced a high risk of making "false positive" errors and accordingly should use a "rule of reason" standard that would enable courts to weigh evidence of procompetitive benefits against anticompetitive harms.[105] The Court applied this principle to remake the antitrust treatment of tying practices in a 1984 case, *Jefferson Parish Hospital District No. 2 v. Hyde*.[106] The Court effectively rejected the existing per se rule against tying—which, in the patent-licensing context, can be dated from the Court's 1942 decision in *Morton Salt Co. v. G. S. Suppiger Co.*[107]—by clarifying that a court could only deem tying an antitrust violation if it found that the defendant exerted pricing power in the tying-product market (typically, the patented product) and the practice had a substantial anticompetitive effect in the tied-product market (typically, the unpatented complementary good). This substantially more demanding standard for imposing liability in turn influenced courts' application of the closely related patent-misuse doctrine to licensing practices. In a 1986 decision, the Federal Circuit observed that economic analysis "questions the rationale behind holding any licensing practice per se anticompetitive."[108] The court further held that any claim of patent misuse must show that the practice "tends to restrain competi-tion unlawfully" and specifically cited the Supreme Court's *Sylvania* decision for the proposition that rules of per se illegality should be limited to clear-cut antitrust vio-lations.[109] In 1988, Congress essentially codified the Federal Circuit's reasoning by requiring that any party that challenges a tying clause in a patent license on grounds of patent misuse must demonstrate that the patentee has market power.[110] In 1992, the Federal Circuit provided additional guidance, stating that field-of-use restric-tions in patent licenses generally do not raise anticompetitive concerns and therefore should be analyzed under the "rule of reason" standard.[111] These decisions limited substantially the extent to which a plaintiff could bring a patent-misuse claim in circumstances in which there was insufficient evidence of competitive harm to support an antitrust claim.

By the 1990s, it was clear that antitrust law, and its close cousin, the patent-misuse doctrine, had shifted back in the direction of the relaxed approach toward patent licensing that had characterized the legal landscape in the late nineteenth and early twentieth centuries. Any party that challenged a license on grounds of patent misuse or under an antitrust cause of action now faced a substantially higher burden to secure a favorable judgment (or even survive summary judgment) and, in virtually all cases, would be compelled to demonstrate market power as a threshold matter. In 1995, this remaking of the antitrust treatment of patent licensing culminated in the release by the antitrust agencies of the "Antitrust Guidelines on the Licensing of Intellectual Property."[112] The guidelines reflected post-*Sylvania* developments in federal case law that had abandoned the postwar period's "per se illegal" treatment of tying, exclusivity clauses, field-of-use, and other common restrictions in IP licenses. In sharp contrast to the New Deal–inspired view of patents as an "absolute blockade" [113] that insulated incumbents from entry threats, the guidelines rejected any presumption that IP rights create market power, affirmed that IP licensing is "generally procompetitive,"[114] and concluded that, "[i]n the vast majority of cases," antitrust scrutiny of licensing agreements should take place under the rule of reason that required evidence of competitive harm.[115] The bottom-line implication was clear: license agreements were no longer an easy target for patent-misuse or related antitrust claims without substantial proof of market power and competitive harm. This shift in antitrust law and policy mitigated substantially the liability cloud over patent-licensing transactions, which now again offered innovators a viable mechanism for extracting value from R&D investments.

4.3 Summary: A History of Patent Strength in the United States (1890–2006)

I have now presented a reasonably complete description of key historical changes in patent strength—understood to include both patent law and elements of antitrust law that impact patent value. Enforcement of patents and patent-related antitrust law move roughly inversely to each other throughout the period from the late nineteenth century through the early twenty-first century. As patent law provided increased protection, antitrust scrutiny of patentees' licensing practices relaxed, and vice versa. This is not fortuitous: a political, legal, and intellectual environment that is skeptical of the social value of patents will be inclined to invalidate patents and attribute anti-competitive effects to patent licenses without substantial inquiry; conversely, an environment that is more sympathetic toward the social value of patents will tend to have the opposite predilections. Those tendencies support the highly approximate division

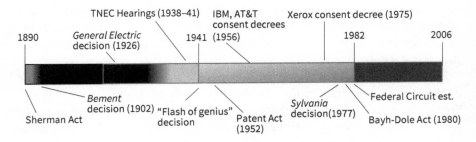

Figure 4.5 An approximate history of patent strength (1890–2006)

Notes: Darker regions approximately indicate stronger patent protection; lighter regions approximately indicate weaker patent protection. Not drawn to scale.

of U.S. patent history in Figure 4.5, which is provided as a visual point of reference. Darker shades indicate higher IP strength; lighter shades indicate weaker IP strength.

This proposed division of U.S. patent history is inherently imperfect insofar as it relies upon a partial set of all legal and other features that can influence the economic value of a patent and, with respect to any particular feature, relies on a limited body of evidence to assess the strength of that feature. However, historical evidence on patenting behavior during this time period provides considerable confidence that the proposed division of U.S. patent history reflects, at a reasonable degree of approximation, actual changes in patent strength. Generally speaking, any shift in patent strength is expected to impact patent value by adjusting innovators' expectations with respect to the likelihood of prevailing in an infringement action, which in turn impacts innovators' expectations that they can monetize R&D value through patent-dependent business strategies. As patent strength increases, innovators anticipate that patents can be enforced more easily and deployed in a greater variety of licensing arrangements; conversely, reductions in patent strength have the opposite effect. Given that proposed relationship, it follows that changes in IP strength should yield predictable changes in the number of patent applications and grants. As courts and agencies reduce patent enforceability, limit patentees' licensing freedom, and consequently enhance expropriation risk, potential patent applicants assign a lower valuation to patents and therefore, everything else being equal, invest fewer resources in patent applications as a strategy by which to earn a return on innovation efforts. Holding constant application fees and examination standards, fewer patents are issued. Subject to the same assumptions, the opposite outcome results when courts and agencies signal increased enforceability, expand patentees' licensing freedom, and consequently reduce expropriation risk.

Historical evidence on patent applications and grants from 1890 through 2006 is consistent with these expectations. As shown in Figure 4.6, the numbers of domestic[116] patent applications and grants (shown in both cases on a per capita basis)[117] largely coincide with the historical movements, as discussed in this chapter, in the selected proxies for aggregate patent strength.

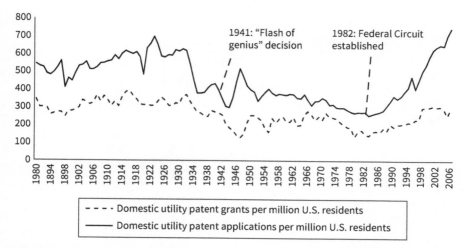

Figure 4.6 Domestic utility patent applications and grants (per capita, 1890–2006)

Notes: Population figures for non-decennial years are estimated. Prior to 1900, the USPTO does not break out data on foreign and domestic patent applications. For that period, the number of domestic utility patent applications is estimated by assuming that the foreign share of utility patent applications is equal to the foreign share of utility patent grants (which is provided by the USPTO for that period). This implicitly assumes that the quality of foreign patent applications is equal to the quality of domestic patent applications and that patent examiners exhibit no bias for or against foreign applicants.

Sources: U.S. Patent and Trademark Office, "U.S. Patent Statistics Chart, Calendar Years 1963–2015" and "U.S. Patent Activity, Calendar Years 1790 to Present"; U.S. Census Bureau.

Notably, the two substantial breaks in patent applications and patent grants coincide closely with, respectively, the two substantial breaks in patent validity rates and the salient judicial decisions or legislative enactments that accompanied those breaks. The proposed start of the weak-patent period during approximately the mid-1930s coincides with a sharp decline in per capita patenting rates, approximately coincident with Supreme Court decisions that had raised the bar for defending patent validity and limited licensing freedom. The proposed start of the strong-patent period is followed shortly thereafter by a significant rise in per capita patenting rates, which occurs concurrently with the establishment of the Federal Circuit in 1982 and the ensuing case-law developments that bolstered protections for patent owners. This provides comfort that the proposed tripartite division of U.S. patent history reflects historical changes in patent strength at a reasonable level of approximation, which, as will be discussed in chapter 5, would be expected to lead to changes in the mix of business strategies adopted by innovators and other firms to extract value from innovation assets.

5

An Organizational History of the U.S. Patent System

In this chapter, I use the proposed tripartite division of U.S. patent history during 1890–2006 as a basis for constructing an organizational history of the U.S. patent system. In doing so, I identify apparent patterns in firms' organizational choices that are consistent in general with the theoretical expectations of the dynamic approach. Specifically, I find that the proposed relationship between three paradigmatic innovation architectures—entrepreneurial, hierarchical, and bureaucratic—and the effective level of patent protection (as impacted by changes in both patent and antitrust law) approximately track structural trends in U.S. technology markets over a period of almost 120 years. Increases in the strength of patent protection coincide approximately with movements from hierarchical and bureaucratic to entrepreneurial innovation architectures; decreases in the strength of patent protection coincide approximately with movements in the opposite direction. To be clear, I do not assert any definitive causal relationship and recognize that other contributing factors influence these structural changes and further empirical work is required to more precisely understand the extent to which IP strength influences organizational choice and market structure in any particular industry or period. Nonetheless, the evidence is highly suggestive over a significant time period and largely consistent with the proposed relationship between IP strength and organizational forms.

The strongest evidence for these proposed relationships is provided by the structural commonalities between the manner in which innovation and commercialization were organized in the late nineteenth and early twentieth centuries, on the one hand, and the late twentieth and early twenty-first centuries, on the other hand. In both time periods, a strong-patent/weak-antitrust regime prevailed, and substantial innovation activity took place in R&D-specialist entities that relied on contractual arrangements with outside investors and other business partners to commercialize and monetize R&D assets. In distinct contrast, during the four decades of a weak-patent/strong-antitrust regime that prevailed from the late New Deal through the 1970s, robust R&D activity persisted for a substantial portion of that period but principally took place in the corporate laboratories of large incumbents with substantial market shares. Additionally, the postwar innovation economy was substantially supported by extensive government funding and faltered once that funding was reduced from its peak in the mid-1960s.

This distinct pattern in the interaction between property-rights strength and organizational structure conforms to the theoretical expectations of the dynamic

Innovators, Firms, and Markets. Jonathan M. Barnett, Oxford University Press (2021). © Oxford University Press.
DOI: 10.1093/oso/9780190908591.003.0006

approach to IP analysis. In periods during which IP strength decreases, innovation shifts toward hierarchical entities that can use scale and scope to capture returns on innovation and partially "bureaucratized" entities that rely on tax-funded transfers to fund R&D. As IP strength increases, transactional choice is restored, and innovators can migrate toward entrepreneurial entities that specialize in R&D and use contractual relationships to execute the commercialization process. Even in cases in which substantial changes in IP strength do not yield substantial differences in total innovation activity, those changes may elicit substantial differences in the organizational structures used to conduct innovation. Those structural effects reflect changes in the viability of different organizational forms as a function of different levels of IP strength.

This relationship between IP rights and organizational form has a normative implication. Even absent any significant decline in total innovation efforts, weak IP rights run the risk of distorting the allocation of innovation capital across firm types, resulting in a skew toward entities that are larger, more integrated, and more established. In turn, this may distort the types of innovation projects that are undertaken, with a skew toward incremental and process innovation (typically favored by larger firms) over more "radical" forms of product innovation (typically favored by smaller firms). Far from lowering entry costs, expanding access, and increasing competitive intensity, diluting or withdrawing IP rights can generate an innovation environment that advantages large incumbents that enjoy the easiest access to non-IP alternatives that can correct for "missing" IP coverage. The result is an implicit barrier to entry by smaller, less integrated, and R&D-intensive firms that are often the most fertile sources of innovation that challenges, rather than merely improves, existing technologies.

5.1 Strong Patents, Weak Antitrust, and the Inventor-Entrepreneur

Economic historians (in particular, Zorina Khan, Naomi Lamoureaux, and Kenneth Sokoloff)[1] have amassed a body of scholarship that documents in great detail the economic effects of strong enforcement of U.S. patents during the mid- to late nineteenth century and the early twentieth century. Those historical studies, which have been insufficiently integrated into the legal academic literature as well as the broader economics literature on patent policy, show that a judicial track record of reliable patent enforcement supplied a credible property-rights infrastructure that fostered the emergence of an independent class of individual inventors. If short on necessary internal capital (the almost universal case), inventors often relied on patents to secure financing from outside investors for commercialization purposes or to extract value through patent assignments and licenses to third parties. Courts' treatment of patents as secure property rights had two positive effects: (i) it induced investors to provide capital to inventors, who then used those funds for product development and commercialization activities, and (ii) it enabled inventors to negotiate licensing relationships with downstream manufacturers and other business partners. A strong-IP regime supplied the necessary legal input for enabling innovation by inventor-founded, R&D-focused entities (in today's parlance, "tech start-ups") with limited internal financing and commercialization capacities. At the same time, a strong-IP regime provided the legal infrastructure for holders of outside capital (in today's parlance, "venture capitalists") to invest in developing and commercializing inventions that had a high risk of technical and commercial failure. In short, IP rights supplied the "glue" that connected idea-rich innovators with capital-rich investors, which in turn enabled innovation to take place in entrepreneurial forms outside the organizational framework of a large incumbent or a state-supported research entity.

5.1.1 The Individual Inventor

From the point of view of industrial organization, the popular history of the American individual inventor of the nineteenth century can be reconstrued as an organizational history of the manner in which robustly enforced patents supported the formation of R&D-intensive entities that could monetize innovation without an end-to-end production and distribution pathway to market. Under a secure patent umbrella, an entrepreneur-innovator can extract value through either (i) patent licenses or assignments to other entities that can more efficiently execute the commercialization process or (ii) financing arrangements with outside investors willing to fund forward integration through some portion of the commercialization sequence. Without a property right, the innovator is unable to execute either of those commercialization pathways and, working backward, must either decline to invest in R&D or seek employment with a large integrated incumbent.

Illustration: The Pioneers of Radio Technology

The critical role played by the patent system in enabling individual inventors to extract a return on their innovations, and thereby incentivize those individuals to invest efforts in R&D outside an employment relationship with a large entity, can be illustrated by the lead role played by individual inventors in the founding years of the radio-communications industry during the early twentieth century.[2] The patent system provided a property-rights infrastructure that enabled markets to form around technological innovations in radio communications. As shown in Table 5.1, the lead inventors (of which only a selected number are shown) universally patented their inventions, which in turn enabled the inventor to monetize his invention through a corporate vehicle backed by outside investors or by "exiting" through a technology transfer to a larger firm. Among these lead inventors, only Guglielmo Marconi succeeded in creating a successful integrated firm (the leader in wireless telegraphy in the United States and the United Kingdom in the early twentieth century), which relied on a patent portfolio accumulated through internal R&D and the

Table 5.1 Leading independent inventors in early radio technology

Date of invention (est.)	Inventor	Principal invention(s)	Patented invention(s)?	Sought to independently commercialize invention(s)?	Licensed or transferred invention(s) (incl. corporate acquisition)?
1896	Marconi	Wireless telegraphy	Yes	Yes	No
1901	Fessenden	Heterodyne circuit	Yes	Yes	Yes (various manufacturers, starting 1917)
1906	De Forest	Triode valve ("Audion")	Yes	Yes	Yes (AT&T, 1917)
1913	Armstrong	Feedback (or "regenerative") circuit	Yes	No	Yes (Westinghouse, 1920; RCA, 1922)
1918	Armstrong	Super-heterodyne circuit	Yes	No	Yes (Westinghouse, 1920; RCA, 1922)
1922	Hazeltine	Neutrodyne circuit	Yes	No	Yes (Independent Radio Manufacturers Assoc., 1923)
1930	Armstrong	Frequency modulation (FM radio)	Yes	No	Yes (various radio manufacturers, starting 1937)

Notes: Dates are approximate. The Marconi corporate group ultimately sold its U.S. operations to Radio Communications of America in 1919; however, this was done under U.S. government pressure in connection with World War I (Maclaurin 1949, 99–104). Hence the table indicates that Marconi's invention was not (voluntarily) transferred.

Sources: Archer (1938, 67–121); Barnett (2015, 172–182); Frost (2010, 62–63); Maclaurin (1949, 31–131); Sterling (2011, 9–12, 95–96, 137–39); Sterling and Keith (2008, 17–20, 23, 55).

acquisition of patents from independent inventors. In other cases, the inventor initially sought to commercialize the invention independently with outside financing and then subsequently licensed or sold the invention to one of the handful of large hardware manufacturers (AT&T, GE, RCA, and Westinghouse). In other cases (such as Edwin Armstrong's development of FM radio), the inventor monetized the innovation through broad nonexclusive licensing to all interested producers. In all these cases, however, an individual inventor operating in a small-firm environment was the source of the foundational innovation, which was then often refined and commercialized by the major producers of communications equipment. Consistent with this general tendency, a history of FM radio technology observes that the large equipment manufacturers "contributed little to FM's core technologies ... though GE and later Zenith helped to both improve and promote them."[3]

It is no accident that patents were universally used by these leading entrepreneur-inventors in the early years of radio communications. Without a patent, the inventor would have been powerless against imitation by large incumbents, which lagged in innovation but far outperformed in production and distribution capacities. (Even with a patent, Armstrong, the inventor of FM radio, was largely powerless to extract royalty payments from RCA, which successfully dragged out an extended infringement litigation with Armstrong under the weak-patent regime that prevailed in the 1940s.)[4] For the same reason, an inventor who lacked a robust patent portfolio could not plausibly expect to attract the risk capital required to bring a nascent technology to a stage of development that was suitable for being licensed or transferred to downstream intermediate users. The leading contemporary history of invention in the radio industry underscores the critical relationship between a secure patent regime, entrepreneurial invention, and the ability to attract investment capital for purposes of commercialization:

> It was the era of the individual inventor; and wealthy businessmen in the United States were surprisingly willing to finance the research of talented inventors.... The American courts were particularly generous in their interpretation of the patent rights of inventors, and the rewards for backing an Edison or a Graham Bell had proved spectacular.[5]

Beyond Radio: The Emergence of the Inventor-Entrepreneur

The radio-communications industry is broadly representative of the process by which invention—in particular, product innovation—was often funded and commercialized during the late nineteenth and early twentieth centuries. Systematic inquiry by economic historians supports this view. Specifically, empirical research shows that individual inventors in the late nineteenth and early twentieth centuries were typically reliant on an active market for selling and licensing patents as a means by which to extract returns on their innovation activities. In a study of 409 "great inventors" who were born before 1886 and were active in the United States, Khan and Sokoloff found that approximately half of them assigned or licensed patents to their inventions.

Additionally, they found that assignment and licensing activities were engaged in most actively by inventors with only primary schooling (which is understood to suggest that these inventors were more financially sensitive and therefore chose not to raise the more significant capital required to undertake forward integration into manufacturing and other downstream functions).[6] In other work, Lamoureaux and Sokoloff used patenting and other data to identify the emergence, during the period 1870–1911, of a population of career inventors who were repeatedly issued patents and frequently engaged in sale and licensing transactions involving patents. Starting around the turn of the century, it became more common for inventors to assign away all their patents to a firm at the time the patent was issued. However, these assignees tended to be firms in which the inventor was a principal or officer, suggesting that the inventor had formed a corporation to own his patents, rather than doing so individually, after which he could elect to license the patents to other entities or independently commercialize the technology.[7]

The classic historical figure of the individual inventor rested on a critical set of institutional inputs. The availability of a market in patents, supported by a reliable legal infrastructure for enforcing those rights, enabled innovative individuals, whether acting individually or through a corporate entity, to earn a livelihood by developing technologies that could be sold or assigned on the open market or commercialized independently by the inventor. Under either business model, patents operated as a mechanism by which individual and small-firm innovators could act as entrepreneurs and earn a return on their R&D efforts outside the boundaries of a large-firm or state-supported entity.

5.1.2 Small Firm/Large Firm Symbiosis

The centrality of the inventor-entrepreneur shifted starting in the early twentieth century, at which time a substantial portion of innovation activity began to move into the hierarchical setting of the corporate research laboratory. Starting in the early twentieth century, leading manufacturing and technology-related firms founded significant research laboratories: General Electric (1900), DuPont (1903), Westinghouse (1906), Bell Telephone (1907), Corning (1908), Eastman Kodak (1912), and Alcoa (1919).[8] The percentage of research personnel employed by the largest firms increased substantially throughout this period: as of 1933, 10 percent of all private research laboratories employed 47.7 percent of all research personnel.[9] While individual and small-firm innovators waned in centrality from a quantitative perspective, they continued to serve an important function from a qualitative perspective as a critical source of R&D inputs in the country's innovation ecosystem. Small firms remained an important source of innovation, as reflected both on the input side by R&D intensity and on the output side by patenting activity.[10] Outside the chemicals industry, the research-employment intensity of small firms (research personnel as a percentage of a firm's total personnel) exceeded that of the largest two hundred manufacturing firms in the United States during 1921–1946. Even the chemicals industry (an especially research-intensive sector) exhibited an increasing rate of research-employment intensity on the part of smaller firms relative to larger firms during this period.[11]

The result in the later years of the first strong-patent regime was a bifurcated market consisting of significant innovation activity by both large industrial laboratories and small technology firms. This was a symbiotic relationship: large firms regularly acquired technologies from outside inventors (and regularly surveyed the outside market for promising inventors),[12] thereby exchanging large firms' advantages in process innovation and scale production for small firms' advantages in product innovation. Leading U.S. firms in technology-intensive markets relied on outside firms as a key source of innovation. An empirical historical study finds that, based on data as of 1921 and 1927, independently acquired inventions accounted for approximately 20 percent of General Electric's patented inventions and were of high average quality (based on citation measures).[13] In the communications industry, the American Bell Telephone Company (a predecessor to AT&T) regularly acquired novel technologies from outside inventors and then developed incremental improvements that were necessary to implement those technologies on an efficient scale.[14] Similarly, a study of innovation by DuPont found that among the twenty-five inventions that accounted for 45 percent of the firm's total sales in 1948, ten had been developed internally, while the remainder had been acquired from, or developed through a joint venture with, an outside innovator.[15] Hence, even as innovation in the aggregate migrated toward corporate research laboratories, the market for ideas continued to operate and did so on the basis of a reasonably secure patent system that could be used to regulate information flows from small-firm innovators to larger production and distribution entities. Both hierarchical and entrepreneurial innovation structures coexisted, a state of affairs that is compatible with, and facilitated by, a strong-IP regime that supports market selection across the full spectrum of organizational structures.

Illustration: Universal Oil Products

Some upstream R&D-focused firms used the patent system as a mechanism for transferring technology not to a single corporate acquirer in a one-off sale transaction but to a pool of downstream firms through an ongoing stream of licensing transactions. This structure delivered remuneration to the upstream innovator entity for its research efforts, incentivized it to undertake future research, and promoted broad access to its technological output in the producer market. Universal Oil Products (UOP), an R&D-specialist firm that was active in licensing production processes to the petroleum industry during the first half of the twentieth century,[16] operated under this business model. UOP owned a valuable patent portfolio that covered a fundamental innovation known as the Dubbs process, which enabled petroleum to be refined as efficiently or more efficiently relative to existing technologies, in par-ticular the Burton process owned by Indiana Standard, a dominant incumbent in the refining market. UOP licensed the Dubbs process widely, together with know-how and technical assistance.[17] Refiners were eager to license the Dubbs process because it countered Indiana Standard's cost advantage due to the Burton process, which Indiana Standard refused to license in markets in which it operated. Interest in licensing the Dubbs process was especially strong among smaller refiners that lacked R&D capacities and otherwise struggled to replicate the process efficiencies of larger firms. As an integrated entity active in the downstream market, Indiana Standard had no incentive to share its technology with direct competitors in the geographic regions in which it operated. By contrast, as an unintegrated R&D specialist, UOP had every incentive to license widely and at reasonable rates in order to maximize its royalty income.[18] (Note that this is the same "low rate, broad base" licensing policy pursued by the lead patent owner in the sewing-machine industry in the nineteenth century, as discussed previously in Chapter 3, section 3.2.3.) In UOP's case, the patent system enabled entry by both an R&D specialist in the upstream portion of the market and, and as an indirect consequence, smaller production specialists in the downstream portion of the market.

5.2 Weak Patents, Strong Antitrust, and Innovation Oligopolies

Starting in the 1930s, the winds of change started blowing from the Supreme Court. As described previously (see Chapter 4, sections 4.1.2 and 4.2.2), the Court issued an increasing number of decisions in which it invalidated patents or limited pat-entees' licensing options, while the antitrust agencies launched an enforcement strategy that would ultimately result in compulsory-licensing orders against some of the country's largest firms. The conventional approach to IP rights anticipates that the weak-patent and strong-antitrust regime that prevailed during the late–New Deal and postwar period should have resulted in a decline in innovation activity, given reduced profit expectations in the absence of secure IP rights. The dy-namic approach to IP analysis has a more nuanced set of expectations. Specifically, it anticipates that (i) firms would respond to the weakening of formal IP rights by adopting alternative non-IP mechanisms for extracting returns on innovation, (ii) R&D investment would therefore not necessarily vary substantially under a weak-patent regime, but (iii) the organizational structures used to carry out innovation and commercialization activities would potentially change significantly. In partic-ular, the dynamic approach anticipates that under a prolonged period of weak IP protection, the U.S. innovation market would evolve toward a mix of transactional structures skewed substantially toward hierarchical and bureaucratic entities. These expectations are largely confirmed in the U.S. innovation economy during the postwar period.

5.2.1 Weak Patents, (Mostly) Strong R&D

Figure 5.1 shows the movement of multiple R&D-intensity (R&D expenditures as a percentage of U.S. GDP) measures during 1953–1980.

The results depart to a certain extent from the expectations of a conventional approach to IP rights and the associated assumption that innovation investment depends closely on the strength of formal IP rights. Despite weak patent protection and vigorous patent-related antitrust enforcement, total R&D investment (private- and government-funded R&D) as a percentage of GDP increased substantially in the early part of the period through approximately 1965; thereafter, it exhibited a steady decline. As can be deduced from the timing of the large increase in federal R&D funding, the initial rise in total R&D intensity is primarily attributable to the massive infusion of R&D funds from the federal government as part of the Space Race and related national security initiatives. Government R&D funding surpassed private R&D funding in 1943, reaching its peak on a percentage basis in 1963, and remained the source of a majority of R&D funding through 1977. The reliance of postwar U.S. innovation through the mid-1960s on government funding is further indicated by the fact that once federal R&D intensity fell starting in the mid-1960s, total R&D intensity fell as well.

The initial rise in R&D investment under a weak-patent regime can be reconciled with a conventional approach to IP rights, since that increase can plausibly be attributed in substantial part to external government R&D subsidies (both direct and indirect), while the decline in R&D intensity starting in the mid-1960s can plausibly be attributed to the partial withdrawal of that subsidy. That is, it is plausible to argue that the market would have exhibited a decline in R&D intensity under the postwar weak-IP regime but for the massive infusion of federal R&D funding. However, the

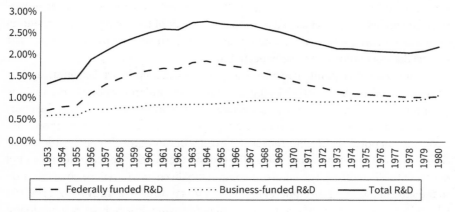

Figure 5.1 U.S. R&D intensities (1953–1980)

Source: National Science Foundation, National Center for Science and Engineering Statistics, National Patterns of R&D Resources (annual series). This figure also appears in Barnett (2021).

conventional approach cannot easily explain the fact that *business* R&D intensity increased moderately throughout this period, within a range of 0.5 to 1 percent of GDP (although not by an amount sufficient to correct for the decline in government funding, which explains the decline in total R&D intensity as that funding declined). A dynamic approach can account for this observation. In response to a weak-patent regime, it would be expected that firms would invest fewer resources in patenting and migrate toward non-IP-dependent mechanisms for extracting returns from innovation. Assuming those alternative mechanisms could be secured at approximately comparable cost by at least some significant group of R&D-capable entities, no material reduction in the total amount of privately funded R&D would be expected to arise absent any other change in relevant economic or other conditions. That outcome is approximately what is observed in Figure 5.1, which shows total and business R&D intensities, and is further consistent with the previously observed decline in per capita patenting during this same period (see Figure 4.6). While there is a significant decline in total R&D intensity during the late 1960s and 1970s (falling from almost 3 to slightly more than 2 percent of GDP), there is no such decline in business R&D intensity (which holds stable at slightly less than 1 percent of GDP), although there is a slowdown in the 1970s that may be associated with generally adverse economic conditions during that decade. Following this interpretation, the decline in patenting during the postwar period does not necessarily indicate a decline in innovation; rather, it principally indicates a shift in the mix of structures used to fund and support innovation.

5.2.2 Weak IP, High Concentration

As discussed previously (see Chapter 4, section 4.2.2), the patent-skeptical policies pursued by both the courts and the antitrust agencies starting in the 1930s were motivated at least in part by the rationale that diluting patent protections would lower barriers for smaller firms that lacked a comparable stock of technology assets, resulting in increased entry, lower concentration, and enhanced competitive intensity.[19] The market did not conform to these expectations.

To illustrate this point, consider the government's antitrust litigation against United Shoe, then the country's leading manufacturer and innovator of shoe-making equipment. After the government prevailed on its monopolization claim, the court issued a compulsory-licensing order with respect to the company's four-thousand-strong patent portfolio in 1953, renewed the order in 1965, and ultimately ordered the dissolution of the company in 1968 on the ground that market concentration had not decreased sufficiently.[20] The failure of compulsory licensing to relieve concentration in the shoe manufacturing equipment industry was typical. In a study of industries in which firms were subject to compulsory patent licensing orders, F. M. Scherer found no evidence that the orders had any statistically significant effect on concentration levels.[21] More generally, the postwar period's weak-IP regime coincided throughout with high concentration levels. Multiple empirical studies, using different measures of concentration, different samples of firms, and slightly different time periods, have found that concentration increased or remained at high levels throughout the postwar decades.[22] These findings are further consistent with other evidence showing that during the 1950s and 1960s, turnover in the Fortune 500 rankings (which rank firms by revenues) was substantially lower as compared to turnover in the 1970s and especially the 1980s.[23] These trends in industry structure and concentration were aptly summarized by an observation made in 1974:

> [T]he indisputable fact of life is that in many industries production is concentrated in a few hands, [and] has been concentrated in a few hands for many decades.[24]

Persistently high concentration levels and stable market leadership under the postwar weak-patent regime are fully consistent with a dynamic understanding of the effects of a weak-IP regime on organizational choices and market structure. That approach anticipates that weakening patent protection compels firms to migrate toward alternative mechanisms for capturing returns on innovation and, as a result, advantages firms that have the lowest-cost access to those mechanisms. Those mechanisms include certain assets that are most easily accessed by larger, more established, and more integrated firms: among others, internal capital resources; production, marketing, and distribution infrastructure; economies of scale; and accumulated goodwill. In the postwar period, that alternative asset portfolio included access to the government-procurement apparatus, which skewed the allocation of funds, and as a result R&D activity, toward larger firms in the defense, aerospace, and communications industries.[25] Larger firms have an inherent advantage in procuring these funds due to the scale economies and specialization efficiencies that generally characterize lobbying and procurement processes (and, in this particular case, the fact that government defense-related projects often involved capital-intensive and labor-intensive systems technologies that were most efficiently undertaken by larger enterprises). This is reflected in part by the fact that 92 percent of all government defense-related procurement expenditures on electronics and communications during 1955–1960 flowed to large firms.[26]

Given the differential entity-specific costs of accessing these non-IP mechanisms for earning returns on R&D (including the lobbying investment required to secure capital from the government), the dynamic approach anticipates that weakening patents may have little effect on total R&D investment (assuming at least some firms can adopt cost-competitive non-IP alternatives) but substantial effect on the distribution of R&D activity by advantaging larger and more integrated firms that have lower-cost access to non-IP alternatives. Even if entrepreneurial forms of innovation have difficulty remaining economically viable in the absence of a secure patent regime, hierarchical and bureaucratic forms of innovation persist and even thrive. These expectations are consistent with certain structural characteristics of the postwar innovation economy. Business-funded R&D intensity remained largely stable (and, during some years, moderately increased), but R&D was concentrated among integrated incumbents that enjoyed large market shares and, in defense-related sectors, access to a steady stream of government funding. Contemporary observers reported that industrial R&D had concentrated in the hands of a relatively small population of large vertically integrated firms.[27] National Science Foundation data confirms these observations, showing that private R&D expenditures were heavily skewed toward larger firms. As shown in Figure 5.2, large firms (defined as firms employing more than one thousand persons) consistently accounted for 90 to 95 percent of total non-federal R&D expenditures in the domestic U.S. economy throughout the postwar period.

The concentration of R&D among a relatively small group of large firms was promoted by the flow of federal R&D funds (especially during the earlier part of the postwar period) that, as discussed previously, represented the majority source of national R&D funding throughout the postwar period. This shift toward a semi-bureaucratic innovation architecture—that is, private R&D partially supported by public funds—promoted the concurrent shift toward hierarchical innovation insofar as federal R&D funding was directed substantially toward large firms in the aerospace, communications, and other defense-related industries. During 1946–1962, two-thirds of federal R&D funds flowed to only twenty large firms.[28] In 1951–1953, small firms received only 17 percent of defense procurement funding; in 1956–1950, they received 18 percent.[29] In 1964, a government report observed: "[The] top 300 manufacturing companies which perform 97 percent of all [f]ederally financed research and development in industry, also perform 91 percent of *all* research and development in industry, regardless of the source of funds … [and] 82 percent of industrial research and development, paid for by their own and other non-Federal funds."[30] As shown in Figure 5.2, this extreme skew in the distribution of R&D activity persisted and was even exacerbated during the postwar period: by 1980, R&D expenditures

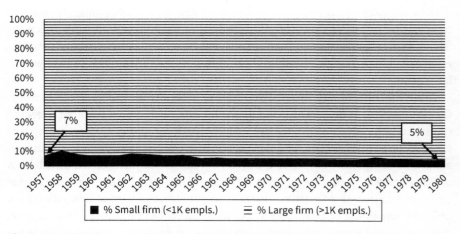

Figure 5.2 U.S. R&D expenditures by firm size (1957–1980, excluding federal funds)
Source: National Science Foundation, "Company and Other (Except Federal) Funds for R&D, by Industry and Size of Company, 1957–98."

by smaller firms as a percentage of total private R&D expenditures (5 percent) had declined relative to 1957 (7 percent).

5.2.3 Weak Patents, Trustified Capitalism

The organizational ecology of the post–New Deal period can be derived in part from the weak-patent and strong-antitrust regime that prevailed during this period. For large integrated firms, the postwar weak-patent regime was a perfectly hospitable, if not strategically preferred, property-rights regime that sheltered and, with federal funding, supported extensive R&D performed by those firms at university-like research facilities. Firms that supported R&D through federal defense funding reportedly did not even regularly seek patent protection, since the funding was delivered under contractual constraints that effectively precluded or challenged the firm from asserting exclusivity over its research output.[31] But there was a social price paid to sustain this "IP lite" innovation model. Firms such as AT&T, DuPont, RCA, and others funded research operations through cash flows generated through dominant market positions protected by a difficult-to-replicate production and distribution infrastructure[32] (and, in defense-related sectors, a skewed allocation of government R&D funding). This suggests that the postwar weak-IP regime advantaged firms that could feasibly construct and maintain internal capital and information markets (supplemented by government subsidy) in lieu of external capital and information markets.[33] By implication, this environment disadvantaged, and may have suppressed entry by, stand-alone R&D entities that rely on contractually based licensing relationships to monetize their R&D investments. The relationship between weak-IP protection, high levels of firm integration, and high market concentration illustrates the fallacy of assuming that a market without IP is free of access constraints. To the contrary, it was the existence of barriers to entry based on incumbents' ample portfolio of non-IP alternatives (including differential access to government funding) that generated the rents necessary to sustain innovation in the absence of robust IP rights.

The Inevitability of Innovation Oligopolies

The link between robust innovation and oligopolistic markets did not go unappreciated. In 1942, Joseph Schumpeter wrote in *Capitalism, Socialism and Democracy*:

> [P]erfectly free entry into a *new* field may make it impossible to enter it at all. The introduction of new methods of production and new commodities is hardly conceivable with perfect—and perfectly prompt—competition from the start ... perfect competition is and always has been temporarily suspended whenever anything new is introduced.[34]

Subject to a handful of dissenters,[35] postwar commentators widely adopted and elaborated upon what came be to known as the Schumpeterian hypothesis, that is, the proposition that large-firm oligopolies had the most robust incentives and capacities to fund R&D, given the combination of high fixed costs and uncaptured knowledge spillovers that would otherwise deter innovation investment.[36] In dramatic language, Kenneth Galbraith wrote in 1952 that "[a] benign Providence ... has made the modern industry of a few large firms an almost perfect instrument for inducing technical change"[37] and again in 1971 that "the entrepreneur no longer exists as an individual person in the mature industrial enterprise."[38] In 1959, an economist stated that "the problem of the small firm consists of its inability to bear the potentially large overhead costs of its own research facilities and workers needed in some types of research,"[39] reflecting the view that large firms were inherently necessary to undertake innovation or, at least, innovation involving substantial fixed costs. More generally, economic historians widely adopted a deterministic narrative according to which the uncoordinated entrepreneurial capitalism of the late nineteenth century had been supplanted by the coordinated oligopolistic capitalism of the postwar period.[40]

This consensus view seemed to have ample empirical support in a postwar economy that exhibited both high levels of market concentration and robust investment in innovation. The university-like research laboratories of dominant firms such as AT&T, DuPont, RCA, and others were rightly credited as fertile sources of technological advancement (although, as discussed previously with respect to AT&T in Chapter 3, section 3.1.2, they may have suffered from certain deficiencies inherent to undertaking and commercializing R&D in large-firm environments that are substantially insulated from competition). Consider IBM, which represented approximately two-thirds of the worldwide computing-hardware market as of 1966.[41] Despite having been subjected to a compulsory-licensing order in 1956, IBM enjoyed a substantial *rise* in the Fortune 500 rankings from number 61 in 1955 to number 9 in 1965, and again number 9 in 1975.[42] IBM's market position was protected by the barriers to entry implied by the financing, technological expertise, and human capital required to launch an integrated computer system of comparable scope, complexity, and capacity. The sums required were gargantuan: IBM invested approximately $5 billion (equivalent to approximately $45 billion in 2019 dollars) in the development and release of its revolutionary System/360 computer system in the mid-1960s.[43] As IBM illustrated, technology markets dominated by a few integrated firms appeared to provide an efficient infrastructure for inducing private industry to bear the costs and risks involved in high-stakes R&D projects. In that environment, patents and other formal IP rights appeared to be a relatively insignificant tool for capturing returns on innovation, compared to the scale economies; production, distribution, and financing infrastructure; and other non-IP mechanisms available to a large firm with a dominant market share.

The Overlooked Costs of Innovation Oligopolies

Postwar economists such as Galbraith applauded the apparently inevitable evolutionary path from entrepreneurial capitalism, in which the individual inventor played a leading role in advancing innovation, to administered capitalism, in which innovation primarily took place within large protected corporations, which were in turn partially subsidized by differential access to government R&D funding and procurement contracts. Yet this laudatory characterization overlooked the fact that Schumpeter's 1942 work—the source of the "Schumpeterian hypothesis"—had observed that organizing innovation within large-firm environments was an *imperfect* solution to the challenge of inducing markets to make R&D investments that were inherently exposed to expropriation by free-riders. Schumpeter recognized that what he called "trustified capitalism"[44] comes at a heavy social price. Namely, the loss of the entrepreneurial function that drives the process of creative destruction in dynamic market economies. Specifically, Schumpeter observed with regret that "[t]he perfectly bureaucratized giant industrial unit not only ousts the small or medium-sized firm and 'expropriates' its owners, but in the end it also ousts the entrepreneur."[45]

This largely overlooked qualification to the Schumpeterian hypothesis narrows considerably the often observed divergence between Schumpeter's 1942 work, *Capitalism, Socialism and Democracy*, in which the large firm primarily drives innovation, with his 1911 work, *The Theory of Economic Development*, in which the individual entrepreneur plays that role. In the earlier work, Schumpeter had expounded at length upon the entrepreneurial function and the challenges it poses to entrenched incumbents, identifying it as the engine behind a dynamic economy engaged in a continuous process of "new combination[s] of means of production."[46] Critically, Schumpeter also placed the *investor* (known as the "capitalist" in early-twentieth-century terminology) at the heart of the innovation ecosystem, given that the entrepreneur-innovator typically relies on risk capital to finance the innovation and commercialization process.[47] In a 1939 publication, Schumpeter clearly set out this connection between innovation and financing: "Capitalism is that form of private property economy in which innovations are carried out by means of borrowed money, which in general, though not by logical necessity, implied credit creation."[48]

Aside from a few passing references,[49] Schumpeter did not to my knowledge address in detail the role of IP rights in the investor-inventor relationship and innovation and commercialization processes. Testifying before the TNEC hearings at almost the same time as Schumpeter's 1942 work appeared in print, the commissioner of the U.S. Patent Office indirectly addressed this point, suggesting that the patent system renders feasible individual invention by spreading the costs and risks among outside investors:

> I think I can present to you indisputable evidence that speculative capital will not back new inventions without the patent protection. And in the final analysis this is the crux and the most important thing in the whole patent question.[50]

More explicitly, it can be argued that a robust patent system can forestall the inevitable triumph of the large firm by enabling entry by vertically disintegrated R&D specialists, who can in turn challenge entrenched incumbents by contracting with third parties for the necessary suite of financing and commercialization inputs. The late–New Dealers who originated the campaign against robust enforcement of patents (and patent licenses) and the postwar policymakers who implemented it most widely did not contemplate this proposition. The TNEC hearings during 1938–1941 and the antitrust enforcement campaign launched by the DOJ under Arnold's leadership at the same time were motivated by the view that patents enabled large incumbents to block entry, impede competition, and preserve market rents. If that is the case, it naturally follows that opening access to incumbents' patent portfolios through compulsory licensing, restraining patentees' licensing capacities through the antitrust laws, and setting a high bar for patent validity would expand entry opportunities and increase competitive intensity.

While this reasoning follows natural intuitions, it runs into an inconvenient fact. While weak-IP/strong-antitrust policies were pursued for several decades from the late New Deal through the 1970s, this period exhibited high market concentration, little turnover in market leadership, and heavy concentration of R&D activity among large firms. The stark discrepancy between theory and evidence suggests that the New Deal and postwar consensus on patent policy suffered from a logical flaw. The dynamic approach to IP rights resolves this puzzle. Removing or weakening IP rights does not necessarily compel firms to open up access to the relevant market; rather, it induces firms to adopt the next-best combination of non-IP alternatives for regulating access and capturing returns on innovation. Those non-IP alternatives are often available at the lowest cost to the largest, most integrated, and most well-established firms. If that is the case, then the late–New Deal and postwar policies to constrain the force of IP rights may have suppressed entry by the firms that those policies purported to assist and entrenched the incumbents that those policies purported to challenge. (This is an empirical analogue to the "inverted" scenario contemplated in the theoretical discussion in Chapter 1, section 1.2.2: reducing IP strength results in increased access costs and reduced IP incentives.) This counterintuitive result can arise to the extent that a weak-IP regime disadvantages entities with more limited access to non-IP alternatives—in particular, entrepreneurial entities that specialize in R&D but lack the means to vertically integrate forward into the commercialization tasks required to reach market. In turn, large integrated firms operate in a sheltered market that is at least partially immunized from the entry threats that might otherwise prompt those firms to undertake more drastic types of innovation projects.

This is an anomalous outcome following the standard incentives/access trade-off and associated conventional approach to IP analysis that equates nominal IP protections with real IP protections. In that framework, reducing formal IP rights should always improve access and open up markets in the short term, which must be balanced against the risk that doing so may unduly depress innovation incentives over the medium to long term. But the anomalous outcome that apparently transpired during a substantial portion of the postwar decades—robust innovation under a weak-IP regime—easily falls within the universe of plausible outcomes following a dynamic framework in which firms respond to reductions in the strength of formal IP rights by adopting non-IP alternatives, which in turn sustains innovation incentives. (I am being somewhat generous in this interpretation of the postwar weak-IP regime, since it supported innovation in substantial part through outside government funding and then faltered once that funding was withdrawn.) Critically, however, different firm types bear significantly different costs in migrating to non-IP alternatives for capturing value from innovation. The absence of strong IP favors firms that can most efficiently adopt IP-like alternatives—in particular, the scale efficiencies, reputational capital, and cost-of-capital advantages that are inherently more available to large established firms. By implication, a weak-IP regime logically suppresses entry by smaller and less integrated firms that can only monetize innovation by transmitting valuable informational assets through contractual relationships with production and distribution partners in the commercialization process. Ironically, weakening IP can strengthen the competitive position of incumbents that can most easily do without it.

5.3 The Patent System Revived

Starting in the early 1980s, several actions reversed the weak enforceability of patents, strict antitrust constraints on patent licensing, and, consequently, the declining per capita patenting rate. As discussed previously, two major legal developments took place during this period. First, the "antitrust revolution," as reflected by judicial decisions starting in the late 1970s and changes in the antitrust agencies' enforcement policies starting in the early 1980s, dramatically reduced the antitrust liability exposure associated with IP licensing (see Chapter 4, section 4.2.3). Second, the "patent revolution," as reflected by enactment of the Bayh-Dole Act in 1980,[51] which enabled recipients of federal research funding to apply for patents on the results of that research, and the establishment in 1982 of the Federal Circuit (see Chapter 4, section 4.1.3), which enhanced patent protection. As a result of decisions by the Federal Circuit shortly after its establishment, patent strength increased considerably, as reflected by a sharp decline in the rate at which courts invalidated patents and an increased readiness among courts to award injunctive remedies and substantial monetary damages against infringers.

The signal to the market from these legal developments was clear: the postwar patent winter had ended. As shown in Figure 5.3 (which is an extended version of Figure 4.6), these legislative and judicial enhancements of patent value were followed by an increase in the number of patent applicants and grants at the USPTO that, after some time lag, restored per capita rates to levels that had not been observed since the early twentieth century. In 1982 (the year in which the Federal Circuit was established), 273 patent applications per million U.S. residents were filed at the USPTO. By 2000, that figure had increased to 584, and by 2005, it exceeded the prior peak of 697 patent applications in 1923. In 1982, the USPTO issued 146 patents per million U.S. residents. By 2000, that figure had increased to 301, and by 2013, it exceeded the prior peak of 394 per capita patent grants in 1916.

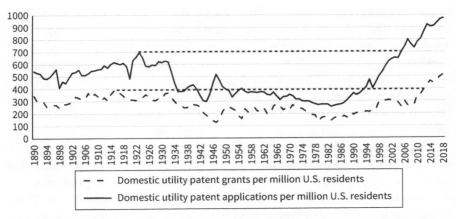

Figure 5.3 Domestic utility patent applications and grants (per capita, 1890–2018)

Notes: Population figures for non-decennial years are estimated or (after 2010) projected. On the calculation of foreign and domestic patent grants during 1890–1899, see note to Figure 4.6.

Sources: U.S. Patent and Trademark Office, "U.S. Patent Statistics Chart, Calendar Years 1963–2015" and "U.S. Patent Activity, Calendar Years 1790 to Present"; U.S. Census Bureau.

Expanded use of the patent system has been accompanied by an architectural shift in U.S. innovation markets consistent with the proposed relationship between patent strength, organizational form, and market structure. Remarkably, substantial portions of the late-twentieth- and early twenty-first-century U.S. innovation economy developed organizational characteristics that bear a strong resemblance to the U.S. innovation economy in the late nineteenth and early twentieth centuries, the last period in which patentees had enjoyed consistently strong levels of protection against infringing users. (Just as remarkably, both periods in turn bear a strong resemblance to the inventor-investor relationships and patent-licensing markets that emerged in Great Britain following the strengthening of the patent system during the mid- to late nineteenth century, as discussed in Chapter 3, section 3.1.1.)

5.3.1 The Decline of Bureaucratic Innovation

Concurrently with the strengthening of patent protection starting in the early 1980s, there has been a shift away from bureaucratic forms of innovation, as illustrated by a sharp decline in the share of total R&D activities financed by the federal government. As shown in Figure 5.4 (which is an extended version of Figure 4.3), federal R&D funding declined from a peak of almost 67 percent of total R&D expenditures in 1964 to less than 25 percent by 2018. Although the decline in federal R&D funding commenced in the mid-1960s and federal R&D funding was first surpassed by business R&D funding in 1979, this trend accelerated starting in the late 1980s and persisted thereafter, aside from a slight increase in the relative share of federal R&D funding

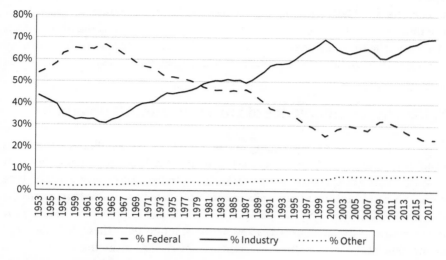

Figure 5.4 U.S. R&D funding sources (1953–2018)

Note: "Other" refers to funding provided by non-federal governmental or nonprofit entities.

Source: National Science Foundation, National Center for Science and Engineering Statistics 2019, National Patterns of R&D Resources 2017–18 Data Update. Data for 2017 and 2018 is preliminary.

during the 2000s. Currently, federal R&D funding constitutes about one-quarter of total U.S. R&D funding, as compared to approximately one-half as of 1980, on the eve of the patent and antitrust "revolutions." Critically, as shown in Figure 5.5 (which is an extended version of Figure 5.1), while the reduction in federal government R&D-funding intensity (federal R&D funding as a percentage of GDP) starting in the mid-1960s was initially accompanied by a decline in total R&D intensity (all R&D funding

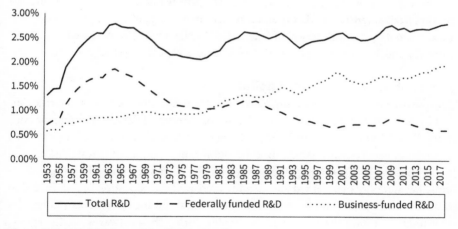

Figure 5.5 U.S. R&D intensities (1953–2018)

Source: National Science Foundation, National Center for Science and Engineering Statistics 2019, National Patterns of R&D Resources 2017–18 Data Update. Data for 2017 and 2018 is preliminary.

as a percentage of GDP), the latter figure recovered starting in the early 1980s. Since that time, total R&D intensity has mostly held constant, increasing slightly on an annual basis due to a concurrent and significant increase in business R&D intensity (business R&D funding as a percentage of total R&D expenditures).

5.3.2 The Re-Emergence of Entrepreneurial Innovation

Concurrently with the strengthening of patent protection (including the relaxation in antitrust scrutiny of IP licensing) starting in the early 1980s, there has been a shift away from hierarchical forms of innovation, as illustrated by the convergence of three developments: (i) increased per capita rates of patent applications and grants, (ii) the rise of venture capital as a principal source of financing for innovation, and (iii) the re-emergence of the small firm as a key source of innovation. These three developments stand at the heart of the entrepreneurial market structure that emerged—or, more precisely, re-emerged—under the strong-patent regime inaugurated in the early 1980s. Not coincidentally, the increase in business R&D intensity occurred concurrently with the growth, starting in the mid-1970s but accelerating starting in the 1990s, of a VC industry to support emerging firms in technology markets. Just as independent sources of capital for individual inventors emerged in the late nineteenth century concurrently with a strong patent system, so, too, the VC industry emerged and grew in the late twentieth century concurrently with the restoration of a strong patent system. Annual investment by VC firms increased from approximately $500 million in 1980 to more than $2.5 billion in 1990 to more than $100 billion in 2000 (during the "Dot Com" boom), falling to approximately $500 million through 2009.[52] As of 2018, VC investment had rebounded and (on a nominal basis) exceeded "Dot Com" levels, reaching almost $131 billion.[53] Through the VC mechanism, internal corporate funding, and other sources, the private market not only filled any gap in total R&D intensity (R&D expenditures as a percentage of GDP) that would have been created by the withdrawal of federal R&D dollars but also increased total R&D intensity and, by 2009, had matched the last historical peak in 1964.

From Public to Private Risk Capital

The postwar innovation economy relied heavily on the allocation of public risk capital by government agencies, either directly or through defense procurement contracts that disproportionately flowed to large incumbents. By contrast, the post-1982 innovation economy is characterized by significant amounts of private risk capital being supplied by VC funds, principally to smaller entrants. Hence, the strong-IP regime has not only maintained and steadily increased the allocation of risk capital to innovation activities but also redirected that capital toward entrepreneurial entities that might not have been economically viable during the postwar weak-IP regime. Remarkably, the VC/start-up model of innovation largely replicates in modern form the "inventor-capitalist" combination that played a critical role in the late nineteenth and early twentieth centuries in the United States (see section 5.1.1 of this chapter) and in the mid-nineteenth century in the United Kingdom (see Chapter 3, section 3.1.1).

It is not accidental that all three periods have been characterized by relatively strong-patent regimes. Patents overcome two transactional hazards that might otherwise impede a VC investment in a promising start-up. First, patents mitigate the initial-stage and mid-stage expropriation risk that might otherwise deter innovators from approaching potential VC investors or disclosing information to a VC investor during the course of their working relationship. While reputational discipline may often deter VCs from acting opportunistically, this may not be effective in all circumstances, and therefore a patent can provide the innovator with a supplemental device for protecting against this risk. Second, patents provide VC investors with at least a partial signal of profit potential that enhances the start-up's ability to secure outside investment at a favorable valuation.[54] This view is well supported by multiple empirical studies showing a correlation between a start-up's patent applications and grants, its valuation by VC investors, and its likelihood of securing VC financing.[55] In one such study, David Hsu and Rosemarie Ziedonis found that a start-up's patent applications have a positive effect on valuation and that this effect is strongest in earlier financing rounds, suggesting that patents alleviate informational asymmetries between investors and innovators.[56] In another study, Josh Lerner found a relationship between patent scope and a start-up's valuation by VC investors, suggesting that the latter may use patent scope as a proxy for a start-up's ability to block imitators following market release of the start-up's product or service.[57] These findings are corroborated by extensive interview evidence in the previously discussed Berkeley study of small-firm patenting practices (see Chapter 2, section 2.2), which describes views among start-up managers that patents facilitate the outside funding process.[58]

From Hierarchical to Entrepreneurial Innovation

It is insightful to compare the years 1966 and 2006, which stand four decades apart and can be used to illustrate the extent to which two dramatically different property-rights regimes yield different types of innovation economies within a relatively short period of time in historical terms. Table 5.2 compares these two reference years based on multiple indicators of innovation performance.

In both years, the U.S. economy exhibits similar levels of total R&D intensity but drastically different percentages of federally funded R&D expenditures, numbers of domestic patent applications on a per capita basis, and the percentage of R&D expenditures attributed to small firms. Based solely on the substantially comparable levels of R&D intensity between these two regimes, it might be concluded that the patent system and the social costs inherent to any IP system are therefore unnecessary to support innovation. Despite substantial differences in per capita patenting rates, which track substantial differences in patent strength, total innovation activity as measured by R&D intensity is largely constant.

Table 5.2 Hierarchical versus entrepreneurial innovation

Indicator	1966	2006
Total R&D intensity	2.71%	2.53%
Federally funded R&D as percent of total R&D funding	63%	28%
Patent applications per 1M U.S. residents	340	743
Small-firm R&D expenditures as percent of total company R&D expenditures	5.36%	23.92%

Note: "Small firms" are defined as firms with less than 1000 employees.

Sources: For total R&D intensity and federally funded R&D as percent of total R&D funding: National Science Foundation, National Center for Science and Engineering Statistics, National Patterns of R&D Resources (annual series); for patent applications per 1M U.S. residents: U.S. Patent and Trademark Office, "U.S. Patent Statistics Chart, Calendar Years 1963–2015," and U.S. Census Bureau; for small-firm R&D expenditures as percent of total company R&D expenditures: National Science Foundation, "Company and Other (Except Federal) Funds for R&D, by Industry and Size of Company, 1957–98"; National Science Foundation/Division of Science Resource Statistics, Industrial Research and Development (Annual Reports, 1999–2007).

That would be an unjustified conclusion in two respects. First, this conclusion ignores the fact that the postwar period's bureaucratic innovation regime relied heavily on federal fund transfers (63 percent of total R&D expenditures in 1966 but only 26 percent in 2006) and therefore gives rise to the social costs inherent to any taxation regime. These costs include not only the burden on the public fisc but the rent-seeking behavior and resource misallocation that are likely to arise once the state, rather than the market, acts as the principal mechanism for supporting and selecting innovation-related activities. Second, and most fundamentally, this conclusion does not address the fact that the two innovation regimes differ in the distribution of innovation activities across entity types. Specifically, the postwar innovation regime was not only bureaucratic but also hierarchical insofar as innovation investment was heavily concentrated among larger firms. During the postwar period, roughly 90 percent of all non-federal expenditures for R&D by the private sector were made by (or paid to) large firms (defined as firms with one thousand employees or more). Starting in the mid- to late 1980s, this long-standing skew in the location of innovation activities was substantially reversed. As shown in Figure 5.6, the share of non-federal expenditures on industry R&D that is represented by small firms (defined as firms with fewer than one thousand employees) grew dramatically from approximately 5 percent in 1980 to 21 percent by 1992, which then increased slightly and reached a peak of approximately 24 percent during 2002–2008 (and moderately declining thereafter to 18 percent as of 2017). Additionally, as shown in Figure 5.7, there was a noticeable increase in the percentage of R&D expenditures constituted by firms having fewer than five thousand employees. These shifts of innovation toward smaller and mid-size firms is consistent with empirical observations that new firms (proxied by firms that had never previously patented) were a major driver behind the general increase in patenting at the USPTO starting in the early 1980s.[59]

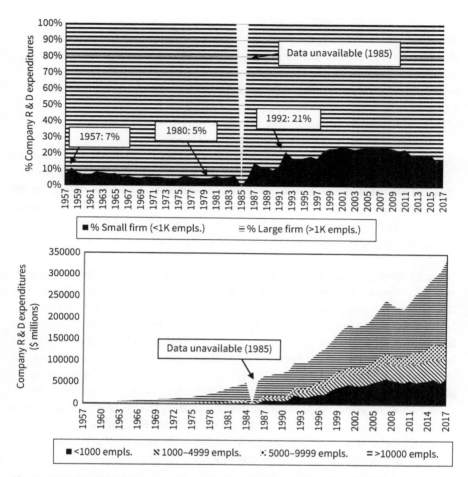

Figures 5.6, 5.7 U.S. R&D expenditures by firm size (1957–2017, excluding federal funds)

Notes: Data was not collected by NSF for 1985. "Company R&D expenditures" refers to all expenditures for R&D performed by companies in the U.S. and funded by all sources except the federal government. Starting in 2008, R&D expenditures are restricted to expenditures paid for by the company.

In Figure 5.7 only, figures are in current dollars. For 1957–1965, the NSF data does not distinguish between firms with "5000–10000 empls." and ">10000 empls." For those years, R&D expenditures were allocated among those categories based on the average percentage allocation among those categories in the five years following 1965.

Sources: National Science Foundation, "Company and Other (Except Federal) Funds for R&D, by Industry and Size of Company, 1957–98"; National Science Foundation, Division of Science Resource Statistics, Research and Development in Industry (Annual Reports, 1999–2007); National Science Foundation, National Center for Science and Engineering Statistics, Business R&D and Innovation (Annual Reports, 2008–2017).

Review

Three key characteristics distinguish the innovation economy that emerged under the post-1982 regime of strong patent protection from the innovation economy that operated under the postwar regime of weak patent protection:

(1) The decline of bureaucratic innovation, as reflected by the roughly inverted mix of federal and private R&D expenditures.

(2) The reduced prominence of hierarchical innovation, as reflected by the substantially decreased share of private R&D expenditures attributable to larger firms.

(3) The rise of entrepreneurial innovation, as reflected by increased per capita patenting rates, the increased share of R&D expenditures attributable to small firms, and the emergence of a VC industry to fund early- and mid-stage firms in technology-intensive markets.

The post-1982 period matches or outperforms the postwar period in terms of total R&D intensity. As shown previously in Figure 5.5, total R&D intensity for the U.S. economy during 1982 through 2017 has been relatively stable, hovering around 2.5 percent, and then increasing starting in the mid-2000s and reaching a peak of 2.82 percent in 2018, the last year for which confirmed data is available. Starting in 1953, the postwar period experienced a steep increase in R&D intensity lasting through 1964, when it peaked at 2.79 percent, and then experienced a steady drop-off through the 1970s, reaching a low of 2.07 percent in 1978. Whereas the postwar period experienced an "R&D boom" during the years of the Space Race (reflecting a dramatic infusion of government funding) and an "R&D bust" in the 1970s (which followed a sharp reduction in government funding), the post-1982 period has maintained a consistently strong level of R&D intensity despite a steady withdrawal of government funding for R&D activities. As such, only the post-1982 strong-IP regime provides a workable model of a mostly autonomous innovation economy that allocates risk capital based primarily on market, rather than political, signals. By reducing reliance on public R&D funding, the post-1982 regime avoided the rent-seeking incentives, fiscal burdens, and, most important, informational limitations inherent to a top-down, politically driven resource-allocation mechanism. Of special importance, the post-1982 strong-patent regime has increased by almost fivefold the percentage allocation of R&D funds to smaller firms, facilitated through the funding mechanism provided by the VC industry. By contrast, the explicit and implicit forms of compulsory licensing that characterized the postwar innovation economy mostly operated to the benefit of the large and protected firms that dominated the computing, communications, and aerospace markets, with the assistance of a steady flow of government funding.

The dominant narrative of the U.S. innovation economy since the establishment of the Federal Circuit has focused on the social losses attributed to the increased litigation, licensing, and other transaction costs associated with the substantial increase in patent applications and issuance. Certainly, increased usage of the patent system introduces certain dispute-resolution and other transaction costs that would not otherwise exist—as would be the case in any formalized system of property rights. Yet it is important to keep in mind the alternative state of affairs. A weak-IP environment gives rise to *other* categories of transaction costs and associated expropriation risks that are inherent to information-intensive relationships involving innovators, investors, and other partners in the commercialization process. Without secure IP rights, those expropriation risks may shift innovation and commercialization activities to the internal capital and information markets maintained by larger and more integrated firms. The hierarchical and semi-bureaucratized architecture of mid-twentieth-century technology markets is consistent with those expectations. When IP rights are strengthened, certain categories of transaction costs increase, but expropriation risk is mitigated and entry becomes economically viable for R&D-specialist firms that rely on contractual relationships with financing and commercialization partners to earn a positive return on innovation. Under a weak-IP regime, all those effects are reversed. The entrepreneurial architecture of late-twentieth- and early-twenty-first-century U.S. technology markets (as well as late-nineteenth- and early-twentieth-century U.S. technology markets), as compared with the hierarchical and semi-bureaucratic architecture of mid-twentieth-century U.S. technology markets, is consistent with those expectations. These architectural shifts matter. In a world with secure IP rights, the research scientist who might otherwise have been a paid employee at Bell Labs can rationally attempt to earn a return on innovation as a VC-backed independent entrepreneur. In chapter 6, I will look more closely at the re-emergence of the innovator-entrepreneur in selected technology markets concurrently with the post-1982 strengthening of the U.S. patent system.

6

Exploding the Supply Chain

Strong Patents and Vertical Disintegration

The tripartite division of U.S. patent history culminates with the restoration of a strong-patent regime, accompanied by a weak-antitrust regime, in the later decades of the twentieth century and continuing at least into the first decade of this century. In this chapter, I examine at a more granular level the manner in which the restoration of a strong U.S. patent regime for approximately two decades starting in the early 1980s likely influenced the organizational structure of key technology markets. In particular, I study three innovation environments that illustrate how a robustly enforced patent system promotes transactional choice and enables entry by R&D-intensive innovator firms into markets that are otherwise dominated by vertically integrated incumbents. These case studies concern (i) the biotechnology market, (ii) the semiconductor market, and (iii) patent-licensing entities in information-technology markets. Each market is a core element of the global knowledge economy and challenges conventional wisdom that presumptively views patents as an entry barrier that shelters incumbents from competition and impedes the circulation of knowledge assets. Intensive patenting in the biotechnology, semiconductor, and certain information-technology markets has been accompanied by a progressive disintegration of supply-chain structures that expands entry opportunities for smaller entities with strong innovation capacities but limited access to the capital and expertise required to establish and maintain an integrated commercialization infrastructure. The result is a virtuous cycle in which upstream R&D-specialist firms and licensing intermediaries transmit patent-protected knowledge assets to downstream firms that specialize in the production and distribution of products and services for end-user markets, which in turn generates revenue flows that support continued investment in upstream R&D that sustains the innovation ecosystem.

6.1 Biotechnology: Integration by Contract

Concurrently with the strengthening of patent protection in the early 1980s, multiple institutional actors in the U.S. patent system took steps to establish a secure property-rights infrastructure for the then-nascent biotechnology industry. In this section, I describe how this legal foundation supported the biotechnology industry's adoption of a vertically disintegrated organizational model for funding and conducting the high-cost, high-risk innovation and commercialization tasks involved in delivering a new biotechnology product to market.

Innovators, Firms, and Markets. Jonathan M. Barnett, Oxford University Press (2021). © Oxford University Press.
DOI: 10.1093/oso/9780190908591.003.0007

6.1.1 The IP Infrastructure for the Biotechnology Industry

The U.S. patent system moved early and fast to provide secure property rights for innovators in the biotechnology industry. On December 2, 1980, the USPTO issued U.S. Patent 4,237,224, "Process for Producing Biologically Functional Molecular Chimeras," to two university scientists, Stanley Cohen and Herbert Boyer, for the recombinant DNA technology that would form the basis for much of the biotechnology industry. In 1982, the Supreme Court upheld the patentability of genetically engineered microorganisms and adopted a broad understanding of patentable subject matter in general.[1] In 1988, the USPTO issued a statement that it considered "non-naturally occurring non-human multicellular living organisms" as patentable subject matter[2] and, on that basis, issued U.S. Patent 4,736,866 for the so-called "Harvard oncomouse" (a mouse that had been genetically altered for purposes of testing anticancer therapies). In 1991, the Federal Circuit upheld the patentability of sufficiently isolated genetic material.[3] Together with the Bayh-Dole Act (enacted in 1980),[4] which lifted restrictions on patenting inventions developed using federal R&D funding, these actions supplied a secure property-rights infrastructure for biotechnological methods and products. By contrast, European jurisdictions exhibited resistance to the extension of patentable subject matter to this field.[5] Even after endorsing patent protection for "biotechnological inventions" in 1998, the European Union still reserved the right of member states to restrict patentability on ethical grounds.[6] It is perhaps no coincidence that the United States pioneered the biotechnology market and continues to represent the majority of biotechnological research and commercial activity.[7]

6.1.2 Patenting Activity in the Biotechnology Industry

From its inception, the biotechnology industry (which encompasses medical treatment, agriculture, and industrial applications across a broad range of product categories) has made intensive use of the patent system to protect and monetize its R&D investments.[8] While researchers have produced varying measures of biotechnology-patenting activity (reflecting the lack of any settled definition of the industry and any straightforward "matching" to USPTO classifications), all such measures observe a largely consistent trend of intensive and growing use of the patent system by innovators in this field. Focusing on medical applications, David Adelman and Kathryn DeAngelis document a steep increase in biotechnology patenting starting in the early 1990s, peaking in 1998, and then moderately declining in the early 2000s.[9] This largely upward trend appears to have continued. In a report that relies on patent classes that reflect a broader definition of the biotechnology industry (as compared to the Adelman and DeAngelis study), the USPTO documents robust growth in biotechnology patenting for the period 2002–2015, reaching a peak grant volume of 12,580 patents in 2015.[10]

6.1.3 The Fallacy of the Biotech Anticommons

The extension of robust patent protection to the biotechnology field was not welcomed by many, if not most, scholarly and policy commentators. Conventional wisdom asserted that high patenting rates in biotechnology and the associated commercialization of science would impede the free-flowing circulation of ideas among researchers who had formerly operated in a zero- or weak-IP regime. An article published in 1998 and thereafter cited 3,439 times (as of August 2020) stated: "[T]he privatization of biomedical research ... promises to spur private investment but risks creating a tragedy of the anticommons through a proliferation of fragmented and overlapping intellectual property rights."[11] However plausible in theory, real-world markets have not conformed to this assertion. The patent-intensive biotechnology market has proven to be a fertile source of treatments derived from academic research that might have remained unexploited in the absence of an effective mechanism by which to establish exclusivity in the marketplace and attract investment capital to support costly and lengthy product development and commercialization activities. Given the low commercialization rates that were observed when federally funded researchers were precluded from seeking patents (see Chapter 4, section 4.2.2), the availability of patents appears to have generated social value by providing a secure pathway through which a start-up can interact with business partners to convert an innovation into a commercially viable product and then shield that product against imitation following market release. In particular, patents have played a critical role in supporting the formation of scientist-founded start-ups, which then typically enter into licensing and other relationships with larger pharmaceutical firms for purposes of executing the testing, production, and distribution tasks required to achieve commercialization. The effects on market entry run counter to the skepticism initially (and, in many cases, still) expressed by scholarly and policy commentators. Between 1976 and 1997, more than 1,100 biotechnology firms entered the market (mostly targeting the human therapeutics segment),[12] as compared to *no* successful entrants in the pharmaceutical industry from 1945 through 1975.[13] Remarkably, as a commentator observed in the early 1990s, "almost every single important invention was done by independent biotechnology companies ... [n]one of the key innovations and developments throughout the [biotechnology] field were made by the large companies."[14]

6.1.4 The Biopharma Alliance Model of Innovation

The biotechnology revolution was both scientific and organizational. As a scientific matter, genetics and molecular-based techniques freed researchers from the chemical-based techniques that required access to the compound libraries that could only feasibly be maintained by large pharmaceutical companies or academic or government research institutes.[15] As an organizational matter, the robust extension of patent protection to biotechnological innovations enabled the secure exchange of valuable information and, as a consequence, provided new firms with the ability to construct a patent-based contractual detour around the entry barrier posed by the exceptionally high capital requirements at the testing, production, and distribution stages of the commercialization process.[16] Historically, the pharmaceutical market had funded and executed each of these steps on the supply chain primarily within vertically integrated enterprises.[17] The biotechnology industry broke up this structure into upstream R&D and downstream testing, production, and distribution components. In the most typical case, a new biotechnology venture is a small scientist-founded enterprise that lacks the capital and expertise necessary to undertake the clinical testing, production, and marketing functions that must be executed to bring a new product to market.[18] Hence, it often, if not usually, secures financing from a VC fund and then enters into a joint venture with a downstream partner with which it exchanges intellectual assets for the regulatory, production, and marketing expertise necessary to execute some or all of the commercialization process.[19] Alliances between biotechnology and pharmaceutical firms grew from an estimated tens of such transactions per year in the early 1980s to an estimated approximately three hundred transactions annually as of 2002.[20]

Figure 6.1 shows a representative "biopharma" supply-chain structure (subject to the disclaimer that particular supply chains may differ in one or more respects).

The figure shows a multipart sequence in which (i) university technology-transfer offices negotiate the outflow of academic research (in many cases, initially funded by a

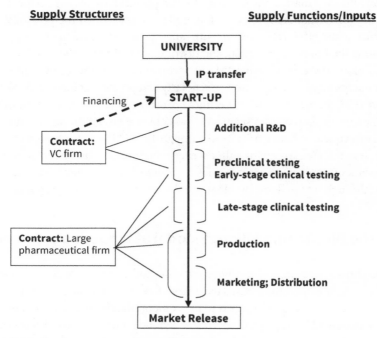

Figure 6.1 Vertical disintegration (biotechnology)

research grant from the federal government) to an independent start-up entity founded by a faculty member, (ii) the start-up bargains with VCs for initial financing, and (iii) the VC-backed start-up bargains with established pharmaceutical (and, more recently, mature biotechnology) firms to fund further R&D and execute the capital-intensive clinical trials, marketing, and distribution functions required to reach market.[21] In a variation on this structure, biotechnology firms sometimes seek funding in the public capital markets after an initial VC investment, which is then followed (if the firm is successful) by a partnership with a downstream pharmaceutical firm.[22] Depending on the relative bargaining power of each party and the stage of development of the biotechnology firm's technology, these "biopharma" alliances can take a variety of more complex forms, in which fewer rights are transferred from the biotechnology firm to its production and distribution partners.[23] In other cases, these arrangements might involve some degree of forward vertical integration by the biotechnology firm into production and distribution or backward vertical integration by the pharma firm into product development.[24]

Patents facilitate information exchange at three critical junctures in the interfirm transactions that are characteristic of the biotechnology market's vertically disintegrated model for executing the innovation and commercialization process:

(1) The transfer of knowledge from the university to the start-up.
(2) The transfer of knowledge from the start-up to a VC firm.
(3) The transfer of knowledge from the start-up to an integrated entity that can act as a commercialization partner.

Without IP protection, each of those knowledge transfers would be fraught with some combination of initial-stage or mid-stage expropriation risk, upstream innovators would likely have difficulty raising sufficient capital to execute the commercialization process, and large integrated pharmaceutical firms would be compelled to integrate backward into upstream research functions.[25] With respect to initial-stage expropriation risk, a patent not only protects the innovator against opportunism by potential VC investors but also can improve the valuation process by permitting the innovator to provide more fulsome disclosure of its technology. That would account for empirical findings that patents increase the likelihood that a biotechnology start-up can secure VC financing[26] and interview evidence that VC firms closely "diligence" a biotechnology start-up's patent portfolio to assess its profit potential.[27] With respect to mid-stage expropriation risk, a patent facilitates the ongoing exchange of knowledge that is inherent to the working relationship between the smaller biotechnology firm and its larger commercialization partner. Finally, with respect to end-stage expropriation risk (which persists even in the case of mature biotech firms that adopt more vertically integrated commercialization structures), a patent plays the well-known function of deterring imitations once the treatment or diagnostic product is launched in the target medical-therapeutic market. These considerations explain why biotechnology start-ups almost universally obtain patents[28] and why patents have been a core element of a biotechnology firm's business model since the inception of the industry.[29]

6.1.5 Illustration: The Genentech/Eli Lilly Alliance

The mechanics of interfirm relationships in the typical life cycle of a biotechnology product and the manner in which IP rights mitigate expropriation risks that might otherwise frustrate efficient information exchange among holders of complementary IP and non-IP assets can be illustrated by examining the transactional structures behind the first commercially released biotechnology product. In 1976, Herbert Boyer, one of the scientists who developed the recombinant-DNA method (on which a patent application was filed in 1974),[30] formed Genentech with VC backing and secured a license from Stanford (the "first-named assignee" of the Cohen-Boyer patent)[31] for purposes of developing synthetic human insulin for the treatment of type 1 diabetes. In 1978, Genentech entered into an agreement with Eli Lilly, a large pharmaceutical firm that agreed to fund Genentech's development of recombinant human insulin in exchange for worldwide production and marketing rights.[32] While Genentech's rights under its license with Stanford were still provisional given that the Cohen-Boyer patent application was still pending at the USPTO, the agreement made explicit reference to those rights (presumably anticipating the contingency in which the patent would ultimately issue, which occurred in 1980).[33] Specifically, the agreement provided that Lilly acquired the right to use certain of Genentech's biological materials and know-how "for the limited purpose of manufacturing, selling and using Recombinant Insulin without regard to Genentech Patent Rights" and further stated that the "Rights granted hereunder shall include the right to practice under any applicable Genentech Patent Right."[34] After FDA regulatory approval (ultimately secured in 1982),[35] Genentech would then be entitled to royalties on Lilly's sales of the product. As suggested by the language of the Genentech-Lilly agreement, Lilly relied to some extent on Genentech's pending patent rights under the license with Stanford (specifically, the expected period of legal exclusivity following market release). Both Lilly and Genentech relied in turn on the ability to enter into a contractual agreement that governed the parties' exchange of Genentech's technology and know-how for Lilly's financing, production, and distribution capacities. Without the security provided by the legal instruments of property rights and contract, Genentech would have faced early-stage and mid-stage expropriation risks in securing and implementing these tailored relationships with larger strategic partners that held the capital and expertise necessary to translate the firm's scientific innovations into technically and commercially viable treatments.

6.1.6 Objection: What about Litigation Costs?

Even granting the enabling function played by patents in promoting biopharma alliances, it may nonetheless be reasonably observed (as the scholarly and policy literature has emphasized) that intensive usage of the patent system imposes litigation-related costs that would not otherwise exist in a weak-IP or zero-IP environment. There are certainly cases in which patent litigation, whether actual or threatened, has had this effect, at least in the short term. The Genentech/Lilly transaction illustrates this concern, since it subsequently gave rise to extensive disputes between Genentech, Lilly, and other parties concerning the synthetic human insulin product.[36] Relatedly, as is true of any other legal entitlement, it is inevitable that some entities will make opportunistic uses of patents for strategic purposes of blocking entry[37] or for financial purposes of extracting settlements that reflect nuisance value rather than any underlying innovative contribution. Even more generally, it could be (and is widely) argued that litigation costs are part of a broader category of dispute-resolution, licensing, and negotiation costs that arise from formal IP rights and, by definition, erect barriers to access that can deter entry by follow-on innovators, resulting in a reduced flow of innovations over time. These reasonable concerns about adverse effects would appear to be especially compelling in the case of "pioneering" patents over fundamental innovations, which could pose a potential roadblock for subsequent innovation in the relevant technological field or industry. Here, too, the Cohen-Boyer patent, which covers a foundational tool in genetic engineering, would appear to provide a concrete illustration of this potential risk.

These observations are entirely reasonable, and any IP policy analysis should take them fully into account. However, they are subject to two important qualifications that are often overlooked.

Only Net Losses Matter

It is critical to keep in mind that transaction costs that are specifically attributable to IP protection only represent a *net* social loss to the extent that these represent costs in excess of the innovation and commercialization gains that would otherwise not been secured in the absence of such protection. Even apparently significant IP-specific litigation and other transaction costs can pale in comparison with the social value that is generated as a result of a secure IP infrastructure that attracts risk capital to innovation activities and supports efficient markets in commercializing and disseminating innovation assets. We can illustrate this point by returning to the previously discussed Marvel "turnaround" transaction (see Chapter 2, section 2.5.3). The costs incurred to negotiate the loan from Merrill Lynch to the distressed Marvel comic-books company and the loan guarantee issued by the third-party insurer that took collateral in Marvel's copyright-protected characters undoubtedly pale in comparison to the billions of dollars in value that were ultimately generated by this infusion of cash, which triggered a sequence of transactions that unlocked the commercial value embedded in Marvel's copyright portfolio. The gains attributable to secure IP rights arise not only from enabling innovators to deter free-riders but also, as is less commonly observed, from enabling the holders of innovation inputs to enter into efficient transactions with the holders of complementary *non*-innovation inputs that are necessary to complete the commercialization process. The Marvel transaction is again illustrative.

Marvel's copyright properties enabled it to induce studios such as Paramount and Universal to invest in the production and distribution of Marvel's first two big-budget motion pictures, an undertaking that only a small number of major studios are equipped to finance and carry out. Without secure IP rights, these transactions would have been economically irrational, both for the investing studios, which would have lacked protection against end-stage expropriation risk following market release, and for Marvel, which would have lacked protection against early-stage and mid-stage expropriation risk in its interactions with sophisticated and well-resourced potential business partners.

Evidence, Not Theory, Ultimately Matters

There is a legitimate concern that strong IP rights, especially in the case of a patent that applies to a fundamental technology, could give rise to transactional and litigation "thickets" that block or otherwise impede follow-on innovation. Perhaps surprisingly, however, there is little compelling evidence that this adverse outcome has actually been realized for any persistent period.[38] As I and others have shown, there appears to be little empirical basis for even widely cited assertions of alleged "patent bottlenecks" in the early aircraft, automotive, and radio-communications markets.[39] This repeated mismatch between theory and evidence concerning IP thickets can be illustrated by biomedical research, which just happens to be the field in which the foundational Cohen-Boyer patent was issued. As noted previously, academic commentators had expressed concern that widespread patenting in the biomedical-research community would generate an "anticommons" in which litigation and other costs would undermine the innovation process.[40] While cogent in theory, this assertion has found little supporting evidence. Multiple empirical studies have failed to find evidence that intensive usage of the patent system has given rise to dispute-resolution, negotiation, or other IP-related costs that have halted or materially impeded biomedical research projects.[41]

The licensing history of the Cohen-Boyer patent is consistent with these findings. The patent was licensed by its owner, Stanford University, for various uses to 468 companies,[42] which in turn sublicensed rights to multiple pharmaceutical or other partners, ultimately yielding, by one estimate, more than 2,400 new drug therapies.[43] The patent-licensing and sublicensing relationships that stood behind those products promoted, rather than impeded, innovation and commercialization activities, resulting in thousands of new medical treatments. This economically and socially attractive outcome contrasts sharply with the low rates of commercialization that were observed during the weak-patent postwar period (see Chapter 4, section 4.2.2), when limitations on asserting legal exclusivity over federally funded research discouraged private parties from undertaking the commercialization investments required to yield a technically and economically viable product. The weak-IP regime that prevailed prior to the enactment of the Bayh-Dole Act saved on litigation and contract-negotiation costs but may have paid a substantially larger price in the form of a reduced flow of new therapies and treatments.

6.2 Semiconductors: Interrupted Integration

The semiconductor industry stands at the heart of the information-technology industry: no PC, smartphone, or other computing and communications devices can work without the chips produced by firms such as Intel, Qualcomm, Nvidia, and others. Since the 1990s, the semiconductor industry has been characterized by both intensive patenting and the emergence of vertically disintegrated structures for funding and executing the innovation and commercialization process. Concurrently, the market has experienced vigorous entry by upstream R&D-intensive firms that specialize in chip design and outsource production and other downstream functions to third parties.

6.2.1 History and Background

The semiconductor industry has its roots in the invention of the transistor in 1947 at AT&T's Bell Labs, a key institutional player in the postwar hierarchical and semi-bureaucratic innovation economy. From a business perspective, AT&T then made a seemingly curious choice. Rather than keeping this landmark technology for its own uses or demanding high licensing fees, AT&T elected to license its invention to all interested parties for a relatively modest one-time fee of $25,000, together with complementary technical know-how, subject to a reciprocal licensing obligation from the licensee.[44] This policy was formalized and made permanent under a 1956 consent decree, in which AT&T was required to offer nonexclusive licenses for all existing and future Bell System patents (including the transistor patent), together with know-how, at a zero royalty in the case of existing patents and at a "reasonable" royalty in the case of future patents, in each case subject to a reciprocal license from the licensee.[45] This order effectively compelled AT&T to maintain approximately the terms that it had already offered to the industry, while, given the reciprocal-licensing obligation, enabling it to access technologies held by its licensees.[46] AT&T's relaxed cross-licensing practices set a model for the industry. In the ensuing decades, leading semiconductor manufacturers regularly exchanged technical information, typically demanded what were perceived to be "below-market" royalties in cross-licensing agreements, and rarely initiated patent litigation.[47] These practices were supplemented in some cases by second-sourcing obligations in defense R&D contracts, which compelled the contractor to share technical designs and process knowledge with another firm.[48] This non-IP-dependent innovation regime relied on the fact that leading U.S. firms generally exhibited three characteristics: (i) roughly comparable patent portfolios, which could be exchanged through cross-licensing relationships at a relatively low evaluation and negotiation cost,[49] (ii) vertically integrated structures for earning returns on R&D through the design, production, and distribution of semiconductors or other products,[50] and (iii) in the 1950s and 1960s, an implicit subsidy through extensive government procurement funding for aerospace and defense-related applications.[51] In this environment, patents were not a critical instrument for extracting returns on innovation.

6.2.2 Vertical Disintegration

Starting in the 1980s, the semiconductor industry moved from a state of affairs characterized by relatively low levels of patenting to substantially higher levels of patenting. This can be seen in Figure 6.2.

The increase in patenting rates coincided with both the establishment of the Federal Circuit in 1982 (and the associated strengthening of patent protections)[52] and entry into the semiconductor market of "fabless" firms that operated under a vertically disintegrated structure in which a firm specializes in chip design but does not acquire production (or "fabrication") capacity.[53] In 1999, fabless firms accounted for slightly more than 7 percent of global integrated-circuit sales; in 2006, they accounted for slightly more than 18 percent; and in 2012, they accounted for almost 28 percent.[54] Fabless firms typically exhibit especially high R&D intensities (ranging from 15 percent and higher for fabless firms such as Qualcomm and Broadcom, which compares to approximately 5 to 7 percent for large integrated electronics manufacturers such as Panasonic, Sony, and LG). Not having to acquire independent production capacity drastically reduces entry costs. Construction estimates for a new chip-production plant currently range from $1.6 billion to $5 billion, which does not include the

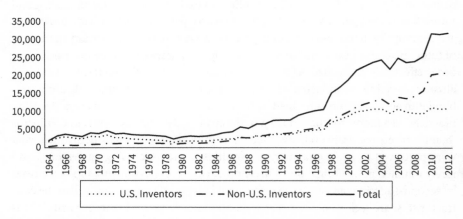

Figure 6.2 Patents issued for semiconductors/other electronic components (1964–2012)

Notes: This figure is based on an approximate concordance developed by the USPTO to match USPTO classifications with NAICS classifications. Data generated by allocating patents on a fractional basis among all relevant NAICS categories.

Source: U.S. Patent and Trademark Office, "Patenting by NAICS Industry Classification—Breakout by Geographic Origin (State and Country) (1963–2012)."

accompanying costs and specialized expertise required to develop the necessary process technologies.[55] The fabless model enables entrants to detour around these capital- and technical-requirements barriers by entering into relationships with third-party suppliers (known as "foundries") that specialize in chip-production services.[56] In a subsequent progression toward even greater vertical disintegration, the semiconductor market includes "chipless" firms such as ARM Holdings, which offer design components (known as "IP cores") that are licensed by fabless and integrated firms to generate new chip designs.[57]

Figure 6.3 contrasts the integrated and unintegrated (fabless) models for organizing supply chains in the semiconductor market. As shown, today even integrated firms adopt a less than fully integrated model with respect to certain functions of the supply chain.[58] Currently, only a handful of chip manufacturers operate under an integrated business model (most notably, Intel and Samsung).[59] This is consistent with theoretical expectations. Given the reduced expropriation risk under a strong-IP regime, transacting parties are free to make organizational choices in response to relevant environmental parameters, which results in a higher degree of transactional diversity than would otherwise be the case.

Just like the "biotechnology revolution," the emergence of the fabless-foundry model in the semiconductor industry is both a technological and an organizational story. As a technological matter, technical achievements in the late 1970s and 1980s (specifically, a design methodology known as "very large-scale integration," or VLSI, and the standardization of certain process technologies) facilitated the separation

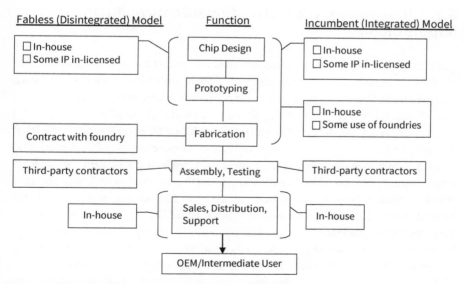

Figure 6.3 Vertical disintegration (semiconductors)

Sources: This figure is adapted from Barnett (2011b, 844), based in part on information in Kumar (2008, figs. 4.8–4.10, 6.1, 6.4, 6.8); Linden and Somaya (2003, 569–70); Nathan Associates (2016, 4–8); Tuomi (2009, 41).

of chip design and production functions.[60] As an organizational matter, the fabless-foundry model realizes the efficiency gains made possible by these technical advances through a combination of patents, contractual constraints, reputational discipline, and technological controls, which together mitigate the two-sided transactional hazards inherent to the exchange of valuable informational assets among technically sophisticated parties. On the side of the fabless firm, patents, coupled with technological, contractual, and reputational protections, protect the firm's chip design against expropriation by the foundry, a sophisticated supplier that could vertically integrate backward into design or share the fabless firm's design with other clients. Consistent with this proposition, Bronwyn Hall and Rosemarie Ziedonis found that chip-design firms are almost five times more likely to patent compared to a broader sample that included large integrated chip manufacturers.[61] On the side of the foundry, patents protect its investment in developing process innovations, which are shared (at least in part) with design-firm clients and could be expropriated by customers, competitors, or departing employees. Leading foundries are under competitive pressure to develop improved process technologies[62] and accordingly exhibit substantial R&D intensities (as of 2018, 8 percent of revenues in the case of TSMC, the world's leading foundry, and 8.6 percent of revenues in the case of UMC, the second-largest foundry) and intensive use of the U.S. patent system.[63] In each of the years 2015–2018, TSMC was ranked among the top ten corporate assignees of U.S. patents.[64]

6.2.3 Illustration: The International Semiconductor Supply Chain

To illustrate further this connection between U.S. patent protections and the organization of semiconductor supply chains, we can examine the relationship between Marvell Technology Group, a fabless semiconductor firm based in Silicon Valley, and TSMC, a leading chip foundry based in Taiwan.[65] Indicative of the fact that it is an upstream R&D-specialist entity, Marvell has an exceptionally high R&D intensity (R&D expenditures as a percentage of sales revenues) of 31.9 percent as of 2018 (which compares with 15.5 percent for Google and 5 percent for Apple).[66] Aside from its Silicon Valley operations, USPTO data (which indicates the residence of named inventors on issued patents) and SEC annual reports show that Marvell maintains R&D operations in China, Israel, Singapore, and Switzerland. To protect these R&D investments, Marvell maintains a significant portfolio of approximately ten thousand U.S. and foreign patents.[67] As previously noted, TSMC makes substantial investments in process R&D, as reflected by an R&D intensity of 8 percent as of 2018 and a portfolio of more than 34,000 U.S. and foreign patents.[68] As in other fabless-foundry relationships, both firms' patent portfolios enable the mutually profitable exchange of valuable informational assets at a reduced level of expropriation risk, which in turn permits each firm to enjoy some share of the resulting specialization efficiencies. Additionally, in Marvell's case, patent protections may enable the firm to protect against the risk of knowledge leakage associated with establishing R&D operations in foreign jurisdictions. (Note that even though patents issued by the USPTO do not have extraterritorial force, they nonetheless exert such force as a practical matter insofar as owners of U.S. patents can seek "exclusion orders" through the International Trade Commission, a U.S. administrative agency, to block the importation of infringing goods that are made outside the United States)

The patent-mediated relationship between Marvell and TSMC is part of a broader vertically disintegrated global supply chain that starts with Marvell's dispersed R&D centers and ends with delivery of the relevant computing or communications device to the U.S. consumer market. The map in Figure 6.4 shows each step in this supply chain, which is simplified for expositional purposes and includes four entities: (i) Marvell, which supplies the R&D inputs in the form of semiconductor chip designs; (ii) TSMC, which supplies the production inputs; (iii) Hon Hai (also known as Foxconn), which supplies the assembly inputs; and (iv) Hewlett Packard (HP),

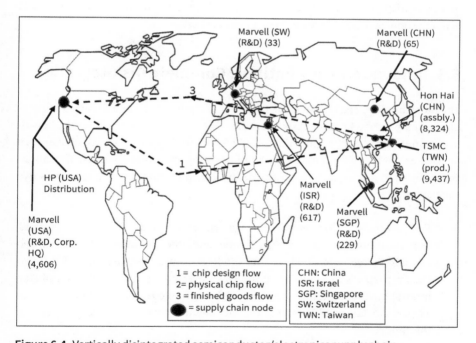

Figure 6.4 Vertically disintegrated semiconductor/electronics supply chain

Notes: Number in parentheses following each entity indicates the number of USPTO patents first assigned to that entity during 2000–2015. In the case of Marvell, these numbers refer to the USPTO patents issued to inventors resident in the relevant country and first assigned to Marvell.

Sources: Adapted from Barnett (2017b, 488, fig. 13). Patent data: U.S. Patent and Trademark Office, "Extended Year Set, Utility Patent Report, Patenting by Geographic Origin (State and Country Breakout by Organization)." Map template: Wikimedia Commons, Creative Commons CCO 1.0, Universal Public Domain Dedication.

which supplies the distribution, marketing, and customer-support inputs. At each step on the supply chain, patent protection can mitigate the early-stage and mid-stage expropriation risk that is inherent to the exchange of commercially valuable informational assets among sophisticated and well-resourced business parties with potentially adverse competitive interests. As part of the R&D process, patents mitigate the expropriation risk to which Marvell is exposed with respect to the employees in its multiple and geographically dispersed R&D facilities, each of which maintains human-capital assets that can migrate to competitors. (Note that the numbers in parentheses in Figure 6.4 indicate the U.S. patents issued to inventor-employees at each facility.) In step (1) (shown in the figure), following completion of the chip-design process at Marvell and its R&D centers, patents mitigate the expropriation risk to which Marvell and TSMC are mutually exposed in the fabless-foundry relationship. In steps (2) and (3) (also shown in the figure), patents mitigate any residual expropriation risk to which Marvell and TSMC are exposed as the physical chip is embedded in a consumer-electronics product by Hon Hai at its assembly facilities in China and then ultimately delivered to HP for distribution to the U.S. consumer market. Like property rights in tangible-goods markets, patents enable firms in technology markets to customize supply chains, achieve specialization efficiencies, and deliver products to market at the lowest possible cost.

6.3 Innovation-Only Entities: Complete Disintegration

The biotechnology start-up and the fabless chip-design firm can be viewed as paradigm examples of a broader class of entities that adopt high levels of vertical disintegration under a legal regime that provides secure IP protection, which can then be used as the foundation for a rich set of licensing and other contractual relationships. This broader class of vertically disintegrated entities in turn comprises two subclasses:

- *R&D specialists.* These entities engage primarily or entirely in R&D activities; lack significant production, distribution, and other commercialization capacities; and therefore rely on licensing and joint-venture relationships with downstream partners to monetize those R&D investments. This could describe an innovation-intensive start-up, a university technology-transfer department, or a handful of larger R&D-intensive companies that have adopted some version of this model.
- *IP intermediaries.* These entities do not have R&D, production, or other downstream capacities and earn revenues from the licensing of IP-protected assets (or, more typically, portfolios of IP-protected assets), which those entities either own directly or administer on behalf of patent owners. This encompasses a broad array of entities, ranging from firms that acquire patents for opportunistic litigation and licensing purposes to firms that aggregate patent portfolios

for broad-based licensing among a target population of producers and other intermediate users.

In the case of both entity types, patents mediate the exchange of commercially valuable informational assets among potentially adverse third parties and enable firms to earn returns on innovation assets through broad-based licensing among the target-user population. Without secure patent protection, and in the absence of sufficiently potent technological, contractual, and reputational constraints to fill the gap in IP coverage, many of these transactional arrangements would be infeasible due to expropriation risk or would have to be structured through second-best mechanisms that use alternative and less efficient means to mitigate that risk.

6.3.1 Patent-Licensing Entities

Legal and popular commentary relating to vertically disintegrated and patent-intensive entities has focused inordinately on the "patent troll," that is, an entity that opportunistically acquires and litigates patents in order to extract exorbitant licensing fees from cash-rich operational enterprises. The social costs attributed to nuisance patent litigation and licensing demands by some patent-holding entities—the precise number and significance of which continue to be debated[69]—have driven legislative and judicial actions that have weakened protections for all patent holders. Most notably, concerns over "patent trolls" substantially motivated the Supreme Court's 2006 decision in *eBay Inc. v. MercExchange LLC*. As I will discuss subsequently (see Chapter 8, section 8.1.1), the *eBay* precedent has largely precluded "nonpracticing" patent holders from securing injunctive relief against infringers[70] and, in certain cases, has led courts to deny injunctive relief to practicing patent holders in infringement litigations involving multicomponent products.[71] As would be expected in the case of any legal entitlement, there are circumstances in which patents are used for opportunistic purposes in litigation and licensing contexts. However, a narrow focus on these socially unconstructive practices has deflected attention from an arguably larger group of entities that engage in licensing and sale transactions for purposes of either monetizing their R&D investments or, in the case of an intermediary, monetizing other entities' R&D investments. Both activities would be expected elements of any well-functioning market in intangible assets, corresponding respectively to sale, leasing, and brokerage functions in tangible-goods markets. Contrary to standard characterizations, the payment made by intermediate users to the holders of these innovation assets is not properly viewed as a "tax" that depletes social value; rather, this is simply the same mechanism that a price-based system uses in markets generally to allocate resources efficiently.[72]

In the scope of this discussion, I do not intend to review the extensive theoretical and empirical literature concerning the relative social costs and benefits that can be reasonably attributed to entities that engage in "stand-alone" patent-licensing activities. However, it is important to note that there is at a minimum considerable doubt concerning the large social costs that have been widely attributed to entities that fall under the rubric of nonpracticing entities (NPEs) and even greater doubt concerning the extent to which those costs are offset by countervailing social gains attributable to a regime of robust IP rights. In two more recent studies, Chris Cotropia, Jay Kesan, and David Schwartz present evidence showing that the NPE label encompasses a substantial population of firms and other entities that cannot be plausibly described as being presumptively engaged in opportunistic patent acquisition and licensing activities.[73] This heterogeneous population encompasses individual inventors, the technology-transfer divisions of academic research institutions, for-profit R&D-only or "R&D-mostly" enterprises, the licensing divisions of operational companies, and patent aggregation and licensing entities. There is a fundamental difference between, on the one hand, an apparently opportunistic entity that acquires patents solely for purposes of licensing and litigating them against cash-rich targets and, on the other hand, an intermediary that seeks to assemble a patent portfolio for purposes of forming cooperative structures that reduce transaction costs, facilitate information sharing, and expand access to technological inputs among downstream producers. Any policy action that weakens patents for purposes of screening out what may be a small population of "bad" licensing entities runs the risk that it will chill activities by a larger population of "good" licensing entities that constructively disseminate informational assets among a large population of intermediate users. The holders of technologies that could have been patented and licensed through these intermediary structures will then be compelled to adopt integrated organizational structures that do not rely on patents. In other cases, the technology holder will lack the necessary capital and expertise to integrate forward and will decline to enter the market (and, working backward, may decline to innovate in the first place). Contrary to conventional assumptions, the result is a market in which IP strength declines but, given the legal risk associated with licensing-based structures, access to the underlying pool of technological assets declines and entry barriers rise.

Presumptively treating all NPEs as a "patent troll" overlooks important examples where NPEs engage in significant R&D with a constructive social impact. I will provide a necessarily selective list of entities that could fall under certain definitions of an NPE but are almost certainly engaged in R&D, product development, and other activities of constructive social value. These entities have four characteristics in common: (i) the entity was responsible for a fundamental "breakthrough" invention (or responsible for commercializing it), (ii) the invention was made by an individual or group of individuals (rather than a large firm), (iii) the invention was patented, and (iv) with the exception of the example below of photocopying technology, the entity's monetization process relied on a patent-licensing model. (As will be discussed, the commercial development of photocopying technology relied on the inventor's patent portfolio, although the technology was ultimately not monetized through a licensing-based model.) All these products, and associated licensing arrangements, have operated to the benefit of consumers and cannot be plausibly associated with the types of opportunistic practices engaged in by "patent trolls." These examples include:[74]

- *Wisconsin Alumni Research Foundation.* This early example of a university technology-transfer entity (founded in 1925) licensed a patented food-irradiation process that is credited with the elimination of vitamin D deficiency (rickets). The process had been invented by Harry Steenbock, a University of Wisconsin researcher.[75] Today it manages a portfolio of more than 1,900 technologies, has been granted (as "first assignee") almost 2,000 patents at the USPTO since 2000, and continues to manage patent licensing on behalf of the University of Wisconsin–Madison.

- *Battelle Memorial Institute.* This nonprofit applied-research institute was founded in 1929, has been granted (as "first assignee") more than 2,750 patents at the USPTO since 2000, and has approximately 3,200 employees as of 2020. Battelle played a key role, starting in the 1940s, as a source of both capital and technical expertise in the development of photocopying. The foundational technology was invented by Chester Carlson, an individual inventor, but required additional technical improvements over two decades from Battelle (and later the Haloid Corporation, to be renamed Xerox) until the first commercial release in 1959. While photocopying technology was ultimately monetized through a vertically integrated production and distribution model, Carlson's patents were critical in supporting a royalty-based license to Battelle and the subsequent acquisition by Haloid.[76]

- *Dolby Corporation.* Starting in the mid-1960s, Ray Dolby, an individual inventor, pioneered and widely licensed analog and digital noise-reduction and other audio technologies that are currently used widely in movie theaters and a wide variety of consumer audio and other electronics devices throughout the course of recent technology history, including recording-studio equipment, cassette tape recorders, DVDs, motion-picture production, and digital television.[77] Today the Dolby Corporation owns more than 8,100 patents on a worldwide basis, which it monetizes through licensing and other contractual transactions with the music and motion-picture industries, theatrical exhibitors, device manufacturers, and other firms in the entertainment and media ecosystem.

- *Qualcomm.* Founded by a group led by scientist-inventor Irwin Jacobs, Qualcomm pioneered the CDMA (code-division multiple access) wireless-communications technology for transmitting rich packages of voice and data. CDMA challenged and outperformed the TDMA (time-division multiple access) technologies that had been adopted by European and U.S. telecom carriers.[78] Qualcomm has widely licensed its technology to several hundred handset and device manufacturers as part of the 3G and 4G wireless-communications standards. The company uses a fabless model in which chip production is outsourced to third-party foundries. The company owns more than 64,000 patents on a worldwide basis.

- *ARM Holdings.* Founded in 1990 as Advanced Risc Machines, a spinoff of Acorn Computer, ARM developed and has widely licensed microprocessor-design architectures that are used by virtually all firms that design semiconductors for mobile computing devices.[79] ARM is sometimes described as a "chipless" firm, meaning that it acts as an input supplier to fabless and other firms that specialize in chip design for the mobile-device semiconductor market. As of 2016 (prior to being acquired by Softbank), ARM owned more than 2,725 patents on a worldwide basis.

It nonetheless may be objected that these productive licensing activities come at a significant social cost that would not be incurred in a legal regime in which patents were absent or less robust. In particular, it can be reasonably argued that entities that hold patents over fundamental technologies could be in a position to exercise pricing power over midstream and downstream users, thereby inflating the social costs attributable to the patent system in the form of increased deadweight losses and reduced access for intermediate and end users. Yet this outcome is by no means inevitable, and there is no reason to believe that "rate gouging" would typically be a licensor's preferred strategy, even in the case in which the licensor holds a critical IP input for the downstream market. So far, we have already encountered three owners of valuable patents or patent portfolios that elected to license their patent or patents widely and at what in retrospect appear to be relatively low rates. These generous licensors include (i) Stanford University, which licensed the Cohen-Boyer patent to hundreds of licensees at what was perceived to be a "below-market" royalty rate, given the technology's exceptional value;[80] (ii) Universal Oil Products, a stand-alone R&D and licensing entity that held the patents to a critical process technology in the petroleum-refining industry in the early twentieth century (see Chapter 5, section 5.1.2); and (iii) Elias Howe, the owner of a "pioneer" patent in the sewing-machine industry in the mid-eighteenth century (see Chapter 3, section 3.2.3). As will be discussed, these same restrained licensing strategies have been adopted by holders of some of the twentieth century's most valuable IP assets. Far from being an outlier case, it appears that IP-licensing markets often converge on pricing levels that deliver significant gains to the entities that originated the relevant technology assets while imposing relatively low access costs on the licensee population of intermediate and end users.

There is a sensible economic reason for IP licensors to favor "low-rate, broad-base" licensing practices that expand the market for the underlying technology. A patentee that lacks downstream commercialization functions and relies primarily on licensing revenue logically has stronger incentives to disseminate its technology widely, as compared to an integrated firm that relies on complementary non-patent assets to extract revenues from innovation. There are several reasons. First, unlike an integrated firm, a stand-alone R&D specialist has no strategic incentive to block entry into the downstream market by competing producers. To the contrary, it typically has incentives to maximize the number of producers from which it can extract a fee. Second, and relatedly, a stand-alone R&D provider typically has incentives to adopt a reasonable-rate strategy that maximizes the base over which it can assess royalties during the limited life of the relevant patent. This motivation to seed adoption is even stronger in information-technology settings that are characterized by both "winner-take-all" effects (meaning a single firm ultimately captures most of the market for a certain period of time) and an initially intense competition among multiple technologies to capture the market. Third, if the patent owner is a repeat-play firm, then it will have an interest in acquiring a reputation for setting royalties that allocate some meaningful portion of market surplus to licensees, which will enhance its ability in the future to secure adoption of new technologies from intermediate and end users. Fourth, low licensing rates discourage patent infringement by minimizing the difference between a user's expected costs of authorized usage (the royalty fee) and unauthorized usage (infringement damages plus legal costs). It is certainly possible to contemplate scenarios in which upstream IP licensors would elect a "high-rate, narrow-base" strategy in order to maximize short-term licensing revenues. However, this would require that (i) the patent holder has a technology that has already been adopted (since a high price would discourage adoption), (ii) there are no actual or potential substitutes to the patented technology (which would limit the patent holder's pricing power), and (iii) the patent holder does not contemplate licensing any future technologies (which would be impeded by a track record of "exorbitant" licensing). Those demanding assumptions may not typically be satisfied in most patent-licensing environments.

6.3.2 The Modern Patent Pool

The rationally altruistic licensing strategy of a profit-maximizing IP-licensing entity can be illustrated by MPEG LA, widely regarded as the pioneer and still-leading firm in the formation and administration of patent pools in information-technology markets. Founded in 1996, MPEG LA assembles portfolios of patents that are essential to a technology standard but held by multiple entities and then licenses (or, more precisely, sublicenses) the portfolio as a package to a larger group of device manufacturers and other licensees. As of 2015, MPEG LA had organized 12 pools involving 200 licensors and 4,421 licensees.[81] MPEG LA's most successful pool, the MPEG-2 patent pool (which covers audio-video compression technology used in DVD players, set-top boxes, and internet transmission), included 1,034 patents issued by 57 countries and 27 licensors in North America, Europe, and East Asia and had licensed its technology to approximately 1,420 licensees.[82] As shown in Figure 6.5, MPEG LA licenses out the patent pool, retains a transaction fee, and then allocates the royalties among the licensors (which must also pay license fees at the same rate to access the pooled technology) based on the number of patents each licensor contributed to the pool. Critically, the pool uses an "open" structure insofar as any party that is willing to pay

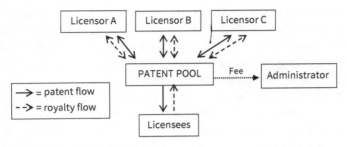

Figure 6.5 Open administered patent pool
Source: Adapted from Barnett (2014, 14, fig. 1).

the licensing fee can obtain a license, as distinguished from "closed" structures in which the pooled technology is only licensed among the licensors.

The patent-pooling structure alleviates transaction-cost obstacles that might otherwise pose a barrier to dissemination of a technology standard characterized by large numbers of patents held by multiple dispersed entities. This type of contractual innovation explains in large part why widely voiced concerns over "thickets" in patent-intensive information-technology markets have generally not materialized, as evidenced by the remarkable growth, rapid adoption, and quality-adjusted price declines in consumer-electronics markets.[83] A simple comparison of the price and computing and communications functions of a 1981 IBM PC ($1,565, equivalent to more than $4,000 in 2017 dollars) with the price and computing and communication functions of a smartphone in 2017 in the U.S. market ($328) provides a shorthand illustration of the remarkable technical and economic performance of the information-technology markets.[84]

In MPEG LA's case, the prospect of a thicket invited a transactional entrepreneur to devise a contractual mechanism by which the relevant rights could be aggregated and licensed to all interested parties. At the same time, a patent pool inherently raises the risk of licensor collusion over royalty rates. This legitimate concern is mitigated by the fact that the intermediary's incentives are not inherently aligned with the potentially collusive intentions of the licensor-patentees. As a third-party administrator, MPEG LA forms pools repeatedly in response to the formation of new technology standards and, as such, has strong incentives to preserve a favorable track record with both existing and future licensors and licensees. With respect to licensors, MPEG LA typically faces competition at the formation stage from other pools or must attract owners of substantial patent portfolios that might otherwise elect to license individually outside any pool. With respect to licensees, MPEG LA seeks to maximize its long-term royalty stream and therefore has an interest in maintaining goodwill among its client base of downstream licensee-manufacturers, especially since MPEG LA has no economic stake in the downstream product markets. Consistent with these theoretical expectations, there is no evidence that MPEG LA has exploited its position to impose an "exorbitant" licensing tax on the market, thereby inflating the price of consumer goods. Based on published royalty rates (as of 2012), the total royalty burden that an original-equipment manufacturer in the PC market would owe to all relevant MPEG LA patent pools constituted an estimated 0.31 percent of the retail price of the end products in which the licensed technology was embedded.[85]

Since the antitrust agencies lifted a de facto prohibition on patent-pooling structures in the late 1990s,[86] these structures have been implemented by for-profit administrators (and, in some cases, industry consortia) in multiple information-technology markets. As shown in Table 6.1, each pool corresponds to a technology standard and provides a licensing-based knowledge-transmission mechanism that enables device producers and other intermediate users to access a portfolio of standard-relevant patents held by dispersed owners.

Patent pools generate two types of efficiency gains. First, the pool substitutes a single licensing transaction for potentially tens of such transactions, enabling the formation of a market in disembodied informational assets that links tens of licensors with hundreds to thousands of licensees. Second, given the commitment to nonexclusive licensing, the pools ensure that any intermediate user can access the required technology inputs subject to payment of the licensing fee, which is most likely far lower than the costs that any such firm would incur to develop a non-infringing substitute technology. It may nonetheless be argued that the patent-pool mechanism is only a solution to a problem—namely, the prospect of a transaction-cost thicket—that would not exist but for increased patenting activity in information-technology markets. As noted previously, there are certainly litigation and licensing-related burdens that are specifically attributable to any robustly enforced system of IP rights. Yet it is important to keep in mind that the alternative state of affairs under weaker or zero IP protection is *not* a public domain in which the same volume and quantity of

Table 6.1 Patent pools in information-technology markets (selected)

Standard	Pooling Entity	Product Category
MPEG-2	MPEG-LA	Video codec. Used in cable TV-set-top boxes, DVD players, digital cameras, Blu-ray players, digital TV.
H.264	MPEG-LA	Video codec. Used in Blu-ray and DVD players, mobile broadcast video, game consoles, high-definition TV.
AAC	Via Licensing	Audio codec. Used in MP3 players.
1394 (Firewire)	MPEG-LA	Serial bus interface for data transfer.
Bluetooth	Bluetooth SIG	Near-field wireless communication.
Wi-Fi (802.11)	Via Licensing	Wireless local area networks (LAN)
Blu-ray	One-Blue	Blu-ray discs and players.
Blu-ray	Premier BD	Blu-ray discs and players.

Source: Adapted from Barnett (2014, 12–13 tab. 2).

innovation is generated and then made available to all users free of access restrictions. A dynamic approach to IP rights anticipates that any reduction in IP strength would necessarily alter the mix of appropriation mechanisms that firms can most profitably use to capture returns on innovation, which would in turn induce shifts in firm and market structure that give rise to *other* categories of social costs. In particular, a shift to weaker IP protection necessarily restores the expropriation risk that is inherent to information exchanges and may therefore compel firms to fund and commercialize innovation within integrated structures, or with a limited group of reputationally validated business partners, rather than through a contractually governed network consisting of (as in MPEG-LA's case) tens of IP licensors and thousands of IP licensees. The result may be an environment in which litigation and related transaction costs are reduced but supply chains inefficiently reintegrate, which in turn suppresses specialization gains, increases the capital requirements to achieve entry, shelters incumbents from competitive discipline, and may ultimately distort the allocation of resources across innovation projects.

PART III

POLITICS

The Market Rents of Weak Intellectual-Property Rights

7
Why Incumbents (Usually) Prefer Weak Intellectual-Property Rights

Natural intuitions, popular commentary and some scholarly commentary often follow a "good guy/bad guy" narrative in which large incumbents always prefer stronger IP rights to block entry and maximize pricing power. This populist narrative appears in enforcement campaigns by the DOJ Antitrust Division in the late New Deal, was a recurring motif in the TNEC hearings during 1938–1941, motivated the antitrust agencies' pursuit of compulsory licensing orders against some of the country's largest firms in the postwar period, and now re-appears in contemporary advocacy for "patent reform." Following this narrative, weakening IP rights always opens up access to informational assets, reduces barriers to entry, and enhances competitive intensity. The dynamic approach to IP analysis, however, suggests a more complex relationship between IP rights, access costs, and entry barriers. Outside the pharmaceutical industry, that approach anticipates that weaker patent protections tend to shelter larger and more integrated firms against the competitive threat posed by more innovative but smaller entrants. The reason derives from the fact that larger firms tend to have lower-cost access to non-patent mechanisms for extracting returns from innovation, in which case it is expected that they would either be largely indifferent to patent protections (since they can mimic those protections through lower-cost non-IP alternatives) or would strategically disfavor them in order to increase smaller firms' entry costs. For the same reasons, it should be expected that smaller and, especially, substantially unintegrated firms (and investors in those firms) would tend to favor stronger patent rights as a necessary tool by which to overcome incumbents' lower-cost access to non-IP assets for capturing returns on innovation.

The divergence between the expectations of the popular narrative and the dynamic approach can be assessed to a meaningful extent by examining the IP-policy preferences of larger and more integrated firms, on the one hand, and smaller and less integrated firms, on the other hand, in different technology industries. In this chapter, I undertake that exercise. This inquiry strongly supports the dynamic approach and the proposed relationship between IP strength and organizational form. With the anticipated exception of the biopharmaceutical industry, larger and substantially integrated incumbents tend to oppose increases in patent strength (or, at least, do not advocate in favor of such increases), while smaller and less integrated entrants (and their financial backers) tend to take the contrary position. This behavior is remarkably constant across history. Senior management at Bell Labs and Ford Motor Company testified in the TNEC hearings in the late 1930s that patents

Innovators, Firms, and Markets. Jonathan M. Barnett, Oxford University Press (2021). © Oxford University Press.
DOI: 10.1093/oso/9780190908591.003.0008

were not especially critical and were not typically a precondition for undertaking research.[1] By contrast, the National Association of Manufacturers (NAM), which principally represented the interests of small and medium-size firms,[2] lobbied against the TNEC's proposals for compulsory licensing. The NAM argued that "[c]ompulsory licensing would be most damaging to small business and independent inventors.... Large corporations would be given an additional weapon to use in acquiring the inventions of independent inventors and small businessmen to whom patent protection is vital."[3] In 2002, the chief intellectual-property counsel of Cisco, one of the world's leading information-technology firms, testified before Congress: "Everything we have done to create new products would have been done even if we could not obtain patents on the innovation and inventions contained in those products."[4] By contrast, as I will discuss in greater detail, smaller R&D-intensive firms, VCs, and the technology-transfer offices of research universities have resisted legislative efforts to reduce patent protections.[5]

In this chapter, I present three bodies of evidence that demonstrate a largely consistent divergence in patent-policy preferences between, on the one hand, smaller, less integrated firms located at upstream points on the supply chain, which tend to favor stronger patent protection, and, on the other hand, larger, more integrated firms located at mid- and downstream points on the supply chain, which tend to favor weaker patent protection. First, I describe two historical episodes concerning policy debates over patent rights in certain industries: the assertion of patent rights by individual inventors in the railroad industry during the late nineteenth century and the pursuit of patent protection by independent software developers in the 1960s and 1970s. In both cases, larger and more integrated firms resisted strong patent rights, while the opposite was the case for smaller and less integrated firms. Second, I present data on amicus briefs filed in Supreme Court litigation relating to patent-law issues during 2006–2016, which supplements existing research starting in 1986. For the three decades since 1986, all available data identifies a consistent entity-specific policy divide (with the familiar exception of the biopharmaceutical industry): large integrated firms tend to support weaker patent rights, while R&D-focused and less integrated firms tend to support stronger patent rights. Third, I show how large integrated firms have undertaken "IP giveaway" licensing and other business strategies designed to devalue or effectively eliminate IP protections across a whole class of technologies without any change in the IP protections that are nominally still available as a matter of statutory or case law.

7.1   Railroads versus Individual Inventors

During the 1870s, the U.S. railroad industry lobbied for legislative reforms, and pursued litigation strategies, to curtail patent-infringement suits and generally weaken patent protections.[6] The railroads presented a narrative that bears a striking resemblance to the narrative promoted by Silicon Valley's large technology companies today. The railroads claimed to be victimized by "patent dealers"—that is, individual inventors or, more commonly, "speculators" who had acquired patents issued to individual inventors—that sought to extract allegedly exorbitant damages awards and licensing fees. The railroads and individual inventors had dichotomous models for extracting returns on R&D, which reflected starkly different costs of accessing complementary non-patent assets for extracting returns from innovation. Railroads were integrated operations that earned revenues through a complex bundle of services and products, could not be easily challenged due to technical and capital requirements, and therefore derived little incremental value from patent protection. By contrast, for individual inventors, the patent system was a necessary tool to acquire sufficient bargaining leverage in order to negotiate with firms that were shielded by these non-patent entry barriers and had sufficient know-how to replicate inventions observed in the marketplace. Without a patent, an individual entrepreneur such as George Westinghouse, the inventor of the air brake (a key innovation that substantially improved rail safety), would have run straight into an especially severe form of Arrow's information paradox. As a sophisticated and well-resourced entity, any railroad would likely have been able to implement an invention that was disclosed to it by an outside inventor. Armed with a patent portfolio, Westinghouse exerted a credible litigation threat (which he carried out when necessary)[7] and was able to induce the railroads to purchase the air brake (rather than simply copy it).[8]

From the railroads' perspective, however, strong patent rights held by individual inventors posed threats in the form of both increased technology-input costs and, given the costs and errors inherent to any formalized litigation system, exposure to opportunistic patent-infringement litigation. As Steven Usselman has shown, the railroads vigorously addressed these threats through two strategies. First, the railroads formed trade associations that gathered information on technical improvements, which created a pool of "prior art" that railroad defendants could then use to invalidate, or narrow the claims asserted in, a plaintiff's patents.[9] Second, the railroads engaged in litigation that targeted three key parameters of patent strength: (i) damages, (ii) claim construction, and (iii) patentability. With respect to damages, the railroads sought to overturn the "savings" doctrine, which instructed courts to calculate patent-infringement damages based on the cost savings enjoyed by the infringer relative to the next-best available non-infringing technology and had the effect of increasing damages awards for patentee plaintiffs. In 1871, the railroads achieved success: the Supreme Court adopted a standard for determining infringement awards that generally reduced damages relative to the savings doctrine.[10] With respect to claim construction, the Court delivered another win for the railroads in an 1873 decision that limited the scope of a patent on a fundamental "double-acting" brake technology that had been asserted against the railroads. More important, the Court expressed generally a preference for a narrow construction of patent claims, stating: "[I]f the advance towards the thing desired [the claimed invention] is gradual and proceeds step by step, so that no one can claim the complete whole, then each is entitled only to the specific form of device which he produces, and every other inventor is entitled to his own specific form, so long as it differs from those of his competitors and does not include theirs."[11] With respect to patentability, the Court in 1883 issued another defendant-friendly decision, holding that patent protection is reserved for those who make a "substantial discovery" and should not be awarded "for every trifling device," on the ground that this had given rise to "a class of speculative schemers ... [who] lay a heavy tax upon the industry of the country."[12]

In the aggregate, these decisions from the highest court delivered the result that had been sought by the railroads as users of externally supplied technological innovations. Given the unfavorable legal climate, patent holders were discouraged from undertaking litigation or were compelled to negotiate lower licensing rates given a substantially weakened threat of patent litigation.[13] The reduction in patent strength not only reduced the railroads' R&D input costs but, consistent with the theoretical expectations of the dynamic approach, was followed by a change in how innovation was conducted in the railroad industry. Thereafter, the railroad industry tended to adopt a hierarchical innovation architecture: technical improvement became routinized, with a focus on standardization and cost-reducing process improvements and reduced interest in the highest-stakes forms of product innovation.[14] By implication, the weakened IP regime may have suppressed an entrepreneurial innovation culture in which capital markets have incentives to direct resources toward smaller R&D-specialist entities, which in turn tend to select innovation projects that seek to displace, rather than merely improve upon, existing technologies.

7.2 Software Patents

In the 1960s, the Patent Office began to receive patent applications for software programs, which it generally resisted, triggering appeals by applicants in the USPTO's internal administrative tribunals and the federal courts.[15] This development elicited a vigorous policy debate in which leading hardware manufacturers such as IBM, Burroughs, and Honeywell opposed the extension of patent protection to software.[16] In 1966, a presidential commission (including computer-industry executives) formally recommended against patent protection for software.[17] Large hardware manufacturers' opposition to software patents most likely stemmed from the fact that they typically sold software as an unpriced component of a hardware/software/services bundle.[18] This was true of IBM, the largest computer-hardware manufacturer, which sold a bundled package of hardware, software, and related services until 1969, after which it offered certain software applications (but not operating-system software) on a separately priced basis.[19] Additionally, hardware manufacturers anticipated that extending patent protection to software could require them to pay licensing fees to independent software developers (which would also be expected to offer the same software to competing hardware manufacturers or to users directly).[20] This raised the possibility that a firm that held the IP rights to a critical software application could capture the bulk of the surplus value generated in a particular computing or communications environment. (This premonition was accurate: Microsoft Windows would capture a large portion of the value embedded in the PC market, while IBM would ultimately capture little.)

Following the dynamic approach, the bundling model used by IBM and other computing-hardware manufacturers can be understood as a response to a weak-IP environment. Absent secure IP rights, firms are compelled to monetize software development by bundling it with a suite of hardware and support services over which exclusivity could be secured—precisely the market in which systems-technology firms like IBM enjoyed a long-held advantage. In that legal environment, stand-alone software providers were limited to earning positive returns through three avenues: (i) contracting to develop customized software programs for business customers, (ii) contracting to develop operating systems and other software for hardware-systems manufacturers, or (iii) being acquired by a large hardware firm.[21] Consistent with the expectations of the dynamic approach to IP analysis, weaker or zero patent protection in this industry raised entry barriers for stand-alone software providers and advantaged integrated incumbents that enjoyed lower-cost access to non-IP alternatives. Martin Goetz, the recipient of what is sometimes described as the first software patent, appreciated this point: "Back in the 1960s … computer companies were giving away their software when they sold the computer…. [S]elling against free software is difficult. That's the reason I tried to get a patent."[22] Similarly, in a case in 1974 involving the patentability of software programs, Judge Giles Rich identified the economic considerations behind large-firm incumbents' resistance to extending patent protection to software. Specifically, he referred to "the collective forces of major hardware (i.e., computer) manufacturers and their respective associations who, for economic reasons, did not want patents granted on programs for their machines."[23]

This bifurcation of preferences concerning software patents between, on the one hand, integrated hardware manufacturers and, on the other hand, stand-alone software suppliers is illustrated by the positions expressed in amicus briefs filed with the Supreme Court in four cases during 1972–1981 in which the Court addressed the patentability of software: *Gottschalk v. Benson*,[24] *Dann v. Johnston*,[25] *Parker v. Flook*,[26] and *Diamond v Diehr.*[27] (See Table 7.1.) Integrated computer-equipment manufacturers (such as IBM, Honeywell, and Burroughs) and the trade association representing those manufacturers (the Computer and Business Equipment Manufacturers Association, or CBEMA) expressed opposition to the extension of patent protection to software programs. Concurrently, IBM even sought (unsuccessfully) to secure the revocation of a software patent issued by the U.K. patent office in 1974.[28] By contrast, small specialized software providers and the trade association representing those firms (the Association of Data Processing Service Organizations (ADAPSO)), supported this extension.[29] It is noteworthy to compare the small size of most members of ADAPSO (two-thirds of which had annual revenues less than $1 million as of 1978)[30] with the much larger size of the hardware manufacturers (for example, Burroughs, Honeywell, and IBM, which independently filed briefs in *Gottschalk v. Benson*, reported annual revenues of approximately $2.1 billion, $2.9 billion, and $18.1 billion,

Table 7.1 Amicus briefs in Supreme Court software-patentability litigation (1972–1981)

Year	Case	Briefs Filed for Patentability	Briefs Filed against Patentability
1972	*Gottschalk v. Benson*	ADAPSO; independent software firms; Iowa State Univ.; Mobil Oil	Business Equipment Mfrs. Assoc.; Burroughs; Honeywell; IBM
1976	*Dann v. Johnston*	ADAPSO; independent software firms	CBEMA
1978	*Parker v. Flook*	ADAPSO; independent software firms; Mobil Oil	CBEMA
1981	*Diamond v. Diehr*	ADAPSO; Chevron; Halliburton Services (energy-services company)	CBEMA; National Semiconductor

Notes: Briefs filed by intellectual-property law associations are omitted (these all favored patentability). ADAPSO refers to Association of Data Processing Service Organizations. CBEMA refers to Computer and Business Equipment Manufacturers Association.
Sources: For full case citations, see References—Judicial Opinions and Administrative Rulings. All briefs sourced through the Westlaw database.

respectively, in 1978)[31] that filed briefs in the case opposing the extension of patent protection to software. Equally noteworthy is the fact that the technology-transfer arm of a research university (Iowa State University) aligned with independent software providers in supporting the extension of patent protection. Structurally speaking, this alignment of interests is expected: an academic technology-transfer department and a stand-alone software provider are both R&D specialists that require a secure IP right to extract revenues on their intellectual assets.

These entity-specific differences in revealed preferences for IP protection for software are consistent with the theoretical expectations of the dynamic approach. Integrated manufacturers that embedded software within a bundle of complementary assets had little need for IP protection and strategic reasons to oppose it. By contrast, stand-alone software providers had few or no such assets and therefore sought some form of secure IP to monetize their R&D investment through direct sales to end users (which would trigger end-stage expropriation risk) and licensing transactions with intermediate users such as hardware manufacturers (which posed early-stage and possibly mid-stage expropriation risks). Incumbents' resistance was successful for about a decade. Courts' decisions effectively blocked the extension of patent protection until the Supreme Court upheld patent protection for certain software applications in *Diamond v. Diehr*, decided in 1981.[32] In an opinion authored by the same Judge Rich who had previously identified the "economic reasons" behind hardware firms' opposition to software patents, the Federal Circuit supplied a more expansive basis for software patents in its 1994 decision, *In re Alappat*.[33] As Adam Mossoff has observed,[34] current skepticism toward software patents fails to appreciate that the extension of some robust form of IP protection for software provided the institutional predicate for today's markets in which hardware and software applications are commonly debundled and priced separately. This not only benefits consumers through increased product variety but also promotes component-specific entry into markets that would otherwise be sheltered by the high capital and expertise requirements to construct end-to-end hardware and software bundles.

7.3 Advocacy and Lobbying Behavior (1986–2016)

Supreme Court patent litigation attracts amicus briefs from interested constituencies, which provide insights into those constituencies' policy preferences. Over the three-decade period extending from 1986 through 2016, there is a remarkable consistency in the relationship between the demand for patent rights (as expressed in amicus briefs) and organizational form. In general, larger and more integrated firms tend to express views consistent with a preference for weaker patents, while the converse is true for smaller and less integrated firms. The standing qualification to this pattern is the biopharmaceutical industry, in which all firms prefer stronger forms of patent protection, irrespective of size or level of integration. In this section, I review existing studies on advocacy behavior during this period and then present data on amicus briefs filed at the Supreme Court during 2006–2016. In the aggregate, the following discussion comprehensively surveys patent-policy preferences as revealed through amicus brief filings in all patent-related Supreme Court cases during 1986–2016.

7.3.1 Existing Studies

David Orozco and James Conley examined amicus briefs filed in patent cases before the Supreme Court during 1986–2008. They found that firms that were larger (defined as having more than five hundred employees) and active in industries characterized by innovations having a large number of patentable elements (for example, information technology) tended to oppose strong patent rights. The opposite outcomes prevailed among firms that were smaller and active in "discrete" innovation industries characterized by products having a small number of patentable elements (for example, pharmaceuticals).[35] Similarly, in a study of amicus briefs filed at the Supreme Court and the Federal Circuit involving patent-related cases during 1989–2009, Colleen Chien found that public corporations filed briefs favoring the patentee only 32 percent of the time; by contrast, universities favored patentees 75 percent of the time, and patent-holding companies favored the patentee virtually all the time. The opposition to strong patent protection was especially consistent in the case of "high-tech" and financial-services companies: among all amicus briefs filed by those companies in patent-related litigation at the Supreme Court and the Federal Circuit during 1989–2008, only 36 percent favored the position of the patentee.[36]

In related research, Jay Kesan and Andres Gallo studied lobbying behavior during 2007–2008 in connection with congressional deliberations over proposed reforms to the Patent Act. Consistent with widespread impressions, they found that large information-technology firms tended to lobby to reduce patent damages, to raise the threshold for obtaining patent protection, to limit the ability to obtain injunctive relief, and to expand opportunities for third parties to challenge issued or pending patents.[37] Other scholars have observed that financial-services firms similarly expressed support for these reforms (and, in particular, lobbied successfully for a new administrative post-grant review procedure for business-method patents).[38] In contrast, the same reforms were opposed by the pharmaceutical industry and a variety of weakly integrated innovation entities, including the biotechnology industry, small businesses, and patent-holding firms.[39] Additionally, as others have reported, VC firms, which supply the risk capital to support small-firm innovators, and academic research institutions, which are structurally analogous to an upstream, R&D-intensive, for-profit entity, have similarly resisted legislative proposals to weaken patent protections.[40]

7.3.2 Supreme Court Amicus Briefs (2006–2016)

To build upon and update the existing body of research, I collected all amicus briefs filed in the twenty-nine Supreme Court cases that principally involved patent-law issues and were decided during the ten-year period from January 1, 2006, through December 31, 2016. A few notes on methodology: The total sample includes 680 amicus briefs, which were "filed" (understood to mean filed directly or signed) by 1,539 individuals or entities. The total number of filers is larger than the total number of briefs filed, because a single amicus brief is often filed by multiple entities or individuals. To determine the party favored by the brief, I relied on the brief's opening statement of its position.[41] For purposes of the data presented here, each filer on a particular brief is treated individually, except in the case of a brief filed by a group of individuals (usually university professors), who are treated as a single filer. I assigned each filer to an "entity type" and to the industry in which it primarily operates (or, in the case of a trade association, the industry that it primarily represents). Compared to existing studies, I achieve more granular identifications of the IP-policy preferences of various industry and sub-industry segments, which yield valuable insights as described. Table 7.2 presents the principal findings.

In general, the dynamic approach anticipates that firms that are likely to have lower-cost access to non-IP instruments for extracting returns on innovation will be indifferent to, or strategically oppose, strong patent protection; firms that are likely to have higher-cost access to non-IP instruments will express the opposite set

Table 7.2 Amicus briefs in Supreme Court patent litigation (2006–2016)

Entity Type	No. Briefs "Filed"	Favors Patentee	Favors Alleged Infringer	Favors Neither Party
All firms (business entities)	740	30%	56%	14%
Fortune 500 firms	266	21%	65%	14%
Non–Fortune 500 firms	469	36%	50%	14%
Public firms	478	24%	62%	14%
Private firms	262	43%	44%	13%
Biopharmaceutical	89	75%	19%	6%
Medical devices and diagnostics	59	51%	34%	15%
Medical care/insurance/drug retailers	57	11%	88%	2%
Information and communications technology (all)	388	10%	75%	15%
ICT—platforms	77	1.3%	87%	12%
ICT—semiconductors	39	21%	72%	8%
Financial services (excluding venture capital)	47	11%	81%	9%
Venture capital	26	100%	0%	0%
Universities and other research entities (including technology-transfer departments but excluding individual academics)	82	96%	1%	2%
IP-licensing entities (excluding academic technology-transfer departments)	55	80%	5%	15%

Notes: Filer's status as a Fortune 500 or public/private firm was determined in each case as of the year in which it filed the relevant brief. To determine industry type, I relied on information disclosed in the company's annual report or website and, as necessary, patents "first assigned" to the filer or information in the trade press. Percentages for each row may not always sum to exactly 100 due to rounding. "IP-licensing entities" encompasses information-technology companies that have active R&D capacities, primarily earn revenues through IP licensing, and do not maintain any significant production, distribution, or other non-licensing capacities.

Source: Briefs primarily sourced through the Westlaw database. A more limited version of this table for 2008–2014 appeared in Barnett (2016, 34 tab. 1).

of IP-policy preferences. Relatedly, I anticipate that firms will tend to favor stronger patents to the extent that they originate new technologies, while those preferences will be reversed in the case of firms that primarily apply new technologies that are developed by others. These expectations are largely confirmed by the IP-policy preferences revealed through amicus briefs filed in Supreme Court patent-related litigation.

Firm Size

At the most general level, it is important to note that business entities in the aggregate exhibit a strong preference for alleged infringers over patentees, favoring the latter only 30 percent of the time. This runs directly counter to the common perception that "Big Business" favors strong patents as a barrier against competitive entry. Among business entities, the preference for alleged infringers over patentees intensifies as a firm grows in size, to the extent that size is measured by inclusion in the Fortune 500 (which ranks firms based on annual revenues) or (more imperfectly) by being listed on a public market. Firms that are included in the Fortune 500 have a somewhat weaker preference for patentees, favoring them only 21 percent of the time, as compared to non–Fortune 500 firms, which favor patentees 36 percent of the time. To the extent that public firms tend to be larger than private firms, there is a comparable indication that size tends to imply a more intensive level of IP skepticism: public firms favor the patentee only 24 percent of the time, as compared to 43 percent of the time in the case of private firms. The biopharmaceutical industry is the unsurprising exception to larger firms' preferences for weaker patent protection, favoring patentees 75 percent of the time. While I do not distinguish among firms in the biopharmaceutical industry based on size, this preference for patentees' interests almost certainly extends to large pharmaceutical firms that operate under integrated business models and, as is widely observed, are heavily reliant on strong patent protection. As discussed previously (see Chapter 1, section 1.2.5), the large disparity between the costs of R&D and commercialization, on the one hand, and the costs of imitation, on the other hand, coupled with a long commercialization time lag and low likelihood of success, implies that even large and vertically integrated firms lack adequate non-IP capacities by which to delay free-riding and capture a sufficient return in the absence of secure patent protection.

Level of Integration

There appears to be an approximate correlation between a firm's level of integration and its IP-policy preferences. For this purpose, I assess integration qualitatively based on how a particular entity, or an industry in which an entity operates, primarily extracts returns on its innovation assets, whether through licensing or other contractual relationships, integration into products or services, or otherwise, as described in its annual report, firm website, or scholarly and trade sources relating to that firm or that firm's industry segment. The IP-policy preferences conveyed by amicus brief filings indicate a disparity between entities that primarily extract revenues on innovation through licensing-based business models and entities that do so primarily through vertical integration into production and distribution or, as is especially relevant in certain software, search, and online market segments, "horizontal" (or systems-level) integration with complementary products and services.

Financial Services

The relationship between IP policy preferences and organizational form can be illustrated by comparing financial-services firms, which favor the patentee only 11 percent of the time, with VC firms and universities (including technology-transfer departments), which favor the patentee 100 percent and 96 percent of the time, respectively. Financial-services firms such as banks and credit-card companies operate under horizontally integrated business models in which financial innovations are typically developed internally and then monetized within a difficult-to-replicate bundle of services and supplementary know-how offered to business and individual customers, complemented by the provider's reputational goodwill.[42] The financial-services industry has undertaken vigorous (and successful) lobbying efforts against financial-method patents. In 1998 and 1999, the Federal Circuit issued decisions that rejected the view that nontechnical business methods necessarily fall into the category of "abstract ideas" that courts treat as non-patentable subject matter.[43] This in turn led to both an increase in the issuance of business-method patents and widely publicized litigations to enforce these patents against large financial institutions.[44] The financial-services lobby responded and achieved rapid success in 2000, when Congress enacted an amendment to the patent statute that provided for a prior-user defense against business-method patents, and the USPTO instituted a "second look" review mechanism for those patents.[45] By contrast, VC funds back start-ups that have valuable intellectual assets but are not vertically or horizontally integrated and are therefore exposed to larger, established firms that may replicate the functionality of a new product and then embed it within an existing production, marketing, and distribution infrastructure. University technology-transfer entities, which extract revenues through a licensing-based business model, exhibit similar strong-IP policy preferences, favoring the patentee 96 percent of the time. This is unsurprising: an academic research institution is a stand-alone R&D entity that relies on patents in order to earn revenues through licensing and other business relationships, given the absence of any meaningful technological, legal, or economic ability to integrate forward into downstream production or distribution capacities.

Information and Communications Technology

Unsurprisingly, firms that operate in the information and communications technology (ICT) market favor the patentee only 10 percent of the time, indicating a strong preference for weaker patent rights that is consistent with the policy views expressed by the industry's trade associations concerning patent reform. If we break down the pool of ICT filers into more narrowly defined segments, some interesting, if subtle, differences in IP-policy preferences can be observed. Firms that have significant platform-based businesses (seventy-seven filers in total) favor the patentee only 1 percent of the time, which reflects the fact that a platform-based business model provides an especially rich and difficult-to-replicate set of complementary capacities that can be used to monetize internal innovation assets or, as will be discussed in Chapter 8 (see section 8.2.2), sometimes thrives by appropriating IP assets developed by others. By contrast, there is less consensus in the semiconductor industry, where filers (thirty-nine in total) favor the patentee 21 percent of the time, suggesting that there is a significant portion of the industry that operates under a business model that performs best under stronger IP protection. The apparent lack of consensus over IP-policy preferences within the semiconductor industry most likely reflects the fact that, as discussed earlier (see Chapter 6, section 6.2), some portions of the industry operate under vertically integrated models (and therefore are prone to favor weaker forms of patent protection), while other portions of the industry operate under licensing-based models that rely on secure patent rights.

Supply-Chain Position

There appears to be an approximate correlation between a firm's location on the technology supply chain and its IP-policy preferences. Firms that occupy lower levels of the supply chain, and therefore tend to be net users of existing technology, prefer weaker IP rights, which lowers the costs of obtaining technology inputs from upstream suppliers. Those preferences are reversed in the case of upstream firms that occupy higher levels of the supply chain, tend to be net sources of new technologies, and sometimes operate under weakly integrated models that rely on licensing and other vertical arrangements with intermediate users to monetize their R&D investments. This relationship between supply-chain position and IP-policy preferences can be observed by comparing the biopharmaceutical and medical-device and diagnostics industry, on the one hand, and medical care and medical insurers, on the other hand. Firms in the former group tend to be net technology producers and, as expected, mostly favor the patentee, although the medical-device and diagnostics sector does so less consistently than the biopharmaceutical sector, favoring the patentee 51 percent of the time, as compared to 75 percent of the time in the case of biopharmaceutical firms. (The lower percentage of medical-device and/or diagnostics firms that favor the patentee most likely reflects the fact that some diagnostics firms appear to have extensive laboratory operations and, hence, may be net technology users.) By contrast, firms in the medical care, insurance, and retail drug industry, which are almost certainly net technology users, only favor the patentee 11 percent of the time.

7.4 Strategic Destruction of Intellectual Property

To change the strength of any given element of the patent system, or any other body of IP law, is a costly exercise, requiring extensive investment in lobbying and litigation activities, with little assurance of achieving a positive return on that investment. Firms have another option by which to adjust the *effective* strength of the relevant IP regime, even without any change in the *nominal* level of IP strength. As observed initially by Robert Merges, firms may have business reasons to acquire or develop a valuable technology and then distribute it at no charge, effectively waiving IP protections that could otherwise be used to exclude third parties.[46] Less drastically, the firm can distribute the technology at a low fee and subject to few technological or contractual constraints. Technology history supplies a surprisingly large number of cases in which firms have expended substantial amounts on developing a valuable technology and then distributed it at no charge (or a substantially "below-market" charge) into the market, effectively waiving IP protections available as a matter of law, either entirely or partially. Table 7.3 lists some notable giveaways, starting with AT&T's giveaway of the transistor as discussed previously (see Chapter 6, section 6.2).

These giveaways of valuable technology assets can have a powerful effect on the effective IP regime in the relevant market. Assuming no significant quality differences across competing products, a firm that adopts an IP-giveaway strategy pressures competitors to do the same, which then shifts the point on the relevant product and services bundle at which all firms can extract positive revenues. Without any change in IP protections as a matter of law, all competitors are effectively compelled to waive those protections as a matter of practice, pushing the price for the relevant technology to zero across the entire market but also compelling all providers to develop a complementary asset from which a positive revenue flow can be generated. The result is an effective change in the property-rights structure of the relevant technology market

Table 7.3 Technology giveaways

Year(s)	Firm(s)	Technology	Extent of Giveaway
1940–1984	Bell Labs (AT&T)	Transistor and related technologies	Low royalty with technical know-how, subject to cross-licensing obligation. Practice formalized in 1956 consent decree.
1980	Xerox, DEC, Intel	Ethernet local-area-network technology	Zero royalty.
1996	Intel	Universal Serial Bus (USB) technology	Zero royalty, subject to reciprocity condition.
1998	IBM, Intel, Ericsson, Nokia, Toshiba	Bluetooth	Zero royalty.
1998	Microsoft	Internet Explorer browser	Released at zero incremental charge, bundled with Windows operating system.
2008	Google	Android operating system	Open-source, zero royalty. Early release of updated versions to OEMs subject to contractual limitations.

Sources: On the transistor, see Levin (1982, 75–76); on Ethernet, see von Burg (2001, 4–5); on USB, see Intel (n.d., 5–7); on Bluetooth, see Han and Liu (2008, 32).

that operates to the advantage of firms that have the lowest-cost access to excludable complementary assets that can substitute for IP protections. As I will discuss, this "IP commoditization" strategy can be extraordinarily punishing for firms that only have a comparable competitive advantage in the portion of the supply chain in which the price has been reduced to zero.

7.4.1 Internet Explorer: The Browser Giveaway

Probably the most well-known example of an IP-commoditization strategy is Microsoft's response to Netscape's pioneering internet browser, the Netscape Navigator product that was released in 1994. As discussed in Chapter 2, section 2.2, Microsoft responded to Netscape by investing several hundreds of millions of dollars in developing its own browser, Internet Explorer, and then including it in the Windows package at no incremental charge to users. As a result, Netscape was compelled to reduce the price of certain versions of Netscape Navigator from approximately $40 to zero.[47] In short order, Netscape's market share fell from market leader to laggard to a nominal participant. The reason is straightforward. Under zero-price conditions, Microsoft could still capture positive revenues through its difficult-to-replicate complementary asset package consisting of the Windows operating system and the allied ecosystem of Windows-compatible software applications. By contrast, Netscape was a stand-alone entity that had a thin suite of complementary products and services from which to extract revenue in lieu of the foreclosed revenue stream from its primary asset, the browser. Microsoft's giveaway to end users had compelled Netscape to give away *its* crown jewel asset, which then shifted the locus of competition to a market segment in which Microsoft had a difficult-to-beat advantage. The commoditization effect of Microsoft's strategy continues to govern the effective property-rights structure in the browser market even today. To my knowledge, there is no general-use browser product available at a positive price in the consumer market.

7.4.2 Linux: The Operating-System Giveaway

The Linux operating system (or, more specifically, the Linux "kernel") supplies a more recent application of this technology-giveaway strategy—in this case, at Microsoft's expense. To appreciate this strategy, some background on the Linux kernel's licensing regime is necessary. The Linux kernel (the most critical part of an operating system) is distributed at no charge under a type of open-source license[48] that provides for free distribution and modification of the licensed code but requires that any distribution of the code (including any "derivative" modifications) take place on the same open-source terms. The result is that a portion of any third-party software (such as Google's Android operating system) that integrates Linux code may be subject to these open-source terms, which could then limit the third party's ability to assert exclusivity and sell the software as a stand-alone product. This is effectively a partial waiver of the copyright protections that apply to the Linux code, although the ability to enforce the open-source terms of the license with respect to derivative applications developed by third parties ultimately relies on the fact that the license is anchored in a copyright that protects the original code.

Many academic and other commentators have lauded this self-replicating free-distribution mechanism as an alternative and workable software-development model that relies on contributions from volunteer programmers and avoids the deadweight losses and access costs inherent to proprietary software development by for-profit firms.[49] Yet empirical studies of open-source projects have found that roughly half of all contributing programmers are employed or sponsored by for-profit firms or nonprofit foundations.[50] In 2005, a commentator stated in an IBM journal: "[T]he often quoted notion that such [open-source] software is written primarily by people working *gratis* for the general good is false."[51] The Linux project illustrates this observation. As of 2009 and 2017, Linux Foundation data showed that approximately 70 percent and 85 percent, respectively, of code contributions to (and an even larger percentage of "sign-offs" on code contributions to) the Linux operating system were made by employees of technology firms.[52] The utopian characterization of open-source software projects also ignores the fact that the most successful open-source projects typically rely on significant outside funding in order to construct the necessary infrastructure to support development and adoption activities.[53] It is perhaps not coincidental that the Linux project achieved significant market penetration concurrently with securing outside financial and other support from large technology companies.[54] IBM has been the most prominent of those sponsors, having announced in 2000 that it had invested $1 billion in the Linux project.[55]

IBM's support of the zero-priced Linux operating system followed Microsoft's own playbook in the browser market in its competition with Netscape. IBM is a leading firm in the server-hardware market, which had used Microsoft Windows as its dominant operating system. Whereas Microsoft enjoyed a competitive advantage in the operating-system segment of the server market, IBM enjoyed a competitive advantage in the hardware segment. By distributing a zero-priced operating-system product with comparable functionality, it appears that IBM sought to commoditize the operating- system segment, induce customers to migrate away from Microsoft Windows, and shift the principal point of revenue extraction to the hardware segment in which IBM enjoyed a stronger competitive position. Like the Microsoft-Netscape interaction in the browser market of the late 1990s, the IBM-Microsoft interaction in the server-operating-system market in the early 2000s illustrates how a firm can use a giveaway strategy to modify a market's *effective* property-rights structure even without any change in the IP rights that are formally available. Contrary to the standard incentives-access trade-off, this is a case in which IP strength was effectively reduced but entry costs may have increased, since any subsequent entrant would be compelled to assemble a bundle of at least two complementary products in order to compete effectively in the market.

7.5 Review

Academics and policymakers have generally operated under the assumption that strong IP rights necessarily entrench incumbent firms, which is a social cost that must be weighed against the increased innovation investment that may arise under stronger IP rights. This assumption no longer holds true once it is appreciated that certain firms—in particular, larger and more integrated firms—can match (or out-match) the IP rights supplied by the state by deploying non-IP mechanisms for capturing returns from innovation. If that is the case, then those firms are expected to be indifferent to changes in the strength of IP rights supplied by the state or may strategically advocate for weaker IP rights in order to erect an entry barrier to smaller and less integrated firms that cannot adopt non-IP mechanisms at a comparable or even any feasible cost. The revealed policy preferences of firms that invest in advocacy and lobbying efforts to influence the IP-policy trajectory are consistent with these theoretical expectations. With the anticipated exception of the biopharmaceutical industry, larger and more integrated firms tend to support weaker IP rights, ranging from railroads in the late nineteenth century, to hardware manufacturers in the 1960s and 1970s, to technology platforms in the early twenty-first century. By contrast, smaller and less integrated firms, and the investors that back those firms, tend to support stronger IP rights, as a necessary means by which to extract revenues from innovation in the absence of capital-intensive production and distribution capacities. If that is the case, then it is reasonable to rethink whether reducing the strength of IP rights necessarily lowers entry barriers and increases competitive intensity. In an important set of circumstances, just the opposite appears to be the case.

8

Organizational Perspectives on Intellectual-Property Reform

The current period in U.S. patent history can be approximately dated from the Supreme Court's 2006 decision in *eBay Inc. v. MercExchange LLC.*[1] That decision, together with subsequent decisions by the Supreme Court, enactment of the America Invents Act by Congress in 2011, and enforcement actions by the antitrust agencies, suggests that the U.S. patent system may be entering a fourth historical stage characterized by demonstrably weaker patent protection as compared to the robust property-rights regime that had been in place since the establishment of the Federal Circuit and the passage of the Bayh-Dole Act in the early 1980s. Historically, this period bears some resemblance to the early to mid-1930s, during which time the federal courts, led by the Supreme Court, transitioned from a relatively strong to a relatively weaker application of patent protections. I apply the dynamic approach to IP analysis to show how current advocacy and lobbying efforts concerning proposed and enacted patent reforms can be understood as largely a conflict between entities that tend to follow mostly entrepreneurial or mostly hierarchical models for funding and executing the innovation and commercialization process. Consistent with historical trends, large integrated firms in technology markets (outside of biopharmaceuticals), including firms that operate under horizontally integrated platform-based models, have been the principal advocates for weakening patent rights, while R&D-specialist entities, and their financial backers, have been the principal advocates for maintaining secure levels of patent protection. As a normative matter, a dynamic approach to recent patent reforms suggests that these changes may have simply enhanced the dominant position of large integrated incumbents—especially incumbents that operate leading platforms in certain information-technology segments—while erecting entry barriers to smaller, less integrated, and R&D-intensive firms that have historically played a critical role in the U.S. innovation economy.

8.1 Rolling Back the "Patent Revolution"

There can be little disagreement that policymakers—broadly understood to include courts, regulatory agencies, and federal legislators—have taken a series of steps over approximately the past decade that have materially weakened legal protections for patent holders. These changes have been led by a series of decisions by the Supreme Court, which have rejected or qualified prior decisions by the Federal Circuit that had

Innovators, Firms, and Markets. Jonathan M. Barnett, Oxford University Press (2021). © Oxford University Press.
DOI: 10.1093/oso/9780190908591.003.0009

strengthened patent protections relative to the "patent winter" that extended from the late New Deal through the 1970s. The Supreme Court's patent-skeptical trajectory has been accompanied by legislative action by Congress and policy statements and enforcement actions by the antitrust agencies that have further weakened patent strength. As summarized in Table 8.1, these actions have challenged patent owners' ability to deter infringement and, as a consequence, place at risk the property-rights infrastructure behind licensing transactions and other secondary markets in patent-protected knowledge assets. This rollback of patent rights is perhaps best captured by

Table 8.1 The patent rollback (2006–2018)

Year	Case/Action	Institutional Actor	Patent Feature Affected	Key Impact
2006	*eBay Inc. v. MercExchange LLC*	Supreme Court	Remedies	No "automatic" permanent injunction. Court has discretion under multifactor equitable standard.
2007	*KSR Int'l Co. v. Teleflex Inc.*	Supreme Court	Non-obviousness	Raises threshold for meeting nonobviousness requirement for patentability.
2007	FTC/DOJ Report on "Antitrust Enforcement and IP Rights"	FTC/DOJ	Remedies	Casts doubt on whether owner of a standard-essential patent is entitled to seek injunctive relief.
2011	America Invents Act	Congress	Patent validity	Expands opportunities for third parties to contest patent validity through administrative tribunals.
2012	*Mayo Collaborative Services v. Prometheus Labs, Inc.*	Supreme Court	Patentable subject matter	Rejects patentability of certain medical diagnostic inventions.
2013	*In the Matter of Motorola Mobility LLC and Google Inc.*	FTC	Remedies	Conditions approval of acquisition of patent portfolio on acquirer's agreement not to seek injunctive relief for standard-essential patents.
2013	*Ass'n for Molecular Pathology v. Myriad Genetics Inc.*	Supreme Court	Patentable subject matter	Rejects patentability of certain isolated genetic sequences.
2014	*Alice Corp. v. CLS Bank Int'l*	Supreme Court	Patentable subject matter	Casts doubt on patentability of software inventions involving generic computer implementation.
2018	*Oil States Services, LLC v. Greene's Energy Group, LLC*	Supreme Court	Patent validity	Upholds constitutionality of administrative mechanism to challenge patent validity.

Source: For full case citations, see References—Judicial Opinions and Administrative Rulings.

the 2018 Supreme Court decision *Oil States Services, LLC v. Greene's Energy Group, LLC*, in which the Court explicitly held that patents are best understood as the "grant of a public franchise," rather than as property rights (although it did suggest that patents may nonetheless be deemed "property" for certain limited purposes).[2]

8.1.1 The *eBay* Effect

Decided by the Supreme Court in 2006, *eBay Inc. v. MercExchange LLC*[3] involved a patent-infringement suit against the online auction website, eBay, by an entity that owned, in the Court's words, a "business method patent for an electronic market designed to facilitate the sale of goods between private individuals by establishing a central authority to promote trust among participants."[4] The patent owner had sought unsuccessfully to enter into a license with eBay, as it had already done with other firms. The *eBay* case took place against the background of a public perception that patents were sometimes being used for opportunistic purposes, as illustrated by an infringement suit brought by a patent-holding company against BlackBerry, then the leading cell-phone provider, which had resulted in a $612.5 million settlement payment to the patentee.[5] In its final decision, the Court overturned Federal Circuit precedent and rejected the historical presumption that a patentee is entitled to injunctive relief once it has defended patent validity and shown infringement. Rather, the Court held that a judge must weigh four factors before granting an injunction and, in some cases, could deny injunctive relief against an infringing defendant.[6] This effectively granted courts the ability to grant a judicially imposed compulsory license insofar as a patent plaintiff that was denied injunctive relief would be restricted to monetary damages for continuing infringement. The Court's majority opinion rejected any "categorical rule" that would deny injunctive relief to patent owners that operated under licensing-based business models,[7] while a concurring opinion authored by Chief Justice John Roberts suggested that courts should in general conform to the long-standing practice of granting injunctions to patentees who successfully defend validity and show infringement.[8] However, a concurring opinion authored by Justice Anthony Kennedy suggested that lower courts should take into account patentees' business model, making reference to "an industry" in which "firms use patents not as a basis for producing and selling goods but, instead, primarily for obtaining licensing fees."[9]

The lower courts have largely followed Justice Kennedy's concurring opinion. A study by Christopher Seaman of patent-litigation outcomes for the seven-and-a-half-year period after the *eBay* decision found that nonpracticing patent owners had a limited chance of securing injunctive relief (approximately 16 percent of the time on average), a remedy that courts largely reserved for operating businesses.[10] This de facto two-tier-remedies regime based on a patent owner's entity type effectively puts in place a modified working requirement, a concept that had been specifically rejected by the Court in 1908[11] and is not contemplated by the patent statute. While practicing patentees largely operate under a remedy regime consisting of injunctive relief against future infringement and monetary damages for past infringement, nonpracticing patentees largely operate under a remedy regime consisting of only monetary damages for both past and future infringement. Even in the case of practicing patentees, the Seaman study found that the likelihood of securing injunctive relief, rather than only monetary damages, had diminished materially (from nearly 100 percent to 80 percent of cases in which the patentee defends validity and shows infringement).[12] The expanding scope of the "*eBay* effect"—that is, the increasing population of patentees that are practically ineligible for injunctive relief—was illustrated vividly by the headline patent litigation in 2014 between Apple and Samsung, in which Apple, despite prevailing on validity and infringement, failed to secure in the district court even a "sunset" injunction (an injunction with a staged "phase-in" period).[13] Although the decision was reversed on appeal a year later,[14] it nonetheless reflects the increased willingness of federal courts to deny injunctive relief even in classic "head-to-head" patent disputes involving operational firms in technology-intensive markets.

8.1.2 The *Mayo/Alice* Effect

In retrospect, the *eBay* case signaled the end of the strong-patent regime that had been launched by the establishment in 1982 of the Federal Circuit and the shutdown injunction issued in Polaroid's 1986 infringement litigation against Kodak's instant-camera division, an order that is almost impossible to contemplate being issued in today's legal and policy climate. Subsequent decisions by the Supreme Court have further weakened patent protections by reducing the scope of patentable subject matter, which in turn induces defendants in infringement litigation to challenge the validity of an asserted patent on subject-matter grounds under section 101 of the Patent Act.[15] If successful, this is an especially effective strategy, since patentable subject matter is generally treated as a question of law rather than of fact,[16] which means that an alleged infringer can potentially secure dismissal at an early stage in the litigation before an extensive and costly discovery process. However, until relatively recently, this strategy was generally not likely to succeed. The principal reason was the Supreme Court's 1980 decision in *Diamond v. Chakrabarty*,[17] in which it had broadly defined patentable subject matter as being "anything under the sun that is made by man."[18] Today it is similarly impossible to contemplate the Court making such a statement. In the software, biotechnology, and medical diagnostic fields, the Court rendered decisions in 2010, 2012, 2013, and 2014 that cast substantial doubt on the patentability of substantial portions of inventive output in those markets.[19] In a 2014 decision, *Alice Corp. v. CLS Bank International*,[20] which applied the test for patentability set forth in the Court's 2012 decision in *Mayo Collaborative Services v. Prometheus Labs, Inc.*, the Court potentially placed at risk tens of thousands of patents covering software-related applications across a wide range of industries. Initial data indicates that this risk has materialized to some extent. From July 2014 (one month after *Alice* was decided) until June 2018, courts applied the *Alice* decision and related precedents in 692 litigations involving challenges to patent validity on subject-matter grounds. In that sample, courts reached a finding of invalidity 65.8 percent of the time (60.8 percent at the district court level and 87.5 percent at the Federal Circuit).[21] Construed in "positive" terms, this means that district courts upheld the validity of patents challenged on subject-matter grounds (under the *Alice* precedent) 39.2 percent of the time; by contrast, the previously discussed study by Henry and Turner had found that district courts upheld the validity of contested patents (on any grounds) 74.3 percent of the time during 1983–2006 and 45.8 percent of the time during 1939–1983.[22] This is a strong indicator that the U.S. patent system is moving toward a historically weaker level of patent protection.

8.1.3 The PTAB Patent Discount

Judicial skepticism toward robust patent protection has been complemented by similarly minded actions taken by the legislative branch. In 2011, Congress enacted the America Invents Act (AIA).[23] Among other provisions, the AIA enables any third party—including parties that would otherwise have no standing to bring a legal action against the patentee in district court—to contest the validity of an issued patent on grounds of obviousness or lack of novelty (corresponding to sections 102 and 103 of the Patent Act), based on "prior art consisting of patents or printed publications," by filing a petition through the *inter partes* review (IPR) mechanism at the Patent Trial and Appeals Board (PTAB).[24] In addition to elimination of the "case or controversy" standing requirement, the IPR proceedings differ from a district court litigation insofar as the challenger need only prove unpatentability by a preponderance of the evidence, rather than the "clear and convincing" standard used in patent litigation in federal district court.[25]

These petitioner-friendly features reflect the key policy motivation behind the IPR mechanism, which was expressly designed to correct for the perceived underperformance of the USPTO's examination mechanism in screening out low-value patent applications. If that view is correct, then the PTAB would be judged a success. From 2014 through 2017, approximately 60 to 75 percent of IPR petitions were "instituted" annually (akin to surviving a motion to dismiss in civil litigation), with the rate stabilizing at approximately 60 percent for 2017 and 2018.[26] After institution, approximately 75 to 80 percent of challenged claims were ultimately invalidated on an annual basis during 2014–2018, with the rate stabilizing at approximately 75 percent for 2017 and 2018.[27] The high rates at which challengers achieve invalidation raise concerns that the IPR mechanism is erroneously screening out higher-value patents. Relatedly, owners of higher-value patents may now be discouraged from taking legal action to enforce a patent, since doing so would likely prompt the accused infringer to initiate a PTAB challenge, imposing additional legal fees and potentially resulting in invalidation of the patent against all potential infringers. This concern is especially salient

in the case of individual and small-firm patent owners, which may lack sufficient resources to fund a two-pronged litigation in the PTAB and federal district court, especially if the infringer is a well-resourced firm that can litigate almost indefinitely
(and, given the *eBay* effect, may often face no credible threat of injunctive relief). On
this point, it is noteworthy that the top ten petitioners at the PTAB during 2018 included some of the world's largest technology firms, such as Apple, Microsoft, Google,
Samsung, Intel, and Huawei.[28] The PTAB mechanism undoubtedly renders the patent
system a less attractive mechanism by which to extract returns on R&D, relative to all
other appropriation strategies, and this is especially the case for smaller firms that may
often rely most heavily on the patent system to extract returns on innovation.

8.1.4 The Antitrust Campaign against Standard-Essential Patents

Since approximately the mid-2000s, U.S. antitrust agencies have issued policy statements and taken enforcement actions that have substantially reduced the value of
"standard-essential" patents (SEPs) in the smartphone and related information-
technology markets. In particular, the FTC, the DOJ's Antitrust Division, and the
USPTO expressed concern, both separately and together, in policy statements
released in 2003, 2007, 2011, and 2013 that SEP owners could use the threat of an injunction to extract exorbitant royalties from producers and other firms that had made
substantial investments in standard-compliant equipment and infrastructure.[29] In
the 2013 report, the DOJ and the USPTO,[30] as well as the FTC in consent decrees issued in 2013,[31] expressed the view that SEP owners should be deemed to have waived
their right to seek an injunction and could even be subject to antitrust liability for
violating this implied waiver. In approximately contemporaneous infringement litigations involving SEPs, three U.S. district courts held in 2012 and 2013 that an SEP
owner may not seek an injunction (except possibly in the scenario where the alleged
infringer refuses to negotiate or pay a royalty rate that is consistent with the SEP owner's commitment to "fair, reasonable and nondiscriminatory" (FRAND) licensing).[32]
Additionally, the judges in two of those cases assessed (or, on appeal, upheld) attor-
neys' fees against the *patentee* for seeking an injunction.[33] While the Federal Circuit
has specifically rejected any "no-injunction" rule for SEP owners, it, too, has held
that an SEP owner can only seek injunctive relief if the infringer demonstrates unwillingness to accept or negotiate a FRAND-compliant license.[34] In late 2019, DOJ
Antitrust and the USPTO jointly abandoned this position on SEPs[35] (which followed
a similar policy shift announced by DOJ Antitrust in November 2017),[36] but the FTC
continues to endorse this view strongly, as exemplified by its antitrust suit against
Qualcomm (which prevailed on appeal in August 2020, after an FTC win at the district court level), a leading SEP owner in the smartphone market.

The sum-total effect of these developments means that a substantial portion of
the patents issued in the wireless-communications and related IT markets—and, in

particular, patents that have been issued to the key innovators behind the smartphone ecosystem—now effectively operate under a liability-rule regime in which no injunctive threat can be credibly asserted. This special treatment of SEPs effectively extends the "*eBay* effect" to a quantitatively and qualitatively significant population of patentees that are now precluded from seeking injunctive relief against infringing parties. For a well-resourced device producer that can fund litigation on an almost indefinite basis, its preferred course of action may now be to infringe and invite the IP owner to incur the costs of bringing suit. Unless a court finds willful infringement (a relatively infrequent occurrence), the producer's worst-case scenario is most likely a reasonable royalty damages award close to the license fee that it would have negotiated voluntarily (plus legal fees), while its most likely scenario is a settlement payment negotiated in the shadow of the truncated range of potential litigation outcomes under an almost-no-injunction patent regime.

8.1.5 Bolstering Trade-Secret Protection

There is one exception to the organizationally driven divide in IP-policy preferences.[37] In 2016, the U.S. Congress passed the Defend Trade Secrets Act (DTSA),[38] which provides for a federal cause of action against misappropriation of trade secrets. The DTSA largely tracks existing causes of action against misappropriation of trade secrets under state law but provides trade-secret claimants with an additional avenue for bringing litigation in cases of alleged misappropriation and may foster national uniformity in the treatment of trade-secret misappropriation. The DTSA enjoyed bipartisan support, passing in the House of Representatives by a vote of 410–2 and enjoying unanimous support in the Senate.[39] As noted, the AIA, which weakened patent protections, was generally supported by integrated firms in information- and communications-technology markets while opposed by firms that operate under disintegrated licensing-based business models (and investors in those firms). By contrast, the DTSA enjoyed virtually universal support across technology-intensive industries irrespective of the dominant business model. This uniformity of views is consistent with the organizational approach to IP analysis. For a substantially integrated firm, stronger trade-secret protections naturally support a business strategy that relies on capturing value from innovation activities through internal informational and capital markets. While a less integrated firm generally pursues a business strategy that relies significantly on patents to extract value from innovation through contractual relationships with third parties, it does not do so exclusively and may welcome stronger trade-secret protection, since it provides a tool that the firm may use for informational assets that cannot otherwise meet the requirements for patentability (or that the firm wishes to keep secret for strategic reasons). Alternatively, some technology firms' support for the DTSA may reflect "second-best" IP-policy preferences in a weak-patent environment, which compels those firms to adopt non-patent-dependent integrated structures for extracting value from innovation investments.

8.2 IP Strength, Organizational Structure, and Policy Preferences

The current legal environment occupies a historical twilight zone situated between the strong-patent regime established in the early 1980s and a weaker-patent regime that is currently being put in place by the "patent rollback" starting in the mid-2000s. The dynamic approach to IP rights anticipates that any such change would have disparate implications for firms that operate under different organizational structures for undertaking innovation and commercialization, which in turn would predict disparate policy preferences being expressed by those firms with respect to those changes in IP protection. In the current ongoing regime shift, the population of integrated firms that are advantaged by this shift includes both vertically integrated firms, such as Intel in the semiconductor industry, and "non-vertically" integrated firms (meaning firms that operate in complementary but non-vertically related markets), such as Google in the online search and advertising markets, which have a rich suite of complementary excludable assets and capacities. By contrast, R&D-specialist, substantially vertically disintegrated entities, such as a fabless firm in the semiconductor market or a scientist-founded start-up without independent production capacities in the biotech market, any technology-transfer division of a research university, as well as VCs and other investors in R&D-mostly entities, are all disadvantaged by a weak-patent regime shift, since it undermines those entities' licensing-based and other contractual structures for funding and monetizing R&D investments. The same is true of even large, integrated firms in the biopharmaceutical industry, which require a secure property-rights umbrella to deter imitators that bear drastically lower (and, as a result of government intervention under the Hatch-Waxman Act and related regulatory frameworks, artificially reduced) costs and risks compared to innovators.

In this section, I examine more closely these relationships between IP strength, organizational form, and IP-policy preferences in the case of Qualcomm, Intel (briefly), and Google/Alphabet. Each entity operates under a different organizational structure, which in turn yields differences in the extent to which each entity type is advantaged or disadvantaged by, and has therefore attempted to promote or resist, the downward shift in patent protections since the mid-2000s. More briefly, I also explore an extension of the dynamic approach to the interaction between organizational structure and the strength of copyright protections in content markets.

8.2.1 Disintegration: Qualcomm

Qualcomm provides an especially concrete illustration of the extent to which robust IP rights enable upstream R&D-intensive firms to lower entry costs and employ contractual relationships to enter into mutually profitable relationships with firms that specialize in the downstream functions that are necessary to convert innovation into a viable product for applicable intermediate- and end-user markets. As discussed previously (see Chapter 6, section 6.3.1), Qualcomm was founded in 1985 by a group of university scientists who pioneered the CDMA technology that challenged the then-dominant but less efficient TDMA-based standard. Based on its widely acknowledged superior performance, CDMA was ultimately adopted as the foundational technology for 3G and 4G wireless-communications networks that have enabled the efficient transmission of voice and non-voice data, which in turn have supported novel business models in a variety of industries. While Qualcomm initially designed and manufactured the chips that embodied its technologies, it divested its manufacturing operations and has since operated under a fabless model in which it innovates new chip designs, outsources production to third-party foundries, and then distributes the physical chipset to device producers. More specifically, as shown in Figure 8.1, Qualcomm carries out IP licensing through a subsidiary known as Qualcomm Technology Licensing (QTL) and chipset sales through a subsidiary known as Qualcomm CDMA Technologies (QCT). Formally, QTL enters into licensing contracts with device assemblers, such as Hon Hai Precision Company (also known as Foxconn), which are then reimbursed through wholesale payments by branded device manufacturers such as Apple.

Expropriation Risks and IP-Policy Preferences

It is not surprising that Qualcomm has consistently supported strong patent protections in its advocacy behavior. During 2006–2016, it filed amicus briefs in five Supreme Court patent-related litigations and supported the patentee in each case. Qualcomm's vertically disintegrated business model relies on its patent portfolio at three critical points in the technology supply chain. First, Qualcomm relies on patents in order to safely disclose some of its technology to competitors and other entities that participate in the standard-setting organizations through which leading

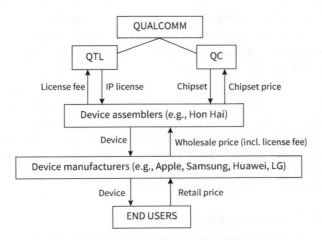

Figure 8.1 Qualcomm's (mostly) licensing-based revenue model
Source: The figure is based in part on information in Qualcomm (2018).

information-technology firms agree on the common standards for a new technology field. Second, Qualcomm relies on patents in order to safely enter into contractual relationships with third-party providers of the chip-production functions that are necessary to embed a new chip design in a physical chipset. Following the fabless model discussed in Chapter 6, section 6.2, Qualcomm specializes in chip design and enters into contractual relationships with foundries that specialize in chip production. Third, Qualcomm relies on patents in order to safely enter into licensing relationships with original-equipment manufacturers that integrate the chips into devices for end users, for which Qualcomm requires remuneration to earn a return on the R&D investment that underlies those products.

Absent patent protection, Qualcomm would be exposed to substantial expropriation risk at each of these three key transactional points, given counterparties' technical sophistication and financial resources. The ability to disclose technological assets under a secure property-rights umbrella has favorable effects on the market as a whole. First, the standard-setting process is the mechanism for achieving interoperability among competing communications devices, which in turn promotes the network effects that drive market growth and facilitates entry by new producers and other firms that can simply conform to the existing standard, rather than having to assemble a competing end-to-end technological design. Second, the foundry relationship between chip designers and chip producers dramatically lowers the capital requirements for entry into the semiconductor market by relieving any chip-design firm from having to raise the capital necessary to support the infrastructural investment required to construct a new fabrication facility (as of 2011, estimated at $1.5 to $3 billion).[40] Third, licensing relationships between upstream IP owners and downstream device producers dramatically lower the technical requirements for entry into the production segment of the market by enabling any prospective producer to gain access to all required technology inputs through a simple licensing transaction. According to its 2018 annual report, Qualcomm has licensed its CDMA-related and LTE-related technologies to several hundred firms worldwide,[41] which may account in part for both the robust entry rates and relatively rapid turnover in the global handset-production market since its inception. While Apple and Samsung currently dominate the U.S. market, they are rapidly losing market share outside the United States to Chinese entrants such as Huawei and Xiaomi, just as companies such as Nokia and BlackBerry that once dominated the market suffered rapid losses of market leadership and have now exited it entirely.[42] Contrary to conventional expectations, this appears to be a market in which patents, and patent licenses, decrease access costs for intermediate users and, as a result, lower entry barriers into the downstream production market. (This is another illustration of the "inverted" scenario contemplated in the theoretical discussion in Chapter 1, section 1.2.2.)

The Myth of the All-Powerful SEP Owner

Given that Qualcomm's technology currently is a critical input for any 3G- or 4G-enabled mobile communications device, it may nonetheless be objected (and is commonly argued) that Qualcomm is (and other similarly situated SEP owners are) in a position to assess "exorbitant" royalty rates that discourage entry into the production market and increase prices in the consumer market. Two factors, however, constrain the rate-setting power of the owner of even a critical IP asset. First, in general, a "high" royalty rate is self-defeating to the extent that it inhibits adoption by device producers or retail consumers, which in turn depresses market growth and limits the royalty base from which licensing fees can be extracted. This is especially true in platform-technology markets where product value relies significantly on network effects, which in turn requires seeding and sustaining a strong critical mass of initial and continuing adopters. Second, in the particular case of the smartphone market, the pricing power of an IP owner is disciplined to the extent that it derives a significant portion of its licensing revenues from a small handful of device producers that occupy strongly branded distribution positions in the end-user market. Largely omitting any consideration of these qualifying considerations, the view that upstream innovators such as Qualcomm are in a position to assess "exorbitant" royalty rates has been adopted and promoted by competition regulators ranging from China to the European Union to the United States (the exception being the DOJ Antitrust Division since a policy shift announced in November 2017).[43] This regulatory campaign culminated in the FTC's antitrust litigation against Qualcomm, which was filed in 2017 and resulted in a finding of liability and an expansive remedy being issued by the district court in 2019.[44] If the remedy had been implemented (in August 2020, the FTC lost on appeal in the U.S. Court of Appeals for the Ninth Circuit),[45] it would have required Qualcomm to renegotiate hundreds of existing licenses with device producers around the world and offer licenses to its direct competitors in the chip-supply market.

This regulatory consensus, and the far-reaching interventions that it has sought to implement, rest on a surprisingly thin body of empirical evidence. If the regulatory (and much of the academic) consensus were correct, we would expect to observe a smartphone market that suffers from declining output, increasing prices, and meager entry as a result of the heavy burden imposed by profit-maximizing IP licensors. In actuality, the smartphone market has rapidly expanded, prices (adjusted for increased functionality) have fallen, adoption has extended across a broad range of income segments, and entry into the production market has been robust. Contrary to claims that SEP owners assess in the aggregate double-digit royalty burdens on device producers in the smartphone and related markets,[46] empirical studies have determined that the total estimated aggregate royalty burden paid to all IP licensors represents on average single- to mid-digit percentages of the price paid by consumers.[47]

This apparently restrained pricing strategy on the part of dominant patent owners should not be surprising. We have already observed this "generous" behavior in the case of Elias Howe, the pioneer patentee in the sewing-machine industry in the mid-nineteenth century; Universal Oil Products, the owner of a key petroleum-refining technology in the early twentieth century; and the owners of the Cohen-Boyer patent in the biotechnology industry in the late twentieth century. A broad-base, low-rate licensing strategy is consistent with the economic self-interest of an upstream R&D-specialist firm that has no strategic incentive to block entry in the downstream product market. Contrary to standard assumptions, it is the nonpracticing patentee (defined loosely to include firms that do not operate in the customer-facing end-user market) that often has the strongest incentives to maintain a "low" royalty rate in order to maximize access by downstream producers and other intermediate users. Additionally, a repeat-play licensor seeks to maximize long-term revenues by securing widespread adoption of the relevant standard (usually in the face of competition from alternative standards), generating network effects that drive end-user adoption and expand the royalty base, deterring infringement by producers that may risk paying damages in lieu of a royalty fee perceived to be "excessive," and developing a track record of "reasonable" rate setting to promote adoption of its future innovations for subsequent technology standards (3G, 4G, 5G, and so on). Given these considerations, a patent-enabled monetization strategy based on vertical licensing relationships between upstream innovators and downstream implementers would appear to generate significant efficiency gains from broad technology dissemination but meager efficiency losses in the form of negotiation and litigation costs and increased device prices for end users. The virtuous combination of declining quality-adjusted prices, expanding output, and continuous innovation in patent-intensive information-technology markets is fully consistent with this view.

Regulators, and commentators who are sympathetic to the regulatory consensus, might nonetheless respond that the market would have grown even faster but for the "licensing tax" imposed by upstream patent owners. This hypothetical "what if" argument exhibits strong symptoms of what Harold Demsetz famously called the "Nirvana fallacy"[48]—namely, the tendency to compare observed outcomes against a theoretical state of affairs that is more efficient but not practically feasible. Precisely to avoid this intellectual pitfall, the dynamic approach to IP analysis compares the organizational forms and market architecture that are observed under strong forms of IP protection against the organizational forms and market architecture that would likely arise under some weaker form of IP protection. Without a secure patent infrastructure to support licensing and other relationships involving the exchange of informational assets, vertically disintegrated monetization mechanisms would likely be placed at risk, and competitive forces would then favor large integrated entities that can execute internally much or all of the innovation and commercialization process. While total innovation investment may not necessarily decline (as would be anticipated by the conventional incentive rationale for IP rights), this organizational distortion may give rise to efficiency losses relative to the organizational forms and market structure under a stronger-patent regime. While upstream R&D-specialist firms that thrive under a strong-patent regime must license, and exchange valuable informational assets with, downstream producers and other entities in order to achieve commercialization, this is not the case for integrated entities that can execute this process internally and have little incentive to disclose valuable IP assets to competitors (except to the extent necessary to achieve interoperability objectives in conjunction with other firms, subject to antitrust constraints on horizontal cooperation). The counterfactual market that would arise under a weak-patent regime would certainly be relieved to a certain extent from the litigation and transaction costs associated with a strong-patent regime. However, it would likely suffer from *other* transaction costs inherent to the exchange of informational assets among potentially adverse third parties. In response to those costs, innovation-intensive markets would likely exhibit reduced technology diffusion, higher entry barriers, and reduced market specialization, given that any viable competitor would be compelled to adopt more capital-intensive integrated structures that can extract returns on innovation while minimizing contractual relationships with third parties.

8.2.2 Integration: Intel, Google

The revenue models employed by integrated entities in the information-technology ecosystem differ markedly from Qualcomm's mostly unintegrated, licensing-based model. Contemporary information-technology markets exhibit two types of integrated models: (i) vertically integrated models, exemplified in the semiconductor market by a firm such as Intel; and (ii) non-vertically (or "horizontally") integrated models, exemplified in the search market by a firm such as Google. Both types of integrated structures employ complementary non-IP assets by which to extract returns on innovation even in the absence of secure IP rights over the core informational asset. Intel's model is more straightforward and largely conforms to vertically integrated models in conventional manufacturing industries that maintain mostly self-contained supply chains from innovation through distribution. Intel has a difficult-to-replicate suite of complementary non-IP assets (especially chip-fabrication facilities that necessitate infrastructural levels of capital investment and deep technical expertise) and does not appear to rely on its patent portfolio to generate licensing revenue.[49] Intel's vertically integrated structure accurately anticipates its revealed IP-policy preferences, which generally favor weaker levels of patent protection. In the twenty-nine patent-related Supreme Court cases decided during 2006–2016, Intel filed amicus briefs supporting the alleged infringer in eleven cases and supporting neither party in three cases (it never supported the patentee). By contrast, Google (the focus of the next part of this discussion) employs a non-vertical integration strategy that relies on both (i) internally developed innovations, which it embeds within its existing systems-level technology platforms and typically provides to users at no charge, and (ii) harvesting others' informational assets and delivering those assets at no charge to individual users. Given these "IP-giveaway" business strategies, we can anticipate that Google's revealed policy preferences generally favor weak levels of IP protection. In the twenty-nine patent-related Supreme Court cases decided during 2006–2016, Google filed amicus briefs supporting the alleged infringer in fourteen cases and supporting neither party in three cases (it never supported the patentee). As described in the last part of this section, Google's subsidiary, YouTube, has adopted similar advocacy positions to secure legal changes that weaken copyright protections in content markets.

Google Search and Related Services

Google's revenue model somewhat curiously relies on distributing some of its most valuable technology assets at a zero price. This model involves a cross-subsidization mechanism in which the firm distributes to end users valuable informational assets at no charge in order to promote sales of advertising services and associated user information to paying business users. As shown in Figure 8.2, Google provides giveaways to two different populations: (i) users receive search services and certain other Google applications at a zero price, subject to the right to access and distribute certain user data; and (ii) device manufacturers and telecom carriers receive access to Google applications and upgraded versions of the Android operating system at a zero price, subject to certain contractual commitments. To preserve its competitive position in the zero-price search market and then extract rents in the positive-price advertising market, Google deploys technological mechanisms, contractual instruments, and complementary assets that raise entry barriers into the search market even without the use of formal IP rights. These assets include Google's search algorithms (which may be costly to reverse-engineer on a continuously updated basis); the installed base of billions of end users, advertisers, and developers, who in the latter two cases may incur significant costs in switching to an alternative platform; and the use of contractual mechanisms to govern access to Google's applications by device manufacturers and telecom carriers. In particular, Google provides device manufacturers and telecom carriers with advance access to proprietary Google applications and updates of the open-source Android operating system, all of which are delivered at a zero price subject to "mobile application distribution agreements" (MADAs) under which the recipient agrees to preload certain Google applications, treat certain Google applications as "default" options, and provide preferential display to those applications.[50] Given that those contractual limitations necessarily impose certain costs on device

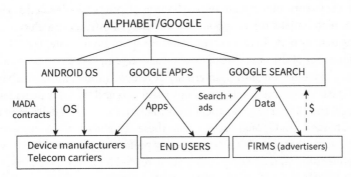

Figure 8.2 Google's multisided giveaway-based revenue model

Notes: Google Apps does not include applications provided by third-party developers on the Google Play site. MADA refers to mobile application distribution agreements. OS refers to operating system.

manufacturers, it would be more precise to say that Google's Android operating system is distributed on a partially free basis.

Google's giveaways support a positive revenue stream by exploiting complementarities between the intermediate-user, end-user, and advertiser markets. Google's unpriced search services and related applications (and information delivered through those services and applications) attract an installed base of device manufacturers, telecom carriers, and individual users, which generate data that can be used to attract paying advertisers. This multisided revenue model anticipates that Google would have weak demand for, or actively oppose, IP rights that might raise manufacturers' and carriers' costs of adopting and maintaining, and end users' costs of using, the search platform, which would in turn limit the user base from which Google can extract advertising sales. For a platform operator such as Google, patents not only provide little marginal value in light of its non-IP mechanisms for extracting value from its search platform but run counter to its giveaway model, which seeks to minimize intermediate users' and end users' costs of adopting and using the platform, which in turn maximizes the pool of user data that can be offered to advertisers.

To appreciate this point, consider a mobile-device user who wishes to access Google's search and other services through the purchase and use of a smartphone device. With respect to its own innovations in search technology (e.g., an improved traffic navigation service), Google can earn returns by embedding them within its existing search platform, which may attract additional users (or may induce existing users to use the platform more frequently), which in turn generates a larger or more targeted pool of data for sale to advertisers. Patents held by chip makers and suppliers of other components in the smartphone-device market increase the royalty overhead of device manufacturers and telecom carriers, which then increases to some extent the cost of devices, wireless subscriptions, and other services sold to consumers. Everything else being equal, any increase in the total costs borne by end users to purchase or use a smartphone device or wireless-communications service (or certain features of that device or service) will limit usage of the search-platform and related technologies through which Google acquires user data for sale to advertisers.

YouTube (Extension to Copyright)

Google's giveaway model is most profitable not only under a weak-patent regime but under a weak-copyright regime as well. Google's ability to attract advertisers to its platform increases as a positive function of the number of users, who are in turn attracted by the maximal quantity and quality of content at the lowest price— preferably, zero. Hence, Google has an interest in minimizing the platform's costs of securing and delivering the informational inputs that flow through its search platform and related applications to end users. Consistent with this objective, Google has facilitated users' ability to distribute and access "free" copyright-protected content through its search platform, YouTube, and other applications. When sued for copyright infringement (mostly under secondary infringement theories), Google has used this opportunity to secure judicial precedents that have reduced substantially its (and other platforms') exposure to copyright-infringement claims. The result has been an effective adjustment of the property-rights regime in content markets such that online-platform operators can take certain relatively low-cost measures (most notably, the notice-and-takedown mechanism) to substantially limit liability exposure for either directly distributing copyright-protected content or facilitating infringement by end users who copy and distribute copyright-protected content through the platform.

Google's (and, in some cases, YouTube's) successes in defending against copyright-infringement claims have generated two categories of precedents that have substantially diluted copyright protections for content owners in digital markets. First, Google has secured expansive judicial understandings of the "fair use" exemption to copyright infringement, which protects both Google and Google's users from infringement liability in certain contexts. In litigations involving challenges to the Google Books project, in which Google made digital copies of millions of copyright-protected books, the court adopted a broad definition of the "fair use" exemption that deemed copying for certain online-search purposes to be a "transformative" use and therefore immune from copyright-infringement liability.[51] Second, Google has secured generous judicial interpretations of statutory safe harbors from secondary copyright-infringement liability for internet platforms, in particular as provided in section 512(c) of the Digital Millennium Copyright Act (DMCA).[52] In a landmark decision involving Viacom (as the plaintiff and copyright holder) and YouTube (as the defendant), a federal court effectively held that online-content hosting sites such as YouTube do not have anything more than a minimal affirmative duty to monitor users' conduct for potentially infringing activity.[53] This decision and others that have adopted similar positions[54] reflect an interpretation of the DMCA in which the lion's share of the burden of policing copyright infringement falls on content owners. While platforms must respond expeditiously to content owners' takedown requests, this is largely an edentulous remedy that has little deterrent force against future infringement, given users' ability to simply repost infringing material. This predicament is illustrated by the fact that large content owners reportedly now typically choose *not* to file a takedown notice and instead elect to receive a share of YouTube's advertising revenue that is deemed to be attributable to the infringing content.[55] While this provides some positive remuneration, the share offered by YouTube is necessarily distorted, given YouTube's outside option to offer exactly zero and compel content owners to continue the "cat and mouse" game of the Section 512(c) takedown procedure.

Google's advocacy of weak copyright derives from the same business rationale, and associated organizational structure, as its advocacy of weak patents. So long as it does not invest extensively in original-content production, a platform operator such as YouTube is advantaged by a weak-copyright regime, which drives down the price of obtaining the content without which the platform has little value for users. In general, the platform's expected revenues increase as copyright enforcement weakens, users' access costs fall, and, as a result, users spend more time on the platform, which generates data that can be sold to advertisers. These IP-policy preferences are reversed in the case of a stand-alone content producer. Like Qualcomm in the technology context, a content producer such as Disney (among others) occupies the top of the supply chain and operates under a business model in which the firm invests in content production and earns a return on that investment through direct sales to consumers in the theatrical, home-video, and streaming markets. Disney therefore relies on secure IP rights (in conjunction with technological mechanisms) in order to deter unauthorized copying and distribution by third parties that have not borne the millions of dollars in production and marketing costs that stand behind an original creative property. A strong-copyright regime is often summarily dismissed in popular discussion and much of the academic literature as a rent-seeking mechanism that inflates profit margins for entrenched and over-rewarded content owners. Yet this same body of commentary has failed to recognize that a weak-copyright regime induces an organizational bias that undermines stand-alone content-monetization models while favoring platform operators that give away content in order to drive sales in a complementary-goods market where the platform has a competitive advantage and can earn a positive return. The fate of Disney in a weak-copyright regime is structurally equivalent to the fate of Qualcomm in a weak-patent regime.

8.3 Normative Lessons from the Apple/Qualcomm Dispute

The contrast between different models for monetizing R&D, and the viability of those models in different property-rights environments, can be illustrated by the sequence of patent-infringement and antitrust litigations involving, on the one hand, Qualcomm, the dominant patent owner and chip-design firm in the global smartphone market, and, on the other hand, Apple, one of the two leading branded-device manufacturers in the U.S. smartphone market, and the FTC, which concurrently brought antitrust litigations against Qualcomm concerning its licensing arrangements with device producers. This landmark sequence of litigations during 2017–2020 illustrates vividly the extent to which changes in IP strength have dramatically different effects on firms that operate under hierarchical or entrepreneurial models for executing the innovation and commercialization process. As a normative matter, these litigations also provide insight into the extent to which a zero- or weak-IP regime can endanger the economic viability of entrepreneurial organizational forms in an innovation ecosystem and, as a result, favor and expand the existing competitive advantages of large integrated firms that do not rely on IP rights to capture returns on innovation.

8.3.1 Background: The Apple/Qualcomm Disputes

Qualcomm and Apple each plays a critical, but different, function in the supply chain that supports the smartphone market. As discussed in section 8.2.1 of this chapter,

Qualcomm's R&D-intensive structure relies on a robust patent infrastructure in order to support a licensing network that extends across a large population of device manufacturers in the wireless-communications markets. By contrast, Apple is a midstream supply-chain participant and focuses on design, assembly, and marketing activities, as reflected by the fact that it does not invest heavily in R&D as compared to other large technology firms. As of 2018, Apple's R&D expenditures constituted 5 percent of its total sales, as compared to 25 percent in the case of Qualcomm, 15.5 percent in the case of Google, and 13 percent in the case of Microsoft.[56] While Apple is rightly credited with the launch and marketing of the iPhone, Qualcomm is generally recognized, as discussed earlier, as being the key innovator of some of the fundamental technologies behind a smartphone's data-transmission capacities. Unlike Qualcomm, Apple does not rely on a robust patent infrastructure, because it holds a rich suite of complementary assets—including brand capital, end-user license agreements, a distribution and marketing infrastructure, and complementary hardware, software, and related services—by which to extract positive returns through the sale of strongly branded hardware in the end-user market. From Apple's perspective, a strongly enforced patent system likely constitutes a net economic burden insofar as it increases the aggregate royalty payments it owes to upstream R&D suppliers such as Qualcomm, which in turn reduces the margins it can earn on device sales to end users.

Qualcomm's licensing-based business model has been the target of enforcement actions by competition regulators in China, the European Union, South Korea, and Taiwan, resulting in some cases in fines of hundreds of millions of dollars. In the United States, this licensing structure has been contested in a related sequence of antitrust, patent-infringement, trade-secret, and contract litigations involving Qualcomm, on the one hand, and Apple and the FTC, on the other hand. At virtually the same time, the FTC and Apple launched suits against Qualcomm in January 2017, based on a mixture of antitrust and, in Apple's case, breach-of-contract theories of liability. In April 2017, Qualcomm announced that Apple had ceased to reimburse its contract manufacturers (formally, Qualcomm's licensees) for the royalties they owe to Qualcomm, which unsurprisingly led the manufacturers to cease payment of those royalties.[57] The litigations between Apple and Qualcomm were resolved in a global settlement announced in April 2019,[58] reportedly involving payment by Apple to Qualcomm of a sum in the range of $5 billion to $6 billion.[59] In May 2019, a federal district court ruled in favor of the FTC in its antitrust suit against Qualcomm and issued a broad remedy that, if it had been upheld (the remedy was struck down on appeal) would have required Qualcomm to renegotiate the terms of its SEP licenses with downstream device producers and enter into new SEP licenses with other chip makers.[60]

8.3.2 Why Organizational Effects Matter

The Qualcomm/Apple disputes (including the FTC litigation) concretely illustrate a direct conflict between business models—in fact, Apple explicitly argued in its court

Table 8.2 Apple/FTC/Qualcomm litigations in U.S. venues (2017–2020)

Start Date	Plaintiff	Defendant	Venue	Principal Cause of Action	Outcome
Jan. 2017	FTC	Qualcomm	Federal court	Antitrust	Trial court held Qualcomm liable. Reversed on appeal.
Jan. 2017	Apple	Qualcomm	Federal court	Breach of contract	Settled.
July 2017	Qualcomm	Apple	Federal court	Patent infringement	Settled.
Aug. 2017	Qualcomm	Apple	ITC	Patent infringement	Terminated with settlement of Apple/Qualcomm dispute.
Sept. 2018	Qualcomm	Apple	Federal court	Trade secret	Settled.

Note: Qualcomm was not formally a plaintiff in the ITC action; rather, it petitioned the ITC to investigate Apple for alleged patent infringement.

Sources: For FTC v. Qualcomm litigation, see *Federal Trade Commission v. Qualcomm Inc.*, 411 F.Supp.3d 658 (N.D. Cal. 2019), *Federal Trade Commission v. Qualcomm Inc.*, 935 F.3d 752 (9th Cir. 2019) and *FTC v. Qualcomm Inc.*, Case No. 19-16122 (9th Cir. Aug 11, 2020); for all other litigations, see Faber and Leswing (2019).

filings that Qualcomm operates an "illegal business model"[61]—that have substantially different levels of dependence on the patent system, which in turn explains each firm's substantially different IP-policy preferences. If that is the case, then it might appear to be a matter of indifference from an economic point of view whether patent strength is adjusted downward, which would favor Apple's consumer-facing and systems-level integrated structure, or upward, which would preserve Qualcomm's R&D-specialist and vertically disintegrated model. That is, different levels of patent strength may have merely distributive effects on the division of market surplus among different participants in the supply chain, without any aggregate efficiency implications for the total amount of social value generated by the market as a whole. This agnostic interpretation can only plausibly be true, however, if there were reason to believe that innovation and commercialization activities can be executed with equal or comparable efficiency irrespective of the organizational structures selected by firms for those purposes. There is no evidence to support this proposition, and the rich diversity of organizational structures for monetizing innovation in technology markets casts strong doubt on even its plausibility. It therefore follows that any deviation from robust patent protection almost certainly induces deviation away from the efficient mix of organizational structures by compelling firms to select from a truncated menu of organizational forms consisting mostly of integrated monetization structures that do not rely on secure IP rights to earn a positive return on innovation.

To explore this point further in the particular context of patent and patent-related antitrust litigations in the smartphone market, it is helpful to construe this market as consisting of three broadly defined elements from "top to bottom":

(1) Chip components and related technology delivered by semiconductor R&D specialists (e.g., Qualcomm).
(2) Hardware, and related assembly, marketing, and distribution services, delivered by manufacturers (e.g., Apple).
(3) Transmission and related support services delivered by wireless carriers (e.g., Verizon).

All of these input categories (and others omitted for the sake of simplicity) are required in order to deliver a technically and commercially viable smartphone device to the end user, which in turn enables a broad range of market transactions that are now a part of everyday life. In the discussion that follows, I consider the likely transactional responses to a reduction in patent protection by firms that occupy levels (1) and (2) of the supply chain, which will in turn generate the organizational architecture for the market as a whole. For the sake of brevity, I omit firms situated at level (3), which are expected to have an approximately similar organizational response to firms situated at level (2).

Qualcomm: Forward Integration

In the event of a substantial reduction in patent protection (including constraints on the ability to enforce patents or patent licenses against downstream users), Qualcomm would likely be compelled to modify or abandon its R&D-focused, licensing-based business model in favor of an integrated model in which it acquired (or, more likely, merged with a company that had) substantial production and distribution capacities in the downstream segments of the technology supply chain. Any such organizational adjustment would enable the firm to exploit non-IP complementary assets to capture returns on the firm's R&D investments through direct sales of hardware, software, or other related services to intermediate and end users. Put simply, Qualcomm would have to look more like Intel, a vertically integrated firm that operates an end-to-end innovation-to-distribution package that monetizes its R&D through the sale of physical chips, or Microsoft, a systems-level integrated firm that bundled a "free" browser with a proprietary operating system and related software applications that cross-subsidize R&D investments across its technology platform. Consistent with this expectation, trade commentators on the semiconductor industry have observed that antitrust regulators' actions have placed at risk Qualcomm's licensing-based model,[62] as illustrated by the district court order issued in the FTC's antitrust suit, which (unless reversed) requires that Qualcomm renegotiate its existing SEP licenses with device makers and offer SEP licenses to its direct competitors in the chip market.[63] This regulatory risk may have been a driving force behind the attempted acquisition in 2018 of Qualcomm by Broadcom,[64] a chip producer that does not rely significantly on

IP-licensing income and had specifically criticized Qualcomm's licensing-based business model as being "not sustainable."[65]

Apple: Backward Integration

In Apple's case, a substantial reduction in patent strength would require no immediate change in its business model. However, it would result in a reduction in the royalties that it pays to upstream chip suppliers such as Qualcomm. This would generate a cost savings that Apple might then elect, depending on competitive conditions in the retail market, either to retain or to pass on to consumers in the form of lower prices. In the longer term, however, Apple would be compelled to vertically integrate backward into upstream chip design if Qualcomm, being one of its largest chip suppliers, were compelled to vertically integrate forward. The reason is straightforward. As noted, a weak-IP regime would induce Qualcomm either to vertically integrate forward into device manufacturing (or some other set of excludable complementary assets) or be acquired by an entity that is already substantially vertically integrated. In either scenario, Qualcomm (and any other upstream R&D specialist) would have a reduced incentive to license to Apple or other device manufacturers with which a newly integrated Qualcomm (or an acquired Qualcomm's parent) would be in direct competition in the device market, subject only to any potential commitments made to standard-setting organizations to achieve technical interoperability. This would require that Apple increase significantly its R&D intensity beyond the current 5 percent level (as compared to 25 percent in the case of Qualcomm and 15.5 percent in the case of Alphabet/Google, as of 2018) and, in the short term, acquire a larger stock of chip-related technology assets from other firms, either directly or through acquisition. Consistent with this expectation, Apple acquired Intel's portfolio of modem-chip patents in 2019, reportedly motivated by the objective of acquiring independent chip-design and production capacities for its smartphone products.[66] The acquisition of the Intel patent portfolio followed Apple's previous efforts to expand its internal chip-design capacities by acquiring PA Semi, a fabless chip-design firm, in 2008[67] and acquiring part of chip maker Dialog Semiconductor in October 2018.[68] These actions are consistent with Apple's strategy with respect to certain other components of the iPhone, which it initially licensed from third-party suppliers and then terminated those relationships once it acquired sufficient capacities to replicate the component in-house.[69] Motivated in part by concern over this type of scenario, Wall Street reportedly places a discount on certain Apple suppliers[70]—an interesting example in which the market apparently identifies and prices in the mid-stage expropriation risk inherent to a technology supply relationship in which the licensee is a dominant device producer and operates in a legal and business environment in which IP owners cannot exert a credible legal threat against a well-resourced infringing user.

Weaker Patents, Higher Entry Barriers

For the sake of argument, I will assume that these predicted organizational responses to a change in the surrounding property-rights environment would not give rise to any material reduction in total R&D investment despite each firm's change in organizational structure (forward integration in the case of Qualcomm, backward integration in the case of Apple). Hence, under the conventional incentive-based case for IP rights, whether or not the state provided stronger or weaker patent protections would then either (i) be a matter of indifference or (ii) be resolved in favor of weaker IP rights, given the deadweight losses and transaction costs associated with stronger IP rights. Under an organizational approach, however, the firms' structural responses to the *other* transaction costs that arise under a weak-IP regime—which would ultimately yield two similarly integrated firms (assuming both survive as separately existing entities)—may give rise to a distorted mix of organizational forms that imply net welfare losses relative to a more secure property-rights environment. In particular, weakening patent protection, and the ensuing reintegration of the supply chain (forward in Qualcomm's case, backward in Apple's case), is likely to give rise to a market structure in which at least some downstream firms may have reduced access to the necessary set of R&D inputs for entry into the device-production market. Currently, Qualcomm acts as the "R&D engine" for the smartphone market by investing heavily in R&D and licensing its innovative output to all firms willing to pay the negotiated royalty rate. If Qualcomm responded to a reduction in patent protection by vertically integrating forward into hardware production and distribution (or merging with a firm that had those capacities), it would have little incentive to license its IP to other firms with which it could then be competing in intermediate-user or end-user markets, subject only to any commitments it may make to standard-setting organizations for purposes of promoting technical interoperability. (Note that a vertically integrated Qualcomm is likely to minimize the extent of those commitments under a weak-IP regime.) This suggests that weakening patent protection for upstream innovators in the smartphone industry may yield a market structure in which innovation is principally confined to a small handful of vertically integrated entities that can independently execute the full suite of innovation and commercialization functions from chip design through launch in the target consumer market. That in turn would erect an implicit barrier to entry by firms that specialize in discrete segments of the relevant supply chain and cannot feasibly assemble a comparable end-to-end technology package. Contrary to conventional expectations, weakening patent protections may simply strengthen the capital- and expertise-requirements barriers that already protect dominant incumbents from the competitive threat posed by innovative but far smaller entrants. That may explain in part why vertically integrated information-technology companies have so vigorously sought to "protect" the public against the purported evils of strong patents.

Objection: What's So Great about Vertical Disintegration?

To be clear, this line of argument does not rely on the view that disintegrated organizational structures, or entrepreneurial ecosystems substantially populated by smaller R&D specialists, are always or even usually the preferred form of organizing the innovation and commercialization process. Rather, the fundamental point is that strong

IP rights are a predicate condition for maximizing firms' ability to choose among the full menu of technologically feasible organizational structures. It may nonetheless be objected that a strong-patent regime itself induces an organizational bias by favoring vertically disintegrated, licensing-based business models for monetizing R&D. This ignores a fundamental asymmetry in the relationship between IP strength and different business models for monetizing R&D investments. Whereas substantially vertically disintegrated structures are only viable in a reasonably secure IP environment, substantially vertically or systems-level integrated structures are viable under either a weak-IP or a strong-IP regime. Under a weak-IP regime, innovator firms are compelled to adopt an integrated business model in order to extract a positive return on their R&D investment. By contrast, under a strong-IP regime, innovators may choose to adopt any preferred level of structural integration when selecting from the full range of technologically feasible business models. As illustrated by the Linux open-source operating system (as discussed in Chapter 7, section 7.4), owners of IP rights (in that case, copyright over the Linux code) may elect to voluntarily relinquish, either partially or fully, control over the informational asset, effectively reducing the de facto level of property-rights coverage in the relevant market. Or an IP owner may choose to engage in a partial waiver of its IP rights, as illustrated by Microsoft's decision to provide access to the application programming interfaces to the Windows operating system in order to induce developers to invest in developing Windows-compatible applications. Or an IP owner may choose to enforce its rights strictly and mostly block outside access, as illustrated by Apple's closed-source operating systems in the PC and mobile-device markets, which are enforced through technological controls and end-user licenses anchored in a secure copyright infrastructure. The diversity of enforcement strategies and associated business models in knowledge-intensive markets demonstrates vividly how strong-IP rights promote transactional agnosticism, enabling monetization strategies ranging from "pure" open-source (rarely, if ever, observed on any significant scale outside publicly funded environments) to "pure" closed-source models. Only a secure IP regime provides innovator firms with the freedom to choose among the full range of structural models for extracting value from R&D investments and, in doing so, provides confidence that the market can converge upon the maximally efficient mix of organizational structures for conducting the innovation and commercialization process.

Conclusion

This book has not been written in a vacuum. For more than a decade, all three branches of the federal government have pursued a remarkably uniform trajectory motivated by the view that the robust patent system that emerged in the early 1980s constituted a policy error that has discouraged innovation by protecting incumbents, blocking entry, and promoting opportunistic patent-litigation and licensing strategies. With some notable exceptions, academic, policy, and popular commentators have generally promoted and applauded this campaign to weaken the force of property rights in innovation markets. The dominant intellectual climate in Silicon Valley, the world's preeminent knowledge-economy cluster, tends to express deep skepticism toward robust IP rights in general and patents in particular. This confluence of views among much of the academic, business, and IP-policy communities has driven enactment of the America Invents Act in 2011, the ensuing implementation of the Patent Trial and Appeals Board, enforcement actions by antitrust agencies against the owners of "standard-essential patents" in the smartphone and related electronics markets, and Supreme Court decisions that have steadily eroded key protections for patent owners. As a result, today substantial categories of patent owners no longer have any reasonable expectation of securing injunctive relief against infringing users, effectively putting in place a compulsory licensing regime in which those patent owners must undertake costly and unpredictable legal actions in multiple venues, often against especially well-resourced defendants (including, in some cases, some of the world's largest companies) that can litigate almost indefinitely. The result in some cases may be settlements that undervalue innovation assets, which in turn may distort prices in secondary markets for licensing and other transactions in IP assets. In certain innovation sectors, courts' unilateral reinterpretations of the scope of patentable subject matter have cast significant doubt over whether certain technology segments—in particular, large categories of software-enabled inventions—can rely on patent protection, and recent decisions by the Federal Circuit have placed at risk the patentability of what would appear to be even "traditional" mechanical inventions.[1] Without exaggeration, the U.S. patent system stands at the precipice of abandoning any meaningful commitment to property rights in the technology markets that drive the innovation economy.

An organizational approach to IP analysis, informed by insights from the somewhat underappreciated history and political economy of the U.S. patent system, casts great doubt whether this policy trajectory serves the broader public interest in a dynamic innovation economy, rather than simply promoting the private interests of firms that operate under integrated structures for funding and commercializing

Innovators, Firms, and Markets. Jonathan M. Barnett, Oxford University Press (2021). © Oxford University Press.
DOI: 10.1093/oso/9780190908591.003.0010

innovation within end-to-end commercialization pathways or systems-based technology platforms. Contrary to the standard incentive justification for IP rights, this approach does not necessarily anticipate any dramatic slowdown in total R&D investment (with the exception of the biopharmaceutical industry) if IP protections continue to be weakened. The mostly robust performance of the U.S. innovation economy during much of the period from the late New Deal through the 1970s is not consistent with any such strong prediction (although the postwar innovation economy's substantial dependence on government funding and the 1970s decline in national R&D intensity do give rise to concern that a weak-IP regime cannot sustain even an externally supported innovation regime over an extended period of time). Rather, the organizational approach expects that the manner in which the innovation and commercialization process is organized under a weak-IP regime would change substantially. That in turn would potentially distort the mix of innovation projects to which resources are allocated. Here, too, the postwar period is instructive. Markets that operate without secure IP rights can often sustain R&D but must do so by shifting toward integrated (and, possibly, government-subsidized) organizational forms to support the innovation and commercialization process. It is therefore unsurprising that today's largest technology firms (outside of the biopharmaceutical industry), which typically operate under vertically or systems-level integrated structures, have been among the most active advocates for dismantling the strong-patent regime that emerged in the early 1980s. It is equally unsurprising that vertically disintegrated, R&D-intensive entities in the biotechnology, semiconductor, and other technology markets; the technology-transfer departments of research universities; and the VC funds that invest in, or enter into business relationships with, those entities have mostly expressed the opposite view.

It might be argued that I have offered a fragile economic case for robust IP rights, given that I anticipate that innovation would continue to proceed under a weak-IP regime at reasonably vigorous levels in most markets (with the important exception of the biopharmaceutical markets), at least for a reasonable period of time. This argument overlooks the fact that the "pretty good" performance of technology markets under weak-IP regimes masks potentially significant efficiency losses that may only be apparent with some time lag. Most fundamentally, a weak-IP regime *necessarily* gives rise to efficiency losses by truncating organizational choice and, as a result, precluding competitive forces from converging upon the maximally efficient mix of organizational structures in any particular innovation market. These losses arise through two principal effects. First, weak-IP regimes raise entry barriers to smaller and less integrated entities that rely on IP-mediated transactional structures to extract a return on R&D in the absence of an end-to-end commercialization infrastructure. Second, and relatedly, weak-IP regimes impede the formation of markets in trading, licensing, and financing informational assets divorced from an existing production and distribution infrastructure. Strong-IP regimes reverse these effects. Both effects are concretely illustrated by the biotechnology and semiconductor markets, which concurrently experienced expanded use of the patent system, increased entry of R&D-specialist firms (biotech start-ups and fabless chip-design firms), and the proliferation of vertically disintegrated and other transactional structures for supporting the innovation and commercialization process. The result in both cases: an economically attractive industry architecture in which innovation is dispersed across R&D-specialist entities and then disseminated through licensing and other transactions among a large population of intermediate users, resulting in a steady flow of new products into the target intermediate- or end-user market. Zero- or weak-IP regimes restore the transactional hazards inherent to informational exchange and, as a result, are likely to generate an innovation environment that advantages incumbents that excel in refining existing technologies, while disadvantaging entrepreneurial mavericks that undertake the highest-risk projects that seek to displace those technologies. In short, weak-IP regimes tend to be conservative; strong-IP regimes tend to be radical. It is the latter, not the former, that are likely to deliver the greatest social return.

Notes

Preface

1. Heald (2005); Kieff (2001, 2005); Merges (2005); Sichelman (2010).
2. Schumpeter ([1911] 1934, 88–89).
3. As this sentence suggests, I generally focus on the extent to which vertical forms of integration can substitute for formal IP coverage as a means by which to erect entry barriers and capture returns on innovation. In Chapter 8, I discuss how horizontal forms of integration (understood to encompass systems-level and platform-based organizational structures) can similarly substitute for formal IP coverage. These alternative forms of integration may be especially relevant in certain software, search-engine, and other online market segments that are salient in current debates over IP law and policy.
4. For leading contributions, see Adelman (1982); Arora and Merges (2004); Bar-Gill and Parchomovsky (2009); Barnett (2004, 2009a, 2011b, 2016, 2021); Burk and McDonnell (2007); Heald (2005); Kieff (2001, 2005); Lee (2012, 2018); Merges (2005); Pisano and Teece (2007); Somaya, Teece, and Wakeman (2011); Teece (1988). Much of the conceptual basis for the literature can be ultimately derived from insights in Teece (1986), which I discuss subsequently (see Chapter 1, section 1.1.2).
5. On the use of the "tax" analogy in IP and IP-related antitrust analysis and policymaking, see Barnett (2020).

Introduction

1. 248 U.S. 215.
2. Schiff (1971, 19–24, 39–41, 85–95, 124–25).
3. Moser (2005).

Chapter 1

1. Copyright Office (2010, 67778).
2. Teece (1986). For additional relevant papers, see Pisano and Teece (2007); Somaya, Teece, and Wakeman (2011); Teece (1988).
3. Luxury automakers have periodically taken action against small-scale makers of "replica" cars; for an example involving Ferrari, see Roman (2014). This is most likely motivated by a concern that failure to take enforcement action against even trivial unauthorized uses of the firm's trademark may be deemed to dilute the mark's "distinctiveness" for purposes of trademark law, which could then challenge the firm's ability to enforce its trademark in more commercially significant circumstances.
4. Cohen, Nelson, and Walsh (2000); Levin et al. (1987); Mansfield (1986). Earlier studies with more limited scope reached similar results; see, e.g., Scherer et al. (1959); Taylor and Silbertson (1973).
5. Vaughan (1956, 63); White (1971, 312–15).

6. A less stylized but more complex analysis would contemplate a graduated range of levels of state-provided IP protection. It is expected that the relationships described here between entity type and "demand for IP" would generally apply across a substantial range of levels of formal IP protection, except at extremely strong levels for which the market could not feasibly provide a cost-comparable IP-like substitute. In real-world environments, extremely strong levels of formal IP protection are most likely not generally feasible, due to enforcement costs, political constraints, and technological limitations.

7. There is an additional "inverted" case. Suppose a market without IP rights but with a powerful but crude non-IP alternative. The holder of a knowledge asset then faces the choice between a zero or an extremely high level of access regulation. Self-evidently, the holder maximizes profits by electing the latter option, since it earns zero returns in the former option. Assume that the state makes available an IP right that the innovator can use to achieve an intermediate level of access regulation at no higher cost relative to the existing non-IP alternative. The innovator would prefer this reduced level of access regulation if doing so increases expected revenues. This could occur if increasing access makes the asset more attractive to buyers or induces sales of a complementary good in which the holder has a competitive advantage. An efficient inverted result ensues: stronger IP rights increase both access to the protected good and expected returns on innovation. By implication, if the state withdraws IP rights, then the innovator will be compelled to return to the more severe non-IP alternative, resulting in an *in*efficient inverted result: a decrease in both the size of the public domain and expected returns on innovation.

8. DiMasi, Grabowski, and Hansen (2016).

9. Rothaermel (2001, 697); Stuart, Ozdemir, and Ding (2007, 481–82).

Chapter 2

1. On the natural advantages of large firms in access to scale economies, brand capital, and internal capital, see Baldwin and Scott (1987, 13–14); Kingston (1968, 23–24; 1984, 83–84; 1990, 58–62); Scherer (1977, 83–84). Roughly the same argument was made in a different context by Alfred Chandler, who famously argued that large firms dominated American industry starting in the late nineteenth century due primarily to managerial and organizational innovations that exploited economies of scale and scope in production, distribution, and marketing (see Chandler 1990).

2. On the role of copyright in supporting open-source licenses and associated business models, see Chapter 7, section 7.4.2.

3. Drucker (1985, 224).

4. Watson and Petre (1990, 2).

5. The following discussion draws on Jewkes, Sawers, and Stillerman (1969, 341–45).

6. Drucker (1985, 44).

7. Wise (1966). For similar market-share statistics, see Brock (1975, 283); Chandler (2001, 93); Flamm (1988, 82).

8. Noam (2009, 283, tab. 12.4).

9. Cooper (2014).

10. The exit was not permanent. Netscape was later resurrected as the Firefox operating system, first released in 2004 through an open-source license by Mozilla, a nonprofit foundation. I discuss the Microsoft/Netscape episode in more detail in Chapter 7, section 7.4.1.

11. Levin et al. (1987, 797); Mansfield (1986, 175). The sample used in the Carnegie Mellon study is larger than the samples in the Levin and Mansfield studies; however, even in that larger sample, the median firm has 3,309 employees and annual sales of $555 million, and the sample excludes any firm that has less than $5 million in sales or employs fewer than twenty people (Cohen, Nelson, and Walsh 2000).

12. The survey's results are most extensively described in Graham et al. (2009). For additional discussion, see Graham and Sichelman (2008); Sichelman and Graham (2010).

13. Graham et al. (2009, 1295).

14. Ibid., 1288–90, 1292–93. There seems to be some divergence between respondents' views of patents as a means for capturing value for innovation and respondents' views of patents as a source of innovation incentives. The study finds that start-up executives in the biotechnology sector "generally provide 'moderate' incentives in the innovation process, whereas software firms report that they generally provide at best 'slight' incentives" (1286). As the study's authors suggest (1287), the divergence between these two findings may reflect the fact that patents' principal function sometimes arises in the commercialization and financing process, as suggested by other findings in the survey.

15. Ibid., 1278–81.

16. For a review, see Hall (2019); Munari, Odasso, and Toschi (2011, 315). For further discussion of this point and related studies, see Chapter 5, section 5.3.2.

17. Graham et al. (2009, 1297–99).

18. Ibid., 1306–7.

19. Ibid., 1281.

20. The Berkeley study addresses these concerns, noting a response rate of 8.7 percent, higher response rates among biotech and medical-device firms as compared to IT companies, and no statistically significant differences within industries among respondent and nonrespondent firms (ibid., 1271–73).

21. Bound et al. (1984, 51); Chakrabarti and Halperin (1991, 79–80).

22. Wessner (2008, 162).

23. Allison et al. (2004, 435, 465–66). The results are based on a sample consisting of all USPTO patents issued during 1963–1999 and every patent lawsuit in U.S. courts terminated during 1999–2000. Similarly, Lanjouw and Schankerman (2003, 145) find that for the period 1978–1999, patents owned by individuals or firms with small patent portfolios are more likely to be asserted in litigation. This effect is strongest among small firms.

24. USPTO Fee Schedule, effective January 16, 2018 (last revised March 1, 2019), https://www.uspto.gov/learning-and-resources/fees-and-payment/uspto-fee-schedule.

25. American Intellectual Property Law Association (2015, 32, 40).

26. Graham et al. (2009, 1311).

27. It might be argued that software is an exception to this tendency insofar as the development costs are sometimes significantly smaller as compared to certain other innovation environments. However, this overlooks the fact that software firms typically rely on copyright to protect the underlying source code (even in open-source models, which still rely on copyright to enforce the open-source license that governs distribution). As I discuss in Chapter 7, section 7.2, revealed IP policy preferences in the earlier years of the software industry are consistent with the proposed inverse relationship between the "demand for IP" and firm size or level of integration. At that time, large hardware manufacturers opposed any form of IP protection for software, most likely because they anticipated that extending

IP protections to software would facilitate entry by specialized software providers that would have incentives to license all hardware manufacturers. By contrast, the trade association representing independent software providers supported patents and other forms of IP protection for software.

28. Coase (1937); Williamson (1975).
29. Arrow (1962).
30. Rampton (2015).
31. For the source of this California cause of action, see *Desny v. Wilder,* 299 P.2d 257 (1956).
32. Economists have developed theoretical models in which the idea submitter can capture a portion of the value of its innovation by threatening to disclose it to a competitor of the recipient. In that case, the idea submitter can claim the difference in expected profits between monopolistic and duopolistic pricing (Anton and Yao 1994). While this strategy forecloses complete expropriation, it still precludes the innovator from fully recovering the value of its innovation.
33. Arora, Cohen, and Walsh (2014).
34. For case-study evidence that some innovators use graduated disclosure mechanisms when raising capital for biotechnology ventures, see Burstein (2012, 232–33).
35. It may be objected that expropriation risk persists to some extent even within the framework of a corporate entity, given the mobility of human capital and the associated leakage of a firm's intellectual capital to actual and potential competitors. Yet the point should not be overstated. Employers have various tools by which to increase employees' exit costs and limit knowledge leakage associated with an employee's departure. First, the employer firm may own unique assets without which the employee cannot earn equal or greater income in any alternative use of the employee's human capital (Holmstrom 1999, 87–89). Second, firms can discourage employee departures through long-term employment agreements and, as is common in U.S. technology markets, deferred-compensation schedules based on the vesting schedules of firm equity grants. Third, firms can constrain to some extent the post-employment use of its informational assets through secrecy precautions, patents, NDAs, invention pre-assignment agreements, and, in most U.S. states, noncompete agreements subject to a "reasonableness" standard. On the last two points, see Barnett and Sichelman (2020).
36. Kortum and Lerner (2001, 26); Lerner (2007, 405–7).
37. For an informal theoretical presentation of this argument, see Long (2002, 625–79); for formal theoretical analysis and empirical evidence, see Conti, Thursby, and Rothaermel (2013); Conti, Thursby, and Thursby (2013); Czarnitzki, Hall, and Hottenrott (2014).
38. Haeussler, Harhoff, and Mueller (2014).
39. Munari, Odasso, and Toschi (2011, 311). For a review of evidence on the "salvage value" of a bankrupt firm's IP portfolio, see Hall (2019, 665–68).
40. This example is also discussed in Barnett (2016, 16). The information is based primarily on Marvel Enterprises Inc. (2005, item 1.01), supplemented by Leonard (2007); Waxman (2007).

Chapter 3

1. This distinction between entrepreneurial and hierarchical innovation architectures has some commonalities with the distinction between entrepreneurial and "routinized"

technological regimes in Winter (1984, 294–97). For related discussion on the movement from managed to entrepreneurial economies, see Audretsch and Thurik (2001, 267–315); and on the distinction between "vertical" and "horizontal" industry architectures as a function of the degree of modularization, see Pisano and Teece (2007, 283–84).

2. For the leading proponents of this view, see Dutton (1984); MacLeod (2007).

3. Dutton (1984, 78–79).

4. Ibid., 62–63.

5. Bottomley (2014, 64), citing Federico (1964, 113), who documents that in 1851, 455 patents were awarded in the United Kingdom, and in 1853, after the patent reform that substantially reduced application fees, 2,187 patents were awarded.

6. The emergence of a professional inventor class is indicated indirectly by an increase in the number of individuals with multiple patents during 1751–1850 (Dutton 1984, 114, tab. 5). The growth of the secondary market is indicated indirectly by an increase in the number of patents that were assigned, out of all patents contested in court during 1770–1849 (ibid., 125).

7. Ibid., 93–94, 124–69. In more recent work, Sean Bottomley shows a similar relationship between a reasonably effective patent regime, the formation of inventor-investor partnerships, and the emergence of an active market in patent licenses and assignments. However, contrary to the historical accounts advanced by Dutton (1984) and MacLeod (2007), Bottomley (2014, 56–73, 169–74, 202–29, 266–83) presents evidence that a reasonably hospitable legal environment and an active market in patent transactions had already emerged by the mid-eighteenth century.

8. Bottomley (2014, 267), who cites Thomas Webster in testimony before a committee of the British House of Lords.

9. *U.S. v. Western Elec. Co.*, 1956 Trade Case (CCH) ¶ 68,246, 71, 139 (D.N.J. 1956).

10. Grindley and Teece (1997, 13).

11. Riordan (2005).

12. Source for data on number of R&D personnel: *Industrial Research Laboratories of the United States* (1975).

13. Author's calculations based on (i) *Industrial Research Laboratories of the United States* (1960, 1965, 1970), for data on R&D-related personnel, and (ii) the Fortune 500 digital archives, for data on total employment. Note that these calculations treat both technical and nontechnical personnel employed at research facilities as "R&D-related personnel."

14. Carrick (1982).

15. Galambos (1992, 111); Noll (1987, 172, 175).

16. Investigation of Concentration of Economic Power (1939, 958) (testimony of Frank Jewett, president, Bell Telephone Laboratories).

17. Noam (1993, 443).

18. Datta (2003, 648–49).

19. Qualcomm Inc. (2018).

20. Datta (2003, 648–49). For similar findings for the period 1967–1985, see Noll (1987, 170–71).

21. Noam (1993, 442–43).

22. Datta (2003, 656–57).

23. Kushida (2015); Rhoads (2005); Riordan (2005).

24. For discussion, see Robinson (1988, 520–29).

25. Stylianou (2011).
26. For discussion of these views, see Pollack (1984).
27. Robinson (1988, 518).
28. Riordan (2005).
29. Crandall (1991, 81).
30. Hazlett (2017); King and West (2002).
31. Farley (2005, 26, 29).
32. Ibid., 28–29.
33. Froehlich and Kent (1990, 151).
34. This is not to say that small firms were entirely precluded from entry during the postwar weak-IP regime. As I note later (see n. 50 in Chapter 6), small firms were the source of some fundamental semiconductor innovations, although these firms then generally vertically integrated forward into production. Watzinger et al. (2020), relying on citation data as a proxy for follow-on innovation, observe that compulsory licensing of AT&T's patent portfolio under the 1956 consent decree (i) had no effect on follow-on innovation in the telecommunications markets in which AT&T enjoyed a monopoly over telephone service and equipment, but (ii) apparently induced follow-on innovation, mostly among smaller and younger firms, in non-telecom markets into which AT&T was prohibited from entering under the consent decree. The first finding is consistent with the dynamic thesis: a holder of complementary non-IP assets (in this case, a statutory monopoly franchise combined with an extensive production and distribution infrastructure) can deter entry even absent legal exclusivity over the underlying technology. The interpretation of the second finding is ambiguous, since it is unknown whether the surge in follow-on non-telecom innovation would have occurred even absent the consent decree. Two nonexclusive counterfactuals are plausible: AT&T might have undertaken such innovation internally or, absent strategic considerations, may have agreed to license follow-on innovators subject to a negotiated royalty (which AT&T had done voluntarily prior to the consent decree by offering a nonexclusive license to the transistor at a "below-market" rate; see Levin 1982, 75–77), especially if this included the same cross-licensing obligation as provided in the consent decree. Assuming one or both counterfactuals in the absence of the consent decree, compulsory licensing principally redistributes wealth to follow-on innovators, while generating an efficiency gain by reducing negotiation and dispute-resolution costs between the first mover and follow-on innovators and imposing an efficiency loss to the extent that the consent decree causes first movers to shift R&D investment away from technology fields subject to compulsory licensing or to capture gains on R&D through secrecy-based strategies that limit informational dissemination.
35. For a similar view of the state as the most extreme form of integrated organization, see Williamson (2005, 54 n. 12).
36. Author's calculations, based on U.S. Department of Commerce (1953).
37. Harbridge House (1968, vi).
38. Smith (1965, 250).
39. Markham (1962, 592–93).
40. Breyer (1970).
41. I am aware of two other commentators who have made similar critiques of this type of IP-skeptical argument. First, William Kingston noted that the "monopoly" instituted by the patent and copyright systems may be preferable, because it counteracts "other kinds of

monopolistic power" (Kingston 1968, 24). Second, Stephen Cheung chastised economists for promoting abolition of the patent system without analyzing how inventors would respond in its absence. The answer: secrecy, which would result in even less access to technological knowledge (Cheung 1982, 1).

42. Khan (2005, 280–83); Liebowitz (2016, 554–56). These authors elaborate upon similar observations by Plant (1934, 171–72).

43. Breyer (1970, 300 n. 79) had argued that the "tacit understanding" among U.S. publishers of works by British authors "seems to have been disregarded fairly often."

44. This is an example of the alternative "inverted" scenario that I described earlier, in which the absence of strong IP rights increases access costs by inducing innovators to move to more powerful (but non-profit-maximizing) access-regulation mechanisms. See Chapter 1, section 1.2.2.

45. Arrow (1962, 619–22).

46. Sources for these arguments, in respective order: (i) Zenger and Lazzarini (2004), (ii) Holmstrom (1993), and (iii) Arrow (1993); McAfee and McMillan (1995).

47. Cohen (2010, 137). For a similar conclusion that R&D productivity declines with firm size, see Sharma (2007, 2). For earlier reviews of the literature (which reach similar conclusions), see Acs and Audretsch (1990, 37–59); Baldwin and Scott (1987, 63–113); Mansfield (1968, 107–110).

48. Acs and Audtresch (1988, 132); Scherer (1984, 293).

49. Based on a sample of firms that appeared on the Fortune 500 list, Scherer (1965) found that the number of patented inventions increases less than proportionally with firm size (as measured by sales). Put differently, smaller firms generate more patents per dollar of sales. For further discussion, see Acs and Audtresch (1990, 42–43).

50. Breitzman and Hicks (2008) (using a database of 1,293 top patenting firms, based on patents issued during 2002–2006); CHI Research, (2003) (finding that, on average, small firms outperform large firms on various measures of innovative contribution, including patenting per employee, citations per patent, and links to cutting-edge technology).

51. Kingston (1990, 58–62); Mansfield (1968, 92–93); Scherer (1991, 32–33). On large firms' predilection for low-risk R&D focused on product improvement, see Nelson, Peck, and Kalachek (1967, 54–55). On large-firm advantages in product development and commercialization, see Freeman (1974, 209).

52. Eckhardt and Shane (2006).

53. Plehn-Dujowich (2013).

54. Methe, Swaminathan, and Mitchell (1996). Relatedly, a detailed study of the typesetting-machinery market finds qualitative evidence that successful entry tends to be achieved by large firms that are diversifying from another industry and already hold a stock of related complementary assets. See Tripsas (1997, 130–34).

55. Enos (1962, 338–41).

56. Jewkes, Sawers, and Stillerman (1969).

57. Arora, Cohen, and Walsh (2014).

58. For discussion, see Chapter 1, section 1.2.5.

59. Investigation of Concentration of Economic Power (1939, 958) (testimony of Frank Jewett, president, Bell Telephone Laboratories).

60. Investigation of Concentration of Economic Power (1938, 262) (testimony of I. Joseph Farley, patent counsel, Ford Motor Company).

61. Ibid.
62. Folk (1942, 175–76).
63. Oxley (1999, 283); Zhao (2006, 1185).
64. Maskus, Saggi, and Puttitanum (2005, 272–73).
65. Smith (2001).
66. Smarzynska (2004).
67. Branstetter, Fisman, and Foley (2006, 325 n. 8); Dedrick and Kraemer (2008, 36).
68. Arora, Ceccagnoli, and Cohen (2007).
69. This paragraph draws on Mossoff (2011).
70. Lampe and Moser (2010).
71. Brandon (1977, 98).
72. Tamilla (2016, 194).

Chapter 4

1. The Chisum treatise on patent law proposes the following division: 1892–1930 as a patent-friendly period; 1930–1950 as a patent-hostile period, which is then somewhat ameliorated by amendments reflected in the 1952 Act; and the period after 1982 as another patent-friendly period (Chisum 1993, §§ OV-9–12, at [1]). William Kingston also proposes a similar division, identifying patents as the primary means of protecting innovation during 1870–1930 and brand capital and secrecy as the primary means during 1930–1990 (Kingston 1984, 83–88; 1990, 63).

2. This point warrants further explanation. Following at least one claim associated with the "Priest-Klein" hypothesis (Priest and Klein 1984), data on litigation outcomes does not reflect changes in applicable law, because prospective litigants respond to any such change in making settlement decisions, and as a result, the pool of cases "selected" to go to trial adjusts and the win/lose rate approximately stays constant. This hypothesis is sensitive to certain predicate conditions being satisfied (especially complete information and symmetric stakes for plaintiffs and defendants). Subsequent empirical findings (which find considerable deviation from the hypothesis) and theoretical analysis recommend a more nuanced approach that anticipates the possibility of partial selection effects to varying extents in any dispute-resolution context (Klerman and Lee 2014, 2016). As will be discussed, available evidence on historical trends in patent-infringement litigation appears to conform roughly to these more complex expectations. There appears to be over time an approximately constant win/lose rate (but not the 50 percent rate typically associated with the Priest-Klein hypothesis), but with significant intervening periods of adjustment following salient changes in applicable law. However, trends in the rates at which courts uphold the validity of a patent are inconsistent with selection effects insofar as these rates shift to and remain at historically lower or higher levels following legal changes that significantly heighten or reduce, respectively, the threshold for defending patent validity. In short, selection effects apply potentially to aggregate outcomes in patent litigation over time but do not appear to apply to at least one significant element of such litigation. For further discussion, see note 30 of this chapter.

3. Khan (2005, 7–10); Mossoff (2009, 349–53).

4. *Davoll v. Brown*, 7 F. Cas. 197, 199 (C.C.D. Mass) (No. 3662), cited by Mossoff (2009, 353).

5. Mayers (1959).

6. These limitations do not appear to give rise to substantive implications, however, given that, as will be discussed, more complete and systematic data in Henry and Turner (2016) covers partially overlapping time periods and identifies similar relative historical trends in validity determinations in appellate litigation. For further discussion, see notes 22–24 in this chapter, including accompanying text.

7. Mayers (1959, 51 app. A). Note that the Mayers study assumes that a patent survives a validity challenge if either (i) a court upholds at least one claim of the contested patent, or (ii) a court finds infringement without specifically determining validity (on the rationale that a finding of infringement necessarily assumes validity). For discussion, see Mayers (1959, 34).

8. Ibid.

9. Ibid., 52 app. B.

10. Schwartz (1964, 1041–43).

11. Ibid., 1029–31.

12. Ibid., 1042–43.

13. 210 U.S. 405 (1908).

14. Mayers (1959, 51 app. A).

15. *Buono v. Yankee Maid Dress Corp.*, 77 F.2d 274, 276 (2d Cir. 1935).

16. *Cuno Engineering Corp. v. Automatic Devices Corp.*, 314 U.S. 84, 91 (1941).

17. *Hotchkiss v. Greenwood*, 52 U.S. (11 How.) 248, 266 (1851).

18. *Picard v. United Aircraft Corp.*, 128 F.2d 632, 636 (2d Cir. 1942).

19. *Mandel Bros. v. Wallace*, 335 U.S. 291, 295 (1948).

20. *Jungersen v. Ostby & Barton Co.*, 335 U.S. 560, 572 (1949) (Jackson, J., dissenting).

21. Federico (1977); Rich (1964); Taylor (2019).

22. Henry and Turner (2016). Note that the Henry and Turner data relies on the "UGA Patent Litgation Datafile" (Henry, McGahee, and Turner 2013), which captures all decisions reported in the *U.S. Patent Quarterly* (USPQ). As described by Henry and Turner (2016, 462), the USPQ includes "all decisions, deemed by editors, to have precedential value or to include noteworthy fact patterns," which covers "nearly all" patent-related appellate decisions and "a big sample of district court decisions." Some scholars nonetheless have concerns about the representativeness of the USPQ patent cases at the district court level. Subject to that qualifying factor, the Henry and Turner study is the most comprehensive and rigorous existing empirical work on changes in patent validity rates in U.S. litigation.

23. Ibid., 455.

24. Ibid., 470.

25. Baum (1974, 762 tab. 3, 782 n. 81), using a sample that includes all appellate cases in which patent validity was an issue and a final determination reached for the period 1921–1973, excluding design and plant patents.

26. Fortas (1970, 571).

27. Henry and Turner (2016, 475).

28. 339 U.S. 605 (1950). The doctrine of equivalents enables patentees to secure liability for certain types of nonliteral infringement, thereby effectively expanding the scope of the patent claims.

29. For an explanation of selection effects, see note 2 of this chapter.

30. Henry and Turner (2016, 476) express doubt regarding whether these litigation patterns reflect selection effects, in part due to the time-lag issue noted earlier. There is additional

room for doubt, given the fact that while win rates did ultimately revert close to historical levels, validity rates remained at historically low levels throughout the postwar period.
This divergence might be explained by a distinction between litigation outcomes and litigation issues. As Rantanen (2012) proposes and Chiang (2016) further discusses, while the
constant win/lose ratio predicted by the Priest-Klein hypothesis might apply to aggregate
litigation outcomes, it does not necessarily apply to individual issues encompassed by a
single litigation. Whereas the Priest-Klein hypothesis anticipates that parties will settle all
"easy" cases in which it is apparent that one party to the litigation has a substantially higher
likelihood of success, it is possible to envision scenarios in which a litigant has significantly
stronger and weaker levels of confidence in prevailing on different issues encompassed by
a single litigation but still has reasonably strong confidence in prevailing in the litigation as
a whole (assuming resolutions of those issues are at least partially statistically independent
events). In short, the precise extent to which selection effects apply in patent litigation (or
particular elements of any such litigation) remains a largely unresolved empirical issue, as
is generally the case in other litigation fields.

31. Cunningham (1995, 218–19); Schwartz (1964, 1025, 1027–28, 1032–33).
32. Cunningham (1995, 217–18).
33. Schwartz (1964, 1025, 1044). This view has been expressed by Chief Justice John Roberts
    of the Supreme Court, who wrote in 2006: "From at least the early 19th Century, courts
    have granted injunctive relief upon a finding of infringement in the vast majority of patent
    cases." *eBay Inc. v. MercExchange LLC*, 547 U.S. 388, 394 (2006). Ironically, as will be dis-
    cussed (see Chapter 8, section 8.1.1), the Court's decision in *eBay* is the reason this state-
    ment is no longer true.
34. *American Hoist & Derrick Co. v. Sowa & Sons Inc.*, 725 F.2d 1350, 1358–60 (Fed. Cir. 1984),
    cert denied 469 U.S. 821 (1984).
35. 564 U.S. 91, 101 (2011).
36. Henry and Turner (2016, 455).
37. Ibid., 470–71.
38. Ibid., 475.
39. Ibid. For similar findings, see Lunney (2004).
40. For an explanation of selection effects, see note 2 of this chapter.
41. See note 30 of this chapter for further discussion.
42. *Smith Int'l v. Hughes Tool Co.*, 718 F.2d 1573, 1581 (Fed. Cir. 1983).
43. Ibid., 1578.
44. *H. H. Robertson Co. v. United Steel Deck, Inc.*, 820 F.2d 384, 390 (Fed. Cir. 1987). Case cita-
    tions in the excerpt accompanying this note have been omitted from the quotation.
45. 447 U.S. 303, 309 (citing S. Rep. No. 1979, 82nd Cong., 2nd Sess., 5 (1952)).
46. *Polaroid Corp. v. Eastman Kodak Co.*, 641 F. Supp. 828, 832 (D. Mass. 1986).
47. Holusha (1990).
48. *E. Bement & Sons v. Nat'l Harrow Co.*, 186 U.S. 70, 91 (1902).
49. *Rubber Tire Wheel Co. v. Milwaukee Rubber Works Co.*, 154 F. 358, 362 (7th Cir. 1907).
50. *Henry v. A. B. Dick Co.*, 224 U.S. 1 (1912).
51. Ibid., 18.
52. Ibid. For skeptical readers, yes, the Court was right in assuming that there were numerous con-
    temporary cases supporting this proposition. See, e.g., *Morgan Envelope Co. v. Albany Paper
    Co.*, 152 U.S. 425, 435–36 (1894) (upholding a tying clause relating to the use of perishable paper

in connection with the purchase of a toilet fixture); *Heaton-Peninsular Fastener Co. v. Eureka Specialty Co.*, 77 F. 288, 301 (6th Cir. 1896) (upholding the patentee's sale of a patented machine conditional upon the purchase of fasteners); *Tubular Rivet & Stud. Co. v. O'Brien*, 93 F. 200, 201-2 (C.C.D. Mass. 1898) (upholding tying clause in patent license); *Edison Phonograph Co. v. Pike*, 116 F. 863, 867 (C.C.D. Mass. 1902) (same); *Victor Talking Mach. Co. v. The Fair*, 123 F. 424, 427 (7th Cir. 1903) (same); *Rupp & W. Co. v. Elliott*, 131 F. 730, 731 (6th Cir. 1904) (same); *Rubber Tire Wheel Co. v. Milwaukee Rubber Works Co.*, 154 F. 358, 363 (7th Cir. 1907) (upholding a resale price maintenance clause in a patent license agreement); *Leeds & Catlin Co. v. Victor Talking Machine Co.*, 213 U.S. 325, 337 (1909) (upholding a tying clause that conditioned purchase of a phonograph on the purchase of records from the seller).

53. *Standard Sanitary Mfg Co. v. U.S.*, 226 U.S. 20, 48 (1912).
54. Ibid., 48–49.
55. 15 U.S.C. § 14.
56. *Motion Picture Patents Co v. Universal Film Mfg. Co.*, 243 U.S. 502 (1917).
57. Ibid., 517–18.
58. *U.S. v. General Electric Co.*, 272 U.S. 476, 491–93 (1926).
59. Ibid., 489.
60. See, e.g., *Waring v. Dunlea*, 26 F. Supp. 338 (E.D. N.C. 1939) (upholding restriction on performance of a musical composition, where notice of the restriction was given to a subsequent purchaser); *Waring v. WDAS Broadcasting Station, Inc.*, 327 Pa. 433, 194 A. 631 (Pa. 1937) (upholding restriction on use of an electrical transcription, where notice was given on the product).
61. 304 U.S. 175, *rehearing denied* 305 U.S. 657 (1939).
62. Wood (1942, 26).
63. Hart (1998, 86).
64. Posner (1970, 371 tab. 3). For additional relevant data, see Calvani and Sibarium (1994, 659).
65. Marcus (1945, 11).
66. 314 U.S. 488 (1942).
67. 316 U.S. 241 (1942).
68. Ibid., 254.
69. *Key Pharmaceuticals, Inc. v. Lowey*, 373 F. Supp. 1190, 1193 (S.D.N.Y. 1974); *Jack Winter, Inc. v. Koratron Co.*, 375 F. Supp. 1, 71–72 (N.D. Cal. 1974); *Dubuit v. Harwell Enterprises*, 336 F. Supp. 1184, 1187 (W.D.N.C. 1971); *Sonobond Corp. v. Uthe Technology, Inc.*, 314 F. Supp. 878, 883 (N.D. Cal. 1970).
70. *Sola Electric Co. v. Jefferson Electric Co.*, 317 U.S. 173, 177 (1942); *U.S. v. Bausch & Lomb Optical Co.*, 321 U.S. 707, 722–23 (1944); *Edward Katzinger Co. v. Chicago Metallic Manufacturing Co.*, 329 U.S. 394, 401–2 (1947); *McGregor v. Westinghouse Electric & Manufacturing Co.*, 329 U.S. 402, 414–16 (1947).
71. *Columbus Automotive Corp. v. Oldberg Manufacturing Co.*, 264 F. Supp. 779, 789 (D. Colo. 1967).
72. Hoerner (2002, 671–72).
73. Wilson (1972).
74. Temporary National Economic Committee (1941, 36).
75. Ibid., 36–37. For the text of President Roosevelt's proposal for compulsory licensing of all patents, see U.S. President (1938).

76. "Third Report of the National Patent Planning Commission" (1945, 603).

77. Atomic Energy Act of 1946, 42 U.S.C. § 2183, § 11, Pub. L. No. 585 (Aug. 1, 1946).

78. National Aeronautics and Space Act of 1958, § 305(a).

79. For a full list, see Barnett (2021).

80. For a fuller discussion of this topic, see Barnett (2021).

81. Bush ([1945] 1960).

82. The DOD was only formally established in 1949. For ease of reference, I use the term to refer to the U.S. military in general.

83. This statement reflects the author's calculations of the sources of federal R&D funding, based on data in Harbridge House (1968, I-3).

84. Markham (1962, 592).

85. Harbridge House (1968: I-43, III-24, III-20, III-21). For the relevant statutory sections, see Atomic Energy Act of 1954 (P.L. 83–703), § 151, 42 U.S.C. § 2181.

86. Author's calculations, based on data in Harbridge House (1968, I-30).

87. Dobkin (1967, 587); Olson (1959, 722).

88. Act of 1910, Pub. L. No. 61–305, 36 Stat. 851, 851–52 (1910), amended by the Act of July 1, 1918, Pub. L. No. 65–182, ch. 114, 40 Stat. 704, 705 (1918).

89. Olson (1959, 737–38); Scherer et al. (1959, 129).

90. Levin (1982, 64–65); Mowery (2009, 145 n. 5); Mowery and Rosenberg (2000, 884–85); Webbink (1977, 97).

91. Harbridge House (1968, I-6, III-7–15, III-20–23).

92. Ibid., I-vi, I-vii, I-ix, IV-1–3, IV-4, IV-16, IV-18.

93. Schacht (2000).

94. U.S. Congress, Senate (1942, 3281–82).

95. U.S. President (1938).

96. Temporary National Economic Committee (1941, 36).

97. For a fuller discussion of this topic, see Barnett (2021).

98. *Hartford-Empire Co. v. U.S.*, 323 U.S. 386, 415 (1945); *U.S. v. National Lead Co.*, 332 U.S. 319, 338 (1947).

99. *U.S. v. Aluminum Co. of America*, 91 F. Supp. 333, 402–10 (S.D.N.Y. 1950).

100. Senate Committee on the Judiciary (1960).

101. *Xerox Corp.*, 86 F.T.C. 364, 364–68 (1975), ¶¶ 14(a)–(c), 15 (ordering compulsory licensing of patents held by Xerox, on antitrust grounds).

102. Hart (1998, 92–93; 2001, 927–28).

103. Bain (1950, 42). For similar views, see Bain (1956, 144–45).

104. 433 U.S. 36, 58 (1977).

105. For a classic exposition of this argument, see Easterbrook (1984).

106. 466 U.S. 2, 18 (1984).

107. 314 U.S. 488 (1942).

108. *Windsurfing Int'l Inc. v. AMF Inc.*, 782 F.2d 995, 1002 n. 9 (Fed. Cir. 1986).

109. Ibid.

110. 35 U.S.C. §§ 271(d)(4)–(5).

111. *Mallinckrodt, Inc. v. Medipart, Inc.*, 976 F.2d 700, 704, 708 (Fed. Cir. 1992).

112. U.S. Department of Justice and Federal Trade Commission (1995).

113. Bain (1950, 42).

114. U.S. Department of Justice and Federal Trade Commission (1995, 2, 16).

115. Ibid., 16.
116. By domestic, I mean patent applicants or grants in which the applicant is a U.S. resident.
117. I note that using a per capita measure based on adult population changes the absolute annual per capita values but does not meaningfully change the directional trends shown in Figure 4.6. Therefore, I have used the per capita measure based on total population given that this is standard in the literature.

Chapter 5

1. See, e.g., Khan (2005); Lamoureaux, Levenstein, and Sokoloff (2004); Lamoureaux and Sokoloff (1999, 2003).
2. This discussion draws on Barnett (2015, 172–182). For extensive historical accounts of this period in the radio-communications industry, see Archer (1938); Maclaurin (1949).
3. Sterling and Keith (2008, 211).
4. For further details, see ibid., 55, 68. RCA engaged in similar tactics in resisting patent-infringement claims brought by Philo Farnsworth, the inventor of the electronic television. For a full account, see Schwartz (2002).
5. Maclaurin (1949, 63).
6. Khan and Sokoloff (2004).
7. Lamoureaux and Sokoloff (1999).
8. For sources, see Froehlich and Kent (1990, 398) (Bell); Hounshell and Smith (1988, 30–34) (DuPont); Petroski (2010, 98–88) (Alcoa, Corning, Westinghouse); Pursell (1990, 136) (Kodak); and Reich (2002, 1) (GE).
9. Mowery and Rosenberg (1989, 61–67).
10. Lamoreaux, Sokoloff, and Sutthiphisal (2011, 236) (presenting data showing that both large firms with industrial research labs and smaller entrepreneurial firms obtained an increasing share of patents during the early twentieth century).
11. Mowery and Rosenberg (1989, 76–77).
12. Lamoureaux and Sokoloff (1999, 41–43); Nicholas (2003, 1023); Nicholas (2009, 5–6).
13. Nicholas (2009).
14. Maclaurin (1949, 160–63).
15. Mueller (1962).
16. The following discussion draws primarily on Enos (1962, 44–96). For shorter discussion, see Barnett (2015, 157–60).
17. Enos (1962, 92–93, 95).
18. In 1931, UOP was acquired by a group of larger integrated firms; however, it continued to operate as a largely autonomous licensing entity that serviced all firms at a uniform royalty and invested in process innovation, with a focus on developing innovations most suited to smaller refiners. In 1943, it again became an independent firm.
19. Hart (1998, 92–93; 2001, 927–28).
20. *U.S. v. United Shoe Machinery Corp.*, 391 U.S. 244, 251–52 (1968); *United Shoe Machinery Corp. v. U.S.*, 266 F. Supp. 328, 334 (D. Mass. 1967); *U.S. v. United Shoe Machinery Corp.*, 110 F. Supp. 295 (D. Mass. 1953).
21. Scherer (1977, 75–78).
22. For 1947–1958, Shephard (1964) found that overall concentration ratios (as measured by values of shipments) had increased since World War II, while intra-industry

concentration ratios had not changed significantly. For 1947–1970, Mueller and Hamm (1974) found that four-firm concentration ratios in a large sample of manufacturing industries had increased moderately. For the same period, Scherer (1980, tab. 4.8) found that concentration increased for consumer-goods industries but declined slightly for producer-goods industries. For 1947–1972, Caves (1980) identified moderately increasing concentration among the two hundred largest manufacturing firms, using measures of concentration based on total value added and assets and sales.

23. Audretsch (1995, 7).
24. Mueller and Hamm (1974, 519–20).
25. On the skew in federal R&D funding toward large firms in the aerospace, communications, and computing industries, see Mowery (1981, 138–39, 145, 175, 304–5). While military procurement in the 1950s did allocate a material percentage of public funding to newer firms in the semiconductor market—accounting for 22 percent of federal R&D contracts in 1959 (Mowery 2011, 163, citing Tilton 1971)—those firms grew into large dominant entities, and the industry tended toward high levels of concentration (Barnett 2020b).
26. Peck and Scherer (1962, 140–41, tab. 5.13).
27. Baldwin (1962, 294) (noting observations and testimony to this effect by scholars in 1956 and 1959); United Nations Economic Commission for Europe (1968, 98) (noting that as of the late 1960s, "the bulk of corporate R and D investment and performance is done by a few large firms in a few industries").
28. Watson and Holman (1967, 380).
29. Peck and Scherer (1962, 138, 142, tab. 5.14).
30. U.S. Congress, House (1964, 59).
31. Scherer (1965, 1101).
32. For related observations, see Mowery (1995, 148, 156–57); Mowery and Rosenberg (1989, 150–51, 156–58).
33. For a related argument, see Hart (1998, 96), who argues that the New Deal attack on patents may have prompted firms to rely on internal R&D, tacit knowledge, and other means to capture gains from innovation.
34. Schumpeter ([1942] 1950, 105).
35. See, e.g., Jewkes, Sawers, and Stillerman (1969).
36. See, e.g., Lilienthal (1952, 69–72); Villard (1958, 483). For a review of the literature that follows Schumpeter's views, see Baldwin and Scott (1987, 64–65); Lamoureaux and Sokoloff (2005, 360).
37. Galbraith (1952, 91).
38. Galbraith ([1967] 1971, 87). For similar arguments, see Galbraith (1952, 93, 96).
39. Baldwin (1962, 294) (citing testimony by D. Hamberg).
40. Graham (2008, 346). I note that Graham describes, rather than endorses, this position.
41. Wise (1966). For similar market-share statistics, see Brock (1975, 283); Chandler (2001, 93); Flamm (1988, 82).
42. All rankings obtained from the Fortune 500 digital archives, http://archive.fortune.com/magazines/fortune/fortune500_archive/full/1975/.
43. Wise (1966).
44. Schumpeter (1928, 384). Another term sometimes used in the literature is "managerial capitalism," as contrasted with "proprietary capitalism" (see Lazonick 1992, 121), or

"bureaucratic capitalism" as contrasted with "entrepreneurial capitalism" (see Baumol, Litan, and Schramm 2007).

45. Schumpeter ([1942] 1950, 134).
46. Schumpeter ([1911] 1934, 74–94).
47. Ibid., 95–115.
48. Schumpeter (1939, 223).
49. In the 1942 work, Schumpeter wrote: "Patent legislation is one of the few instances of legal recognition of the social function of profit in capitalist society" (Schumpeter [1942] 1950, 107 n. 1).
50. Investigation of Concentration of Economic Power (1938, 858) (testimony of Conway P. Coe, commissioner of patents).
51. 35 U.S.C. ch. 30 § 301.
52. Metrick and Yasuda (2011, 12), citing the National Venture Capital Association Yearbooks.
53. Rooney (2019), citing data from the National Venture Capital Association.
54. Munari, Odasso, and Toschi (2011, 318) identify VC firms that use the presence of patents as an initial criterion for determining whether to invest further resources in evaluating a start-up. For related views on the importance of patents in inducing VC investments in start-up firms, see Gruner (2006, 11–12).
55. For a review, see Hall (2019); Munari, Odasso, and Toschi (2011, 315). For one of the underlying studies, see Baum and Silverman (2004), who gathered data on 204 biotechnology start-ups founded in Canada during 1991–2000, finding that a start-up's patent applications have a strong effect on the amount of financing raised.
56. Hsu and Ziedonis (2008). The findings are based on a sample of 370 semiconductor start-ups founded during 1975–1999 and 800 financing rounds through 2005.
57. Lerner (1994).
58. Graham et al. (2009, 1262, 1275–77, 1303–9).
59. Kortum and Lerner (1999, 16–18).

Chapter 6

1. *Diamond v. Chakrabarty*, 447 U.S. 303 (1982).
2. U.S. Patent and Trademark Office (1987).
3. *Amgen, Inc. v. Chugai Pharmaceutical Co.*, 927 F.2d 1200, 1211 (Fed. Cir. 1991).
4. 35 U.S.C. ch. 30 § 301.
5. Dutfield (2016, 206–8); Graff and Zilberman (2004, 4).
6. Directive 98/44/EC of the European Parliament and of the Council of July 6, 1998, on the Legal Protection of Biotechnological Inventions, 1998 O.J. (L 213) 13.
7. IBISWorld (2017).
8. International Trade Commission, Office of Industries (2008, vi).
9. Adelman and DeAngelis (2007, 1730 fig. 1).
10. U.S. Patent and Trademark Office (2015).
11. Heller and Eisenberg (1998, 701). One of the paper's authors has since modified these claims in light of subsequent empirical evidence, taking the view that contractual negotiations may pose transactional obstacles to cumulative innovation in biomedical research, even if patents pose more limited obstacles (Eisenberg 2008).
12. Rothaermel (2001, 691).

13. Pisano (2006, 81–82).

14. Rathmann (1993, 325–26).

15. Gittelman (2016, 6–7, 10–12).

16. Based on the most recent available estimate (DiMasi, Grabowski, and Hansen 2016), the average cost (taking into account the costs of failed projects) to develop a biotechnology product through market release is $2.56 billion prior to approval and, taking into account the costs of approval, $2.87 billion. All amounts are in 2013 dollars.

17. Chandler (2005, 183); Howe (2003, 126).

18. Arora and Gambardella (1990, 361–79, 363–64).

19. Barfield and Calfee (2007, 17, 30, 33).

20. Pisano (2006, 106–7). The author notes that this figure may be an underestimate since it only reflects transactions for which the stage of development was indicated in the signing announcements, which is reported to represent about 50 percent of total transactions.

21. Arora and Merges (2004, 468–69); Pisano (1991, 239–41). For data on alliances between biotechnology firms and pharmaceutical firms, see Lerner and Merges (1997).

22. Shan, Walker, and Kogut (1994).

23. Higgins (2007); Lerner and Merges (1997).

24. For discussion, see Lee (2012, 1545–46; 2018, 1457–59); Pisano (1991, 244–46; 2006, 88); Stuart, Ozdemir, and Ding (2007, 489–94).

25. Burstein (2012, 232–33) provides case-study evidence that even absent patent protection, graduated disclosure mechanisms can in certain circumstances mitigate expropriation risk in the capital-raising process for a biotechnology start-up. Note that even in those circumstances, patents would retain substantial added value by enabling more complete disclosure to investors for valuation purposes and continuing to mitigate mid-stage and end-stage expropriation risk in the remainder of the commercialization process.

26. Haeussler, Harhoff, and Mueller (2014).

27. Graham et al. (2009, 1296, 1304–7).

28. Ibid., 1279.

29. Burrone (2006).

30. U.S. Patent 4,237,224, Process for Producing Biologically Functional Molecular Chimeras (Dec. 2, 1980, continuation in part of Ser. No. 520,961, filed Nov. 4, 1974).

31. Bera (2009).

32. Pisano (2006, 81–82).

33. U.S. Patent 4,237,224, Process for Producing Biologically Functional Molecular Chimeras (Dec. 2, 1980).

34. *In re Recombinant DNA Technology Patent and Contract Litigation,* 850 F.Supp. 769, 771 (S.D. Ind. 1994).

35. Genentech (1982).

36. For discussion, see Holman (2007); Rimmer (2002). On the settlement between Genentech and Lilly, see Genentech (1995).

37. For case-study evidence on this type of strategy in the online-telephone-service market, see Sichelman (2014).

38. Barnett (2015).

39. For the standard source for assertions concerning alleged patent bottlenecks in these industries, see Merges and Nelson (1990). I note that Merges and Nelson articulated these assertions in more tentative form than much of the follow-on literature. For empirical

critiques of these standard assertions, see Barnett (2015) (aircraft, automotive, radio); Howells and Katznelson (2014) (radio); Katznelson and Howells (2014) (aircraft).

40. Heller and Eisenberg (1998).
41. For surveys of the literature, see International Trade Commission, Office of Industries (2008, 2-4-2-5); McManis and Yagi (2014). For leading studies, see Barfield and Calfee (2007, 39–43); Cohen and Walsh (2007, 10–11); Walsh, Arora, and Cohen (2003, 285–86).
42. Feldman, Colaianni, and Liu (2007, ch. 17.22, 1800).
43. Ibid., 1797.
44. Grindley and Teece (1997, 11–12); Levin (1982, 75–77).
45. *U.S. v. Western Elec. Co.*, 1956 Trade Case (CCH) ¶ 68,246, 71, 139 (D.N.J. 1956).
46. Grindley and Teece (1997, 13).
47. Angel (1994, 37–43); Mönch, Uzsoy, and Fowler (2018); Pellens and Della Malva (2018).
48. Mowery (2011, 167).
49. Grindley and Teece (1997, 16–17).
50. On vertically integrated structures in the semiconductor market, see de Heide et al. (2014, 6); Macher and Mowery (2004, 330); Nathan Associates (2016, 9); Tuomi (2009, 29). Certainly, some of the industry's most important innovations emerged from smaller and then-younger firms (for example, the integrated circuit, invented independently by scientists at Texas Instruments and Fairchild in 1958, and the microprocessor, invented by Intel in 1972). However, until the early 1980s, these and other semiconductor firms typically integrated forward into the production and distribution of semiconductor chips (Galetovic 2019). Similarly, Kenney and von Burg (1999, 86–87) observe that minicomputer start-ups that were founded in the 1950s and 1960s in the Boston area vertically integrated forward, in part to protect chip designs.
51. Mowery (2011, 166–69).
52. In 1984, Congress enacted the Semiconductor Chip Protection Act (SCPA), which provided a sui generis form of IP protection for integrated circuit designs. However, the SCPA was never widely used due to chip customization that increased the costs of piracy and market changes that necessitated technical support by the supplier. For discussion, see Radomsky (2000, 1077–81).
53. Ziedonis and Hall (2001).
54. IC Insights (2013). For similar data for the period 1999–2008, see Tuomi (2009, 33–34).
55. Krishnan (2013); McKinsey & Company (2011, 9).
56. Attia, Davy, and Rizoiulières (2001, 145–46); Macher and Mowery (2004, 331); Nathan Associates (2016, 7); Tuomi (2009, 32).
57. ARM Holdings (2016, 13–15); Attia, Davy, and Rizoiulières (2001, 155–58). ARM Holdings (2016, 13–15); Tuomi (2009, 35–38).
58. Nathan Associates (2016, 8); Tuomi (2009, 29–30).
59. Nathan Associates (2016, 7 fig. 3); Tuomi (2009, 29).
60. For further discussion, see Barnett (2011b); Galetovic (2019).
61. Ziedonis (2003); Ziedonis and Hall (2001).
62. Yap and Rasiah (2017, 114, 121–22, 125–26).
63. These figures are disclosed, or based on information disclosed, in the 2018 annual reports of TSMC and UMC.
64. TSMC (2018, 75).
65. This discussion draws on Barnett (2017b, 486–88).

66. R&D intensity figures are disclosed, or based on information disclosed, in the 2018 annual reports filed with the SEC by Alphabet (Google) and Apple and the annual report for the fiscal year ending February 2019 filed by Marvell.
67. Marvell Technology Group (2019, 7).
68. TSMC (2018, 75).
69. For the leading studies cited to illustrate the social costs of patent trolls, see Bessen, Ford, and Meurer (2011); Bessen and Meurer (2014). For a critical review of the evidence on this point, see Risch (2012).
70. For precise data, see Seaman (2016).
71. See, e.g., *Apple, Inc. v. Samsung Electronics Co., Ltd.*, 909 F. Supp. 2d 1147 (N.D. Cal. 2012). Reversed on appeal by the Federal Circuit, the district court ultimately granted the injunction (after a four-year delay); see *Apple, Inc. v. Samsung Electronics Co., Ltd.*, Case No. 12-CV-00630-LHK (N.D. Cal. Jan. 18, 2016).
72. For further elaboration of this argument, see Barnett (2020).
73. Cotropia, Kesan, and Schwartz (2014); Schwartz and Kesan (2014).
74. References for the following examples include specific sources in citations in the following paragraphs, annual reports, entity websites, and company press releases relevant to each entity under consideration. Patent data was sourced through Google Patents.
75. Wiley and Dunek (2017, 104).
76. Myers (2015). For further discussion, see Kearns and Nadler (1992, 25); Xerox (1999).
77. Williams, Isom, and Smith-Peaches (2003).
78. Gilder (2000, 87–94). For a more extensive account, see Mock (2005).
79. Davis (2008).
80. Feldman, Colaianni, and Liu (2007, ch. 17.22, 1800).
81. Barnett (2015, 163 tab. 2).
82. All information accessed through the MPEG LA website, as of August 18, 2014.
83. For further discussion, see Barnett (2017a, 1353–54; 2015, 143–44).
84. Barnett (2020, 24).
85. Barnett (2015, 160–63; 2014, 43–35).
86. The key event was the issuance of a "business review letter" by the Department of Justice, Antitrust Division, in 1997, with respect to the first patent pool organized by MPEG LA. See U.S. Department of Justice (1997).

Chapter 7

1. Investigation of Concentration of Economic Power (1938, 262) (testimony of I. Joseph Farley, patent counsel of Ford Motor Company); Investigation of Concentration of Economic Power (1939, 958) (testimony of Frank Jewett, president of Bell Laboratories).
2. Young (2008, 445–46).
3. National Association of Manufacturers (1946, 14).
4. Barr (2002).
5. Peterson (2009).
6. Usselman (2002, 112–13). The remainder of this discussion draws on Usselman (1991, 1047–75; 1999, 61–101; 2002, 103–98).

7. "Court Decisions in Air Brake Patent Cases" (1898); "Legal Decisions in Air Brake Patent Suits" (1902).

8. Churella (2012, 584); Jonnes (2004, 118).

9. Usselman (2002, 171–72).

10. *Mowry v. Whitney*, 81 U.S. (14 Wall.) 620, 650–51 (1871).

11. *Chicago & N.W. Railway Co. v. Sayles*, 97 U.S. 554, 556–57 (1878).

12. *Atlantic Works v. Brady*, 107 U.S. 192, 200 (1883).

13. Usselman (2002, 170, 174–75).

14. Usselman (1999, 76–80; 2002, 186–89).

15. Con Diaz (2016).

16. On IBM's opposition to IP protection for software and the relationship between its IP-policy position and bundled business model, see Allison, Dunn, and Mann (2007, 1583–86).

17. U.S. Congress, Senate (1967, 20–21).

18. Grad (2002, 64).

19. Ibid., 65–68.

20. Con Diaz (2016).

21. On contract software development, see National Commission on New Technological Uses of Copyrighted Works (1978, 79–80); on software development for hardware firms, see Holmes (1976, 35, 37); on the acquisition of software start-ups by incumbents, see Hall et al. (1983, 33).

22. Arthur (2013).

23. *In re Johnston*, 502 F.2d 765, 774 (1974) (Rich, J., dissenting).

24. 409 U.S. 63 (1972).

25. 425 U.S. 219 (1976).

26. 437 U.S. 584 (1978).

27. 450 U.S. 175 (1981).

28. In the Matter of an Application by IBM for the Revocation of Letters Patent No. 1,352,742 in the Name of Frederick Nymeyer (Royal Courts of Justice of the United Kingdom 1978). The text of the judgment is included as an appendix to Brief Amicus Curiae for Chevron Research Co., *Diamond v. Diehr* (No. 79-1112), Aug. 12, 1980.

29. Mobil Oil, which filed briefs in support of software patents in the *Gottschalk* and *Parker* litigations, and Chevron, which did so in the *Diehr* case, do not fit this pattern, given that both are larger integrated firms. These briefs appear to be motivated by the fact that (i) Mobil had filed a software-related patent (*In re Prater*, 415 F.2d 1378 (C.C.P.A. 1968)), and (ii) Chevron was concurrently contesting the Patent Office's rejection of its patent application for a software-based invention (Brief Amicus Curiae of Chevron Research Corp., *Diamond v. Diehr*, No. 79-112, Aug. 12, 1980, avail. at 1980 U.S. S. Cts. Briefs LEXIS 2168, *1).

30. Brief Amicus Curiae for the Association of Data Processing Service Organizations (ADAPSO), *Parker v. Flook*, S. Ct., No. 77-642, Apr. 7, 1978, at 2 n. 1.

31. Fortune 500 Archives, http://archive.fortune.com/magazines/fortune/fortune500_archive/full/1978/.

32. 450 U.S. 175, 192–93 (1981).

33. 33 F.3d 1526, 1544 (Fed. Cir. 1994).

34. Mossoff (2014, 65–80).

35. Orozco and Conley (2011, 107).
36. Chien (2011).
37. Kesan and Gallo (2009, 1341).
38. La Belle and Schooner (2014, 460–62). For the definition of "covered business-method" patent, see 35 U.S.C. § 121.
39. Barnett (2011b, 855–56; 2009b, 384); Kesan and Gallo (2009, 1341). For the policy position of the National Small Business Association on patent reform, see McCracken (2012).
40. Barfield and Calfee (2007, 63–64).
41. This methodology avoids subjective interpretation but has two imperfections. First, in cases where a brief states that it favors neither party, it may in substance favor one party over the other. Among all filers, 14.2 percent claimed neutrality. Second, this methodology assumes that amicus briefs that favor (or disfavor) the patentee in any particular case support legal positions that imply stronger (or weaker) protections for patentees in general. This is true in my view of all the decisions included in the sample, with the possible exception of *Stanford Univ. v. Roche Molecular Systems, Inc.*, 563 U.S. 776 (2011). In that case, Stanford sued Roche for infringement of patents purportedly covering certain diagnostic kits that had been developed by a firm that Roche had acquired and at which a Stanford researcher had previously worked. Roche sued for joint ownership of the patents on the basis of a contractual agreement with the researcher. Amicus briefs filed in favor of the alleged infringer (Roche) could nonetheless be construed as "pro-patent" insofar as they support the principle that patent-ownership rights vest in the inventor, rather than the employer, subject to contractual agreement to the contrary. A total of twelve amicus briefs were filed in the case, and this point is not expected to affect the overall trends in IP-policy preferences as presented in Table 7.2 and the accompanying discussion.
42. Tufano (1989, 2003). For further discussion, see Barnett (2009b, 403–4).
43. *State Street Bank & Trust Co. v. Signature Financial Group, Inc.*, 149 F.3d 1368 (Fed. Cir. 1998); *AT&T Corp. v. Excel Commc'n, Inc.*, 172 F.3d 1352 (Fed. Cir. 1999).
44. Barnett (2009b, 418–20); La Belle and Schooner (2014, 448–55).
45. Barnett (2009b, 424–25). For the underlying statutory and regulatory sources, see, respectively, First Inventor Defense Act of 1999, 35 U.S.C. §273 (2000); U.S. Patent and Trademark Office (2000).
46. Merges (2004, 200–201). For related discussion, see Barnett (2009b, 431–32); Pisano and Teece (2007, 285–88).
47. Klein (1999, 225 n. 5) describes Netscape's pricing policy as follows: it initially distributed its browser for $0 but during 1995–1997 set a positive price ($40–$50). After Microsoft entered the market, it lowered the price to $0 in January 1998.
48. General Public License Version 2, Free Software Foundation, Inc. § 2(b) (June 1991), http://www.gnu.org/licenses/gpl-2.0.txt.
49. See, e.g., Benkler (2006); Raymond (1999).
50. For review of the evidence, see Barnett (2010, 1808–9).
51. Capek et al. (2005, 257 n. 4).
52. Corbet and Kroah-Hartman (2017, 14–15); Kroah-Hartman, Corbet, and McPherson (2009, 10–12).
53. Barnett (2011a, 1895).
54. Barnett (2010, 1809–11; 2016, 26–27).
55. Barnett (2010, 1810); Wilcox (2000).

Chapter 8

1. *eBay Inc. v. MercExchange L.L.C.*, 547 U.S. 388 (2006).

2. 138 S.Ct. 1365, 1373, 1379 (2018).

3. 547 U.S. 388.

4. Ibid., 391 (stating that a plaintiff seeking an injunction against patent infringement must "demonstrate: (1) that it has suffered an irreparable injury, (2) that remedies available at law, such as monetary damages, are inadequate to compensate for that injury; (3) that, considering the balance of hardships between the plaintiff and defendant, a remedy in equity is warranted; and (4) that the public interest would not be disserved by a permanent injunction").

5. Hughlett (2006).

6. *eBay Inc. v. MercExchange LLC*, 547 U.S. 388, 393.

7. Ibid., 393.

8. Ibid., 394–95 (Roberts, C.J. and Ginsburg, J., concurring).

9. Ibid., 396 (Kennedy, J. et al., concurring).

10. Seaman (2016, 1949).

11. *Continental Paper Bag Co. v. Eastern Paper Bag Co.*, 210 U.S. 405 (1908).

12. Seaman (2016, 1988 fig. 3).

13. *Apple Inc. v. Samsung Electronics Co. Ltd.*, 2014 WL 7496140 (N.D. Cal. Aug. 27, 2014).

14. *Apple Inc. v. Samsung Electronics Co. Ltd.*, 809 F.3d 633 (Fed. Cir. 2015).

15. 35 U.S.C. § 101.

16. I say "generally" because the Federal Circuit has held that a section 101 challenge to a patent's validity on subject-matter grounds can sometimes raise a "genuine issue of material fact making summary judgment inappropriate." See *Berkheimer v. HP, Inc.*, 881 F.3d 1360, 1368 (Fed. Cir. 2018).

17. 447 U.S. 303, 315 (1980).

18. Ibid., 309 (citing S. Rep. No. 1979, 82d Cong., 2d Sess., 5 (1952); H.R. Rep. No. 1923, 82d Cong., 2d Sess., 6 (1952)).

19. *Bilski v. Kappos*, 561 U.S. 593 (2010) (rejecting patentability of a particular financial-method patent and instructing courts not to rely on the "machine-or-transformation" test as the sole test for determining patentability); *Mayo Collaborative Services v. Prometheus Labs, Inc.*, 566 U.S. 66, 67 (2012) (rejecting patentability of certain medical diagnostic inventions); *Association for Molecular Pathology v. Myriad Genetics Inc.*, 569 U.S. 576, 593 (2013) (rejecting patentability of isolated but naturally occurring genetic sequences); *Alice Corp. v. CLS Bank International*, 273 U.S. 208, 221 (2014) (casting significant doubt on patentability of software inventions involving generic computer implementation).

20. 573 U.S. 208, 223 (2014).

21. Mossoff (2019, 4–5) (citing data collected by Robert R. Sachs).

22. Henry and Turner (2016, 455).

23. Leahy-Smith America Invents Act, Public Law No. 112-29, 125 Stat. 284 (2011) (codified in scattered sections of 35 U.S.C.).

24. 35 U.S.C. § 311(b).

25. 35 U.S.C. § 316(e). On the standard for invalidating a patent in federal district court, see *Microsoft Corp. v. i4i Ltd. Partnership*, 564 U.S. 91, 113 (2011).

26. For data through 2017, see Morgan Lewis (2018, 11); for 2018, see U.S. Patent and Trademark Office (2019, 46).

27. Klodowski, Seastrunk, and Galgano (2019).
28. Unified Patents (2019).
29. Federal Trade Commission (2003, ch. 3, pp. 30, 37 and 38); Federal Trade Commission and U.S. Department of Justice (2007, 8, 35 n. 11, 42); Federal Trade Commission (2011, 5, 10, 15); U.S. Department of Justice and U.S. Patent and Trademark Office (2013, 4, 6 n. 13).
30. U.S. Department of Justice and U.S. Patent and Trademark Office (2013).
31. In the Matter of Robert Bosch GmbH, FTC File No. 121-0081, Docket No. C-4377, at 14 (Apr. 23, 2013); In the Matter of Motorola Mobility LLC & Google Inc., FTC File No. 121-0120, Docket No. C-4410, at 4, 7 (July 24, 2013).
32. *Microsoft Corp. v. Motorola, Inc.*, 2013 WL 5373179, at *12–14 (W.D. Wash. Sept. 24, 2013); *Realtek Semiconductor Corp. v. LSI Corp.*, 946 F.Supp.2d 998, 1010 (N.D. Cal. 2013); *Apple Inc. v. Motorola, Inc.*, 869 F.Supp.2d 901, 913-14 (N.D. Ill. 2012).
33. *Apple Inc. v. Motorola, Inc.*, 869 F.Supp.2d 901, 913 (N.D. Ill. 2012), *modified on other grounds*, 757 F.3d 1286, 1332 (Fed. Cir. 2014); *Microsoft Corp. v. Motorola, Inc.*, 963 F.Supp.2d 1176, 1190 (W.D. Wash. 2013), *aff'd by Microsoft Corp. v. Motorola, Inc.*, 795 F.3d 1024, 1049–52 (9th Cir. 2015).
34. *Apple Inc. v. Motorola, Inc.*, 757 F.3d 1286, 1332 (Fed. Cir. 2014).
35. U.S. Department of Justice, U.S. Patent and Trademark Office, and National Institute of Standards and Technology (2019).
36. U.S. Department of Justice (2017).
37. I am grateful to Adam Mossoff for bringing this exception to my attention.
38. Defend Trade Secrets Act of 2016, Pub. L. 114-153, 130 Stat. 376, 18 U.S.C. § 1836 *et seq.*
39. Congress.gov (2016).
40. McKinsey & Company (2011, 9).
41. Qualcomm (2018).
42. For data on entry rates, see Gupta (2015, 893–94); Mallinson (2016, 989). Relatedly, Barnett (2019, 187–89) provides data on substantial turnover in market share in the global handset market during 2007–2016.
43. Delrahim (2017).
44. *Federal Trade Commission v. Qualcomm Inc.*, 411 F.Supp.3d 658 (N.D. Cal. 2019).
45. *Federal Trade Commission v. Qualcomm Inc.*, Case No. 19-16122 (9th Cir. Aug 11, 2020).
46. Armstrong, Mueller, and Syrett (2014); Lemley and Shapiro (2007, 2027).
47. For a review of the leading studies, see Barnett (2019, 2017a). For the studies themselves, see Dedrick and Kraemer (2017, 1) (approximately 5 percent); Galetovic, Haber, and Zaretski (2017, 1532–33; 2018, 266) (3.4 percent); Mallinson (2015) (approximately 5 percent); Sidak (2016, 701) (4–5 percent at upper bound).
48. Demsetz (1969).
49. Intel (2019).
50. For examples, see Mobile Application Distribution Agreement between Google Inc. and Motorola Inc., Dec. 31, 2011; Mobile Application Distribution Agreement between Google Inc. and HTC Corporation, Jan. 1, 2011; Mobile Application Distribution Agreement between Google Inc. and Samsung Electronics Co., Ltd., Jan. 1, 2011. All agreements were filed as exhibits to SEC filings. For further discussion of these agreements, see Edelman (2017).
51. *Author's Guild Inc. v. HathiTrust et al.*, 755 F.3d 87 (2d Cir. 2014); *Author's Guild et al. v. Google Inc.*, 804 F.2d 202 (2d Cir. 2015). Both decisions relied on *Perfect 10 v. Amazon*

et al., 487 F.3d 701, 723 (9th Cir. 2007), which had construed the fair use exemption to cover a search engine's functions with respect to reproducing, distributing, and displaying copyright-protected content, under certain circumstances. Google was a codefendant in the *Perfect 10* litigation.

52. For an influential decision on these points, see *Viacom Int'l v. YouTube, Inc.*, 940 F.Supp.2d 110, 123 (S.D.N.Y. 2013) (broadly construing DMCA § 512(c) safe harbor to exempt content platform from contributory liability even in case of widespread infringement by users, so long as provider does not affirmatively induce infringement, does not have knowledge of specific cases of infringement, and responds expeditiously to content holder's takedown requests).

53. *Viacom Int'l v. YouTube, Inc.*, 676 F.3d 19, 34–35 (2d Cir. 2012); *Viacom Int'l v. YouTube, Inc.*, 940 F.Supp.2d 110, 116–117 (S.D.N.Y. 2013). More specifically, the court held that a platform operator can only fail to qualify for the DMCA safe harbor if it has knowledge of "specific and identifiable instances of infringement" (rather than simply being aware of widespread infringement in general).

54. *UMG Recordings v. Shelter Capital Partners*, 718 F.3d 1006, 1022 (9th Cir. 2013) ("Copyright holders know precisely what materials they own, and are thus better able to efficiently identify infringing copies than service providers ... who cannot readily ascertain what material is copyrighted and what is not"); *Capital Records LLC. v. Vimeo*, 972 F.Supp.2d 500, 524 (S.D.N.Y. 2013), citing *Viacom Int'l Inc. v. YouTube LLC*, 940 F.Supp.2d 110, 116 (S.D.N.Y. 2013) ("[w]hile a service provider may lose safe harbor protection for being willfully blind to infringement, it may not be disqualified for failure to affirmatively seek out instances of infringement"). For a similar view expressed in an earlier decision, see *UMG Recordings, Inc. v. Veoh Networks, Inc.*, 665 F.Supp.2d 1099, 1112 (C.D. Cal. 2009) ("[T]he DMCA does not place the burden of ferreting out infringement on the service provider").

55. Popper (2016).

56. R&D-intensity figures are disclosed, or based on information disclosed in, the 2018 annual reports filed with the SEC by each of the relevant firms.

57. Dillet (2017).

58. Faber and Leswing (2019).

59. Leswing (2019).

60. *Federal Trade Commission v. Qualcomm Inc.*, 411 F.Supp.3d 658 (N.D. Cal. 2019). For the reversal on appeal, see *Federal Trade Commission v. Qualcomm Inc.*, Case No. 19-16122 (9th Cir. Aug 11, 2020).

61. *Apple Inc. v. Qualcomm Inc.*, Redacted First Amended Complaint for Damages, Declaratory Judgment and Injunctive Relief (filed S.D. Cal., June 20, 2017), at 8.

62. Freeman (2018); Mourdoukoutas (2017); Nellis (2019).

63. *Federal Trade Commission v. Qualcomm Inc.*, 411 F.Supp.3d 658 (N.D. Cal. 2019).

64. Cyran (2017); Lohr (2017).

65. Roumeliotis and Bartz (2018).

66. Nellis (2020).

67. Bradshaw (2017).

68. Gurman (2018); Simonite (2017). On the Dialog acquisition, see Byford (2018).

69. Tilley (2017).

70. Bradshaw (2017).

Conclusion

1. See, e.g., *Charge Point Inc. v. Semconnect, Inc.*, 920 F.3d 759 (Fed. Cir. 2019) (apparatus for charging electric vehicles); *American Axle & Manufacturing, Inc. v. Neapco Holdings LLC et al.* (Fed. Cir. 2019), modified by *American Axle & Manufacturing, Inc. v. Neapco Holdings LLC et al.*, Appeal No. 2018-1763 (Fed. Cir. July 31, 2020) (method for manufacturing drive-line propeller shafts for use in automotive vehicles).

References

Acs, Zoltan J., and David B. Audtresch. 1988. "Testing the Schumpeterian Hypothesis." *Eastern Economic Journal* 14, no. 2: 129–40.

Acs, Zoltan J., and David B. Audtresch. 1990. *Innovation and Small Firms*. Cambridge, MA: MIT Press.

Adelman, David E., and Kathryn L. DeAngelis. 2007. "Patent Metrics: The Mismeasure of Innovation in the Biotech Patent Debate." *Texas Law Review* 85, no. 7: 1677–744.

Adelman, Martin J. 1982. "The Supreme Court, Market Structure, and Innovation: *Chakrabarty, Rohm and Haas*." *Antitrust Bulletin* 27, no. 2: 457–80.

Allison, John R., Abe Dunn, and Ronald J. Mann. 2007. "Software Patents, Incumbents, and Entry." *Texas Law Review* 85, no. 7: 1579–625.

Allison, John R., Mark A. Lemley, Kimberly A. Moore, and Derek R. Trunkey. 2004. "Valuable Patents." *Georgetown Law Journal* 92, no. 3: 435–79.

American Intellectual Property Law Association. 2015. *2015 Report of the Economic Survey*. Arlington, VA: American Intellectual Property Law Association.

Angel, David P. 1994. *Restructuring for Innovation: The Remaking of the U.S. Semiconductor Industry*. New York: Guilford.

Anton, James J., and Dennis A. Yao. 1994. "Expropriation and Inventions: Appropriable Rents in the Absence of Property Rights." *American Economic Review* 84, no. 1: 190–209.

Archer, Gleason L. 1938. *History of Radio to 1926*. New York: American Historical Society.

ARM Holdings. 2016. Form 20-F. Filed with the Securities and Exchange Commission, February 2016.

Armstrong, Ann, Joseph J. Mueller, and Timothy D. Syrett. 2014. "The Smartphone Royalty Stack: Surveying Royalty Demands for the Components within Modern Smartphones." http://www.wilmerhale.com/-/media/ed1be41360634d1fa5c3ab08647e8ada.pdf.

Arora, Ashish, Marco Ceccagnoli, and Wesley M. Cohen. 2007. "Trading Knowledge: Exploring the Determinants of Market Transactions in Technology and R&D." In *Financing Innovation in the United States, 1870 to the Present*, edited by Naomi R. Lamoreaux and Kenneth L. Sokoloff, 365–403. Cambridge, MA: MIT Press.

Arora, Ashish, Wesley M. Cohen, and John P. Walsh. 2014. "The Acquisition and Commercialization of Invention in American Manufacturing: Incidence and Impact." National Bureau of Economic Research Working Paper Series 20264.

Arora, Ashish, and Alfonso Gambardella. 1990. "Complementarity and External Linkages: The Strategies of the Large Firms in Biotechnology." *Journal of Industrial Economics* 38, no. 4: 361–79.

Arora, Ashish, and Robert P. Merges. 2004. "Specialized Supply Firms, Property Rights, and Firm Boundaries." *Industrial and Corporate Change* 13, no. 3: 451–75.

Arrow, Kenneth. J. 1962. "Economic Welfare and the Allocation of Resources for Invention." In *The Rate and Direction of Inventive Activity: Economic and Social Factors*, edited by Universities-National Bureau Committee for Economic Research and Committee on Economic Growth of the Social Science Research Council, 609–26. Princeton, NJ: Princeton University Press.

Arrow, Kenneth. J. 1993. "Innovation in Large and Small Firms." *Journal of Entrepreneurial Finance* 2, no. 2: 111–24.

Arthur, Charles. 2013. "Software Patents 'a Bit of a Mess' Says Martin Goetz, the First Man to Get One." *Guardian*, January 24, 2013. https://www.theguardian.com/technology/2013/jan/24/smartphone-patent-wars-intellectual-property.

Attia, Raja, Isabelle Davy, and Roland Rizoulières. 2001. "Innovative Labor and Intellectual Property Market in the Semiconductor Industry." In *Technology and Markets for Knowledge: Knowledge Creation, Diffusion and Exchange within a Growing Economy*, edited by Bernard Guilhon, 137–80. New York: Springer.

Audretsch, David B. 1995. *Innovation and Industry Evolution*. Cambridge, MA: MIT Press.

Audretsch, David B., and A. Roy Thurik. 2001. "What's New about the New Economy? Sources of Growth in the Managed and Entrepreneurial Economies." *Industrial and Corporate Change* 10, no. 1: 267–315.

Bain, Joe S. 1950. "Workable Competition in Oligopoly: Theoretical Considerations and Some Empirical Evidence." *American Economics Review* 40, no. 2: 35–47.

Bain, Joe S. 1956. *Barriers to New Competition: Their Character and Consequences in Manufacturing Industries*. Cambridge, MA: Harvard University Press.

Baldwin, William L. 1962. "Contracted Research and the Case for Big Business." *Journal of Political Economy* 70, no. 3: 294–98.

Baldwin, William L., and John T. Scott. 1987. *Market Structure and Technological Change*. Chur, Switzerland: Harwood Academic.

Barfield, Claude E., and John E. Calfee. 2007. *Biotechnology and the Patent System: Balancing Innovation and Property Rights*. Washington, DC: AEI Press.

Bar-Gill, Oren, and Gideon Parchomovsky. 2009. "Law and the Boundaries of Technology-Intensive Firms." *University of Pennsylvania Law Review* 157, no. 6: 1649–89.

Barnett, Jonathan M. 2004. "Private Protection of Patentable Goods." *Cardozo Law Review* 25, no. 4: 1251–314.

Barnett, Jonathan M. 2009a. "Is Intellectual Property Trivial?" *University of Pennsylvania Law Review* 157, no. 6: 1691–742.

Barnett, Jonathan M. 2009b. "Property as Process: How Innovation Markets Select Innovation Regimes." *Yale Law Journal* 119, no. 3: 384–456.

Barnett, Jonathan M. 2010. "The Illusion of the Commons." *Berkeley Technology Law Journal* 25, no. 4: 1751–816.

Barnett, Jonathan M. 2011a. "The Host's Dilemma: Strategic Forfeiture in Platform Markets for Informational Goods." *Harvard Law Review* 124, no. 8: 1861–938.

Barnett, Jonathan M. 2011b. "Intellectual Property as a Law of Organization." *Southern California Law Review* 84, no. 4: 785–858.

Barnett, Jonathan M. 2014. "From Patent Thickets to Patent Networks: The Legal Infrastructure of the Digital Economy." *Jurimetrics Journal* 55, no. 1: 1–53.

Barnett, Jonathan M. 2015. "The Anti-Commons Revisited." *Harvard Journal of Law and Technology* 29, no. 1: 127–203.

Barnett, Jonathan M. 2016. "Three Quasi-Fallacies in the Conventional Understanding of Intellectual Property." *Journal of Law, Economics and Policy* 12, no. 1: 1–46.

Barnett, Jonathan M. 2017a. "Has the Academy Led Patent Law Astray?" *Berkeley Journal of Law and Technology* 32, no 4: 1313–80.

Barnett, Jonathan M. 2017b. "Patent Tigers: The New Geography of Global Innovation." *Criterion Journal on Innovation*. 2: 429–89.

Barnett, Jonathan M. 2019. "Antitrust Overreach: Undoing Cooperative Standardization in the Digital Economy." *Michigan Technology Law Review* 25, no. 2: 163–238.

Barnett, Jonathan M. 2021 (forthcoming). "The Great Patent Grab." In *Patents, Inventors, and Politics: Historical Perspectives on Current Debates*, edited by Stephen Haber and Naomi R. Lamoreaux. New York: Oxford University Press.

Barnett, Jonathan M. 2020. "The 'License as a Tax' Fallacy." USC Gould School of Law, Center for Law and Social Sciences Working Paper.

Barnett, Jonathan M., and Ted Sichelman. 2020. "The Case for Noncompetes." *University of Chicago Law Review* 87, no. 4: 953–1049.

Barr, Robert. 2002. Testimony at the U.S. Federal Trade Commission/Department of Justice Hearings on Competition and Intellectual Property Law and Policy in the Knowledge-Based Economy, February 28, 2002.

Baum, Joel A. C., and Brian S. Silverman. 2004. "Picking Winners or Building Them? Alliance, Intellectual, and Human Capital as Selection Criteria in Venture Financing and Performance of Biotechnology Start-Ups." *Journal of Business Venturing* 19, no. 3: 411–36.

Baum, Lawrence. 1974. "The Federal Courts and Patent Validity: An Analysis of the Record." *Journal of Patent Office Society* 56, no. 12: 758–87.

Baumol, William J., Robert E. Litan, and Carl J. Schramm. 2007. "Sustaining Entrepreneurial Capitalism." *Capitalism and Society* 2, no. 2: 1–36.

Benkler, Yochai. 2006. *The Wealth of Networks: How Social Production Transforms Markets and Freedom*. New Haven, CT: Yale University Press.

Bera, Rajendra K. 2009. "The Story of the Cohen-Boyer Patents." *Current Science* 96, no. 6: 760–63.

Bessen, James, Jennifer Ford, and Michael J. Meurer. 2011. "The Private and Social Costs of Patent Trolls." *Regulation* 34, no. 4: 26–35.

Bessen, James, and Michael J. Meurer. 2014. "The Direct Costs from NPE Disputes." *Cornell Law Review* 99, no. 2: 387–424.

Bottomley, Sean. 2014. *The British Patent System during the Industrial Revolution 1700–1852: From Privilege to Property*. Cambridge: Cambridge University Press.

Bound, John, Clint Cummins, Zvi Griliches, Bronwyn H. Hall, and Adam Jaffe. 1984. "Who Does R & D and Who Patents?" In *R&D, Patents & Productivity*, edited by Zvi Griliches, 21–54. Chicago: University of Chicago Press.

Bradshaw, Tim. 2017. "The Blessing and Curse of Being an Apple Supplier." *Financial Times*, April 7, 2017. https://www.ft.com/content/3d49b76a-1b76-11e7-a266-12672483791a.

Brandon, Ruth. 1977. *A Capitalist Romance: Singer and the Sewing Machine*. London: Barrie & Jenkins.

Branstetter, Lee G., Raymond Fisman, and C. Fritz Foley. 2006. "Do Stronger Intellectual Property Rights Increase International Technology Transfer? Empirical Evidence from U.S. Firm-Level Panel Data." *Quarterly Journal of Economics* 121, no. 1: 321–49.

Breitzman, Anthony, and Diana Hicks. 2008. "An Analysis of Small Business Patents by Industry and Firm Size." Report prepared for the Small Business Administration, Office of Advocacy.

Breyer, Stephen. 1970. "The Uneasy Case for Copyright: A Study of Copyright in Books, Photocopies and Computer Programs." *Harvard Law Review* 84, no. 2: 281–351.

Brock, Gerald W. 1975. *The U.S. Computer Industry: A Study of Market Power*. Cambridge, MA: Ballinger.

Burk, Dan L., and Brett H. McDonnell. 2007. "The Goldilocks Hypothesis: Balancing Intellectual Property Rights at the Boundary of the Firm." *University of Illinois Law Review* 2007, no. 2: 575–636.

Burrone, Esteban. 2006. "Patents at the Core of the Biotech Business." World Intellectual Property Organization.

Burstein, Michael J. 2012. "Exchanging Information without Intellectual Property." *Texas Law Review* 91, no. 2: 227–82.

Bush, Vannevar. (1945) 1960. *Science—The Endless Frontier: A Report to the President on a Program for Postwar Scientific Research*. Washington, DC: National Science Foundation.

Byford, Sam. 2018. "Apple Buys Part of Chipmaker Dialog for $300 Million." *The Verge*, October 11, 2018. https://www.theverge.com/2018/10/11/17963112/apple-dialog-chipmaker-power-management-acquihire-acquisition.

Calvani, Terry, and Michael L. Sibarium. 1994. "Antitrust Today: Maturity or Decline." In *The Antitrust Impulse: An Economic, Historical, and Legal Analysis*, Vol. 2, edited by Theodore P. Kovaleff, 605–700. Armonk, NY: M. E. Sharpe.

Capek, Peter G., Steven P. Frank, Steve Gerdt, and David Shields. 2005. "A History of IBM's Open-Source Involvement and Strategy." *IBM Systems Journal* 44, no. 2: 249–57.

Carrick, Roger. 1982. "AT&T Likely to Limit Licenses." *InfoWorld*, September 20, 1982.

Caves, Richard E. 1980. "The Structure of Industry." In *The American Economy in Transition*, edited by Martin S. Feldstein, 501–62. Chicago: University of Chicago Press.

Ceccagnoli, Marco, and Frank T. Rothaermel. 2008. "Appropriating the Returns from Innovation." In *Technological Innovation: Generating Economic Results*, edited by Gary D. Libecap and Marie C. Thursby, 11–34. Amsterdam: Elsevier JAI.

Chakrabarti, Alok K., and Michael R. Halperin. 1991. "Technical Performance and Firm Size: Analysis of Patents and Publications of US Firms." In *Innovation and Technological Change: An International Comparison*, edited by Zoltan J. Acs and David B. Audtresch, 71–83. Ann Arbor: University of Michigan Press.

Chandler, Alfred D. 1990. *Scale and Scope: The Dynamics of Industrial Capitalism*. Cambridge, MA: Belknap.

Chandler, Alfred D. 2001. *Inventing the Electronic Century: The Epic Story of the Consumer Electronics and Computer Industries*. New York: Free Press.

Chandler, Alfred D. 2005. *Shaping the Industrial Century: The Remarkable Story of the Evolution of the Modern Chemical and Pharmaceutical Industries*. Cambridge, MA: Harvard University Press.

Cheung, Steven N. S. 1982. "Property Rights in Trade Secrets." *Economic Inquiry* 20, no. 1: 40–53.

CHI Research. 2003. "Small Serial Innovators: The Small Firm Contribution to Technical Change." Report prepared for the Small Business Administration.

Chiang, Tun-Jen. 2016. "Response: Some Realism about the Resilience of the Patent System." *Texas Law Review* 95: 106–13.

Chien, Colleen V. 2011. "Patent Amicus Briefs: What the Courts' Friends Can Teach Us about the Patent System." *UC Irvine Law Review* 1, no. 2: 397–433.

Chisum, Donald S. 1993. *Chisum on Patents*. New York: Matthew Bender.

Churella, Albert J. 2012. *The Pennsylvania Railroad*, Vol. 1: *Building an Empire, 1846–1917*. Philadelphia: University of Pennsylvania Press.

Coase, R. H. 1937. "The Nature of the Firm." *Economica* 4, no. 16: 386–405.

Cohen, Wesley M. 2010. "Fifty Years of Empirical Studies of Innovative Activity and Performance." In *Handbook of the Economics of Innovation*, Vol. 1, edited by Bronwyn Hall and Nathan Rosenberg, 137–40. Amsterdam: Elsevier.

Cohen, Wesley M., Richard R. Nelson, and John P. Walsh. 2000. "Protecting Their Intellectual Assets: Appropriability Conditions and Why U.S. Manufacturing Firms Patent (or Not)." National Bureau of Economic Research Working Paper Series 7552.

Cohen, Wesley M., and John P. Walsh. 2007. "Real Impediments to Academic Biomedical Research." *Innovation Policy and the Economy* 8: 1–30.

Con Diaz, Gerardo. 2016. "Contested Ontologies of Software: The Story of Gottschalk v. Benson, 1963–1972." *IEEE Annals of the History of Computing* 38, no. 1: 23–33.

Congress.gov. 2016. "S.1890—Defend Trade Secrets Act of 2016." https://www.congress.gov/bill/114th-congress/senate-bill/1890/all-actions.

Conti, Annamaria, Marie Thursby, and Frank T. Rothaermel. 2013. "Show Me the Right Stuff: Signals for High-Tech Startups." *Journal of Economics and Management Strategy* 22, no. 2: 341–64.

Conti, Annamaria, Jerry G. Thursby, and Marie C. Thursby. 2013. "Patents as Signals for Startup Financing." *Journal of Industrial Economics* 61, no. 3: 592–622.

Cooper, Sean. 2014. "Whatever Happened to Netscape?" Engadget, May 10, 2014. https://www.engadget.com/2014/05/10/history-of-netscape/.

Copyright Office. 2010. "Federal Copyright Protection of Sound Recordings Fixed before February 15, 1972." *Federal Register* 75, no. 212, November 3, 2010.

Corbet, Jonathan, and Greg Kroah-Hartman. 2017. "Linux Kernel Development Report." Linux Foundation.

Cotropia, Christopher A., Jay P. Kesan, and David L. Schwartz. 2014. "Unpacking Patent Assertion Entities (PAEs)." *Minnesota Law Review* 99, no. 2/3: 649–703.

"Court Decisions in Air Brake Patent Cases." 1898. *Engineering News and American Railway Journal* (May 19): 319.

Crandall, Robert W. 1991. *After the Breakup: U.S. Telecommunications in a More Competitive Era.* Washington, DC: Brookings Institution.

Cunningham, M. A. 1995. "Preliminary Injunctive Relief in Patent Litigation." *IDEA* 35, no. 3: 213–59.

Cyran, Robert. 2017. "Apple Has Deciding Vote in Broadcom-Qualcomm Deal." Reuters, November 9, 2017. https://www.reuters.com/article/us-qualcomm-m-a-breakingviews/breakingviews-apple-has-deciding-vote-in-broadcom-qualcomm-deal-idUSKBN1D92LZ.

Czarnitzki, Dirk, Bronwyn H. Hall, and Hanna Hottenrott. 2014. "Patents as Quality Signals? The Implications for Financing Constraints on R&D." National Bureau of Economic Research Working Paper Series 19947.

Datta, Anusua. 2003. "Divestiture and Its Implications for Innovation and Productivity Growth in U.S. Telecommunications." *Southern Economic Journal* 69, no. 3: 644–58.

Davis, Lee. 2008. "Licensing Strategies of the New 'Intellectual Property Vendors.'" *California Management Review* 50, no. 2: 6–30.

Dedrick, Jason, and Kenneth L. Kraemer. 2008. "Personal Computing." In *Innovation in Global Industries: U.S. Firms Competing in a New World,* edited by Jeffrey T. Macher and David C. Mowery, 19–52. Washington, DC: National Academies Press.

Dedrick, Jason, and Kenneth L. Kraemer. 2017. "Intangible Assets and Value Capture in Global Value Chains: The Smartphone Industry." World Intellectual Property Organization Working Paper 41.

De Heide, Marcel, Oana van der Togt, Noëlle Fisher, and Jos Winnik. 2014. "Study on the Changing Role of Intellectual Property in the Semiconductor Industry—Including Non-Practicing Entities: Final Report." Prepared for the European Commission DG Communication Networks, Content and Technology.

Delrahim, Makan. 2017. Remarks at the USC Gould School of Law's Center for Transnational Law and Business Conference, November 10, 2017. https://www.justice.gov/opa/speech/assistant-attorney-general-makan-delrahim-delivers-remarks-usc-gould-school-laws-center.

Demsetz, Harold. 1969. "Information and Efficiency: Another Viewpoint." *Journal of Law and Economics* 12, no. 1: 1–22.

Dillet, Romain. 2017. "Apple Stops Paying Royalties to Qualcomm." TechCrunch, April 28, 2017. https://techcrunch.com/2017/04/28/apple-stops-paying-royalties-to-qualcomm/.

DiMasi, Joseph A., Henry G. Grabowski, and Ronald W. Hansen. 2016. "Innovation in the Pharmaceutical Industry: New Estimates of R&D." *Journal of Health Economics* 47: 20–33.

Dobkin, James A. 1967. "Patent Policy in Government Research and Development Contracts." *Virginia Law Review* 53, no. 3: 564–653.

Drucker, Peter F. 1985. *Innovation and Entrepreneurship: Practice and Principles.* New York: Harper & Row.

Dutfield, Graham. 2016. *Intellectual Property Rights and the Life Science Industries: A Twentieth Century History.* London: Routledge, Taylor & Francis.

Dutton, H. I. 1984. *The Patent System and Inventive Activity during the Industrial Revolution, 1750–1852.* Manchester, UK: Manchester University Press.

Easterbrook, Frank. 1984. "Vertical Arrangements and the Rule of Reason." *Antitrust Law Journal* 53, no. 1: 135–73.

Eckhardt, Jonathan T., and Scott Shane. 2006. *Innovation and Small Business Performance: Examining the Relationship between Technological Innovation and the Within-Industry Distributions of Fast Growth Firms, Small Business Research Summary No. 272.* Washington, DC: Small Business Administration, Office of Advocacy.

Edelman, Ben. 2017. "Google, Mobile and Competition: The Current State of Play." *CPI Antitrust Chronicle*, Winter 2017.

Eisenberg, Rebecca. 2008. "Noncompliance, Nonenforcement, Nonproblem? Rethinking the Anticommons in Biomedical Research." *Houston Law Review* 45, no. 4: 1059–99.

Enos, John Lawrence. 1962. *Petroleum Progress and Profits: A History of Process Innovation.* Cambridge, MA: MIT Press.

Faber, David, and Kif Leswing. 2019. "Qualcomm Surges after Announcing a Settlement with Apple over Patent Royalties." CNBC.com, April 16, 2019. https://www.cnbc.com/2019/04/16/apple-qualcomm-settle-royalty-dispute-sources-say.html.

Farley, Tom. 2005. "Mobile Telephone History." *Telektronikk* 3/4: 22–34. http://www.private-line.com/wp-content/uploads/2016/01/TelenorPage_022-034.pdf.

Federal Trade Commission. 2003. *To Promote Innovation: The Proper Balance of Competition and Patent Law and Policy.*

Federal Trade Commission. 2011. *The Evolving IP Marketplace: Aligning Patent Notice and Remedies with Competition.*

Federal Trade Commission and U.S. Department of Justice. 2007. *Antitrust Enforcement and Intellectual Property Rights: Promoting Innovation and Competition.*

Federico, P. J. 1964. "Historical Patent Statistics." *Journal of the Patent Office Society* 42, no. 2: 89–171.

Federico, P. J. 1977. "Origins of Section 103." *AIPLA Quarterly Journal* 5, no. 2: 87–116.

Feldman, Maryann P., Alessandra Colaianni, and Connie Kang Liu. 2007. "Lessons from the Commercialization of the Cohen-Boyer Patents: The Stanford University Licensing Program." In *IP Handbook of Best Practices*, ch. 17.22, 1797–1807. http://www.iphandbook.org/handbook/ch17/p22/.

Flamm, Kenneth. 1988. *Creating the Computer: Government, Industry and High Technology.* Washington, DC: Brookings Institution.

Folk, George E. 1942. *Patents and Industrial Progress.* New York: Harper.

Fortas, Abe. 1970. "The Patent System in Distress." *Patent Trademark and Copyright Journal of Research and Education* 14, no. 4: 571–79.

Freeman, Christopher. 1974. *The Economics of Industrial Innovation.* Baltimore: Penguin.

Freeman, Mike. 2018. "FTC Antitrust Case against Qualcomm Puts Business Model under Microscope." *San Diego Union-Tribune*, December 30, 2018. https://www.sandiegouniontribune.com/business/technology/sd-fi-qualcomm-ftc-trial-20181230-story.html.

Froehlich, Fritz E., and Allen Kent. 1990. *The Froehlich/Kent Encyclopedia of Telecommunications.* Vol. 1. Boca Raton, FL: CRC.

Frost, Gary L. 2010. *Early FM Radio: Incremental Technology in Twentieth-Century America.* Baltimore: Johns Hopkins University Press.

Galambos, Louis. 1992. "Theodore N. Vail and the Role of Innovation in the Modern Bell System." *Business History Review* 66, no. 1 (Spring): 95–126.

Galbraith, John Kenneth. 1952. *American Capitalism, The Concept of Countervailing Power*. London: Routledge.

Galbraith, John Kenneth. (1967) 1971. *The New Industrial State*. 2nd rev. ed. Boston: Houghton Mifflin Company.

Galetovic, Alexander. 2019. "Patents in the History of the Semiconductor Industry: The Ricardian Hypothesis." Hoover IP^2 Working Paper.

Galetovic, Alexander, Stephen Haber, and Lew Zaretzki. 2017. "Is There an Anticommons Tragedy in the World Smartphone Industry?" *Berkeley Technology Law Journal* 32: 1527–57.

Galetovic, Alexander, Stephen Haber, and Lew Zaretzki. 2018. "An Estimate of the Average Cumulative Royalty Yield in the World Mobile Phone Industry: Theory, Measurement and Results." *Telecommunications Policy* 42, no. 3: 263–76.

Genentech. 1982. "First Recombinant DNA Product Approved by the Food and Drug Administration." October 29, 1982.

Genentech. 1995. "Genentech and Lilly Reach Settlement." January 5, 1995.

Gilder, George. 2000. *Telecosm: How Infinite Bandwidth Will Revolutionize Our World*. New York: Free Press.

Gittelman, Michelle. 2016. "The Revolution Re-Visited: Clinical and Genetic Research Paradigm and the Productivity Paradox in Drug Discovery." *Research Policy* 48, no. 8: 1570–85.

Grad, Burton. 2002. "A Personal Recollection: IBM's Unbundling of Software and Services." *IEEE Annals of the History of Computing* 24, no. 1: 64–71.

Graff, Gregory D., and David Zilberman. 2004. "Explaining Europe's Resistance to Agricultural Biotechnology." *University of California Giannini Foundation: Agricultural and Resource Economics Update* 7, no. 5: 1–4.

Graham, Martha B. W. 2008. "Technology and Innovation." In *The Oxford Handbook of Business History*, edited by Geoffrey Jones and Jonathan Zeitlin, 347–73. Oxford: Oxford University Press.

Graham, Stuart J. H., Robert P. Merges, Pam Samuelson, and Ted Sichelman. 2009. "High Technology Entrepreneurs and the Patent System: Results of the 2008 Berkeley Patent Survey." *Berkeley Technology Law Journal* 24, no. 4: 1255–328.

Graham, Stuart J. H., and Ted Sichelman. 2008. "Why Do Start-Ups Patent?" *Berkeley Technology Law Journal* 23, no. 3: 1063–97.

Grindley, Peter C., and David J. Teece. 1997. "Managing Intellectual Capital: Licensing and Cross-Licensing in Semiconductors." *California Management Review* 39, no. 2: 8–41.

Gruner, Richard. 2006. "Corporate Patents: Optimizing Organizational Responses to Innovation Opportunities and Invention Discoveries." *Marquette Intellectual Property Law Review* 10, no. 1: 1–79.

Gupta, Kirti. 2015. "Technology Standards and Competition in the Mobile Wireless Industry." *George Mason Law Review* 22, no. 4: 865–96.

Gurman, Mark. 2018. "How Apple Built a Chip Powerhouse to Threaten Qualcomm and Intel." *Bloomberg*, January 29, 2018. https://www.bloomberg.com/graphics/2018-apple-custom-chips/.

Haeussler, Carolin, Dietmar Harhoff, and Elisabeth Mueller. 2014. "How Patenting Informs VC Investors: The Case of Biotechnology." *Research Policy* 43, no. 8: 1286–98.

Hall, Bronwyn H. 2019. "Is There a Role for Patents in the Financing of New Innovative Firms?" *Industrial and Corporate Change* 28, no. 3: 657–80.

Hall, Peter, Ann R. Markusen, Richard Osborn, and Barbara Wachsman. 1983. "The American Computer Software Industry: Economic Development Prospects." *Built Environment* 9, no. 1: 29–39.

Han, Zhu, and K. J. Ray Liu. 2008. *Resource Allocation for Wireless Networks: Basics, Techniques and Applications.* New York: Cambridge University Press.

Harbridge House. 1968. "Government Patent Policy Study, Final Report." Prepared for FCST Committee on Government Patent Policy.

Hart, David M. 1998. *Forged Consensus: Science, Technology and Economic Policy in the United States, 1921-1953.* Princeton, NJ: Princeton University Press.

Hart, David M. 2001. "Antitrust and Technological Innovation in the US: Ideas, Institutions, Decisions, Impacts, 1890-2000." *Research Policy* 30, no. 6: 923-36.

Hazlett, Thomas. 2017. "We Could Have Had Cellphones Four Decades Earlier." *Reason*, June 11, 2017. https://reason.com/2017/06/11/we-could-have-had-cellphones-f/.

Heald, Paul J. 2005. "A Transaction Costs Theory of Patent Law." *Ohio State Law Journal* 66, no. 3: 473-509.

Heller, Michael A., and Rebecca S. Eisenberg. 1998. "Can Patents Deter Innovation? The Anticommons in Biomedical Research." *Science* 280, no. 5364: 698-701.

Henry, Matthew D., Thomas P. McGahee, and John L. Turner. 2013. "Dynamics of Patent Precedent and Enforcement: An Introduction to the UGA Patent Litigation Datafile." University of Georgia Working Paper.

Henry, Matthew D., and John L. Turner. 2016. "Across Five Eras: Patent Validity and Infringement Rates in U.S. Courts, 1929-2006." *Journal of Empirical Legal Studies* 13, no. 3: 454-86.

Higgins, Matthew J. 2007. "The Allocation of Control Rights in Pharmaceutical Alliances." *Journal of Corporate Finance* 13, no. 1: 58-75.

Hoerner, Robert J. 2002. "The Decline (and Fall?) of the Patent Misuse Doctrine in the Federal Circuit." *Antitrust Law Journal* 69, no. 3: 669-85.

Holman, Christopher M. 2007. "The Impact of Human Gene Patents on Innovation and Access: A Survey of Human Gene Patent Litigation." *University of Missouri at Kansas City Law Review* 76: 295-361.

Holmes, Edith. 1976. "IBM Unbundling Cited as Software Industry Impetus." *Computerworld*, May 3, 1976.

Holmstrom, Bengt. 1993. "Agency Costs and Innovation." In *Markets for Innovation, Ownership and Control*, edited by Richard H. Day, Gunnar Eliasson, Clas Wihlborg, and Kenneth J. Arrow, 131-54. Amsterdam: North-Hollands.

Holmstrom, Bengt. 1999. "The Firm as a Subeconomy." *Journal of Law, Economics, and Organization* 15, no. 1: 74-102.

Holusha, John. 1990. "Kodak Told It Must Pay $909 Million." *New York Times*, October 13, 1990.

Hounshell, David A., and John K. Smith Jr. 1988. *Science and Corporate Strategy: DuPont R&D 1902-1980.* New York: Cambridge University Press.

Howe, Timothy F. 2003. "Financing Biotechnology Research: A Firsthand Perspective." In *Science and Cents: Exploring the Economics of Biotechnology*, edited by John V. Duca and Mine K. Yücel, 119-30. Dallas: Federal Reserve Bank of Dallas.

Howells, John, and Ron D. Katznelson. 2014. "The Coordination of Independently-Owned Vacuum Tube Patents in the Early Radio Alleged Patent Thicket." Working Paper.

Hsu, David H., and Rosemarie Ziedonis. 2008. "Patents as Quality Signals for Entrepreneurial Ventures." *Academy of Management Annual Meeting Proceedings.*

Hughlett, Mike. 2006. "BlackBerry Suit Settled." *Chicago Tribune,* March 4, 2006.

IBISWorld. 2017. "IBISWorld Industry Report: Global Biotechnology, Industry Outlook."

IC Insights. 2013. "Research Bulletin: Fabless Suppliers Play Increasing Role in IC Market." May 1, 2013. https://www.icinsights.com/data/articles/documents/542.pdf.

Industrial Research Laboratories of the United States. 1960. Washington, DC: National Research Council of the National Academy of Sciences.

Industrial Research Laboratories of the United States. 1965. New York: R. R. Bowker.

Industrial Research Laboratories of the United States. 1970. New York: R. R. Bowker.

Industrial Research Laboratories of the United States. 1975. New York: R.R. Bowker.

Intel. 2019. 2018 Annual Report and Form 10-K. Filed with the Securities and Exchange Commission, February 1, 2019.

Intel. N.d. "Two Decades of 'Plug and Play': How USB Became the Most Successful Interface in the History of Computing." https://www.intel.com/content/www/us/en/standards/usb-two-decades-of-plug-and-play-article.html.

International Trade Commission, Office of Industries. 2008. *Patenting Trends and Innovation in Industrial Biotechnology*. USITC Pub. 4039.

Investigation of Concentration of Economic Power. 1938. *Hearings before the Temporary National Economic Committee*, Part 1: Economic Prologue, 75th Cong., 3rd Sess., December 1–3, 1938.

Investigation of Concentration of Economic Power. 1939. *Hearings before the Temporary National Economic Committee*, Part 3: Patents, 76th Cong., 1st Sess., January 16–20, 1939.

Jewkes, John, David Sawers, and Richard Stillerman. 1969. *The Sources of Invention*. 2nd ed. New York: W. W. Norton.

Jonnes, Jill. 2004. *Empires of Light: Edison, Tesla, Westinghouse, and the Race to Electrify the World*. New York: Random House.

Katznelson, Ron D., and John Howells. 2014. "The Myth of the Early Aviation Patent Hold-Up: How a U.S. Government Monopsony Commandeered Pioneer Airplane Patents." *Industrial and Corporate Change* 24, no. 1: 1–64.

Kearns, David T., and David Nadler. 1992. *Prophets in the Dark: How Xerox Reinvented Itself and Beat Back the Japanese*. New York: Harper Business.

Kenney, Martin, and Urs von Burg. 1999. "Entrepreneurship and Path Dependence: Industrial Clustering in Silicon Valley and Route 128." *Industrial and Corporate Change* 8, no. 1: 67–103.

Kesan, Jay, and Andres Gallo. 2009. "The Political Economy of the Patent System." *North Carolina Law Review* 87, no. 5: 1341–419.

Khan, B. Zorina. 2005. "The Democratization of Innovation: Patents and Copyrights in American Economic Development, 1790–1920." National Bureau of Economic Research.

Khan, B. Zorina, and Kenneth L. Sokoloff. 2004. "Institutions and Democratic Invention in 19th-Century America: Evidence from 'Great Inventors,' 1790–1930." *American Economic Review* 94, no. 2: 395–401.

Kieff, F. Scott. 2001. "Property Rights and Property Rules for Commercializing Inventions." *Minnesota Law Review* 85, no. 3: 697–754.

Kieff, F. Scott. 2005. "IP Transactions: On the Theory and Practice of Commercializing Innovation." *Houston Law Review* 42, no. 3: 727–58.

King, John Leslie, and Joel West. 2002. "Ma Bell's Orphan: US Cellular Telephony, 1947–1996." *Telecommunications Policy* 26, no. 3/4: 189–203.

Kingston, William. 1968. "Invention and Monopoly." Woolwich Economic Papers 15.

Kingston, William. 1984. *The Political Economy of Innovation*. The Hague: M. Nijhoff.

Kingston, William. 1990. *Innovation, Creativity and Law*. Dordrecht: Kluwer Academic.

Klein, Benjamin. 1999. "Microsoft's Use of Zero Price Bundling to Fight the 'Browser Wars.'" In *Competition, Innovation and the Microsoft Monopoly: Antitrust in the Digital Marketplace*, edited by Jeffrey A. Eisenach and Thomas M. Lenard, 217–53. New York: Springer.

Klerman, Dan, and Yoon-Ho Alex Lee. 2014. "Inferences from Litigated Cases." *Journal of Legal Studies* 43, no. 2: 209–48.

Klerman, Dan, and Yoon-Ho Alex Lee. 2016. "The Priest-Klein Hypotheses: Proofs and Generality." *International Review of Law and Economics* 48: 59–76.

Klodowski, Daniel F., David C. Seastrunk, and Michael R. Galgano. 2019. "Special Report— PTAB IPR Stats over Time for Q2 2019." Finnegan AIA Blog, August 13, 2019. https://www.

finnegan.com/en/insights/blogs/america-invents-act/special-report-ptab-ipr-stats-over-time-for-q2-2019.html.

Kortum, Samuel, and Josh Lerner. 1999. "What Is Behind the Recent Surge in Patenting?" *Research Policy* 28, no. 1: 1–22.

Kortum, Samuel, and Josh Lerner. 2001. "Does Venture Capital Spur Innovation?" In *Entrepreneurial Inputs and Outcomes: New Studies of Entrepreneurship the United States*, edited by Gary D. Libecap, 1–44. Vol. 13 of *Advances in the Study of Entrepreneurship, Innovation, and Economic Growth*. Amsterdam: JAI.

Krishnan, Sanjay. 2013. "Patents in the Semiconductor Industry: A Strategy Perspective." GSA Forum, March 2013. https://www.gsaglobal.org/wp-content/uploads/2019/04/201301_GSA_Forum.pdf.

Kroah-Hartman, Greg, Jonathan Corbet, and Amanda McPherson. 2009. "Linux Kernel Development: How Fast It Is Going, Who Is Doing It, What They Are Doing, and Who Is Sponsoring It: An August 2009 Update." Linux Foundation.

Kumar, Rakesh. 2008. *Fabless Semiconductor Implementation*. New York: McGraw-Hill.

Kushida, Kenji E. 2015. "The Politics of Commoditization in Global ICT Industries: A Political Economy Explanation of the Rise of Apple, Google, and Industry Disruptors." *Journal of Industry, Competition and Trade* 15, no. 1: 49–67.

La Belle, Megan M., and Heidi Mandanis Schooner. 2014. "Big Banks and Business Method Patents." *University of Pennsylvania Journal of Business Law.* 16: 431–95.

Lamoureaux, Naomi R., Margaret Levenstein, and Kenneth L. Sokoloff. 2004. "Financing Invention during the Second Industrial Revolution: Cleveland, Ohio, 1870–1920." National Bureau of Economic Research Working Paper Series 10923.

Lamoureaux, Naomi R., and Kenneth L. Sokoloff. 1999. "Inventors, Firms and the Market for Technology in the Late Nineteenth and Early Twentieth Centuries." In *Learning by Doing: In Markets, Firms, and Countries*, edited by Naomi R. Lamoreaux, Daniel M. G. Raff, and Peter Temin, 19–60. Chicago: University of Chicago Press.

Lamoureaux, Naomi R., and Kenneth L. Sokoloff. 2003. "Intermediaries in the U.S. Market for Technology, 1870–1920." In *Finance, Intermediaries and Economic Development*, edited by Stanley L. Engerman, Philip T. Hoffman, Jean-Laurent Rosenthal, and Kenneth L. Sokoloff, 209–46. New York: Cambridge University Press.

Lamoureaux, Naomi R., and Kenneth L. Sokoloff. 2005. "The Decline of the Independent Inventor: A Schumpeterian Story." National Bureau of Economic Research Working Paper 11654.

Lamoureaux, Naomi R., Kenneth L. Sokoloff, and Dhanoos Sutthiphisal. 2011. "The Reorganization of Inventive Activity in the United States during the Early Twentieth Century." In *Understanding Long-Run Economic Growth: Geography, Institutions, and the Knowledge Economy*, edited by Dora L. Costa and Naomi R. Lamoreaux, 235–74. Chicago: University of Chicago Press.

Lampe, Ryan L., and Petra Moser. 2010. "Do Patent Pools Encourage Innovation? Evidence from the 19th-Century Sewing Machine Industry." *Journal of Economic History* 70, no. 4: 898–920.

Lanjouw, Jean O., and Mark Schankerman. 2003. "Enforcement of Patent Rights in the United States." In *Patents in the Knowledge-Based Economy*, edited by Wesley Marc Cohen and Stephen A. Merrill, 145–79. Washington, DC: National Academies Press.

Lazonick, William. 1992. "Business Organization and Competitive Advantage: Capitalist Transformations in the Twentieth Century." In *Technology and Enterprise in a Historical Perspective*, edited by Giovanni Dosi, Renato Giannetti, and Pierangelo Maria Toninelli, 119–63. Oxford: Clarendon Press.

Lee, Peter. 2012. "Transcending the Tacit Dimension: Patents, Relationships, and Organizational Integration in Technology Transfer." *California Law Review* 100: 1503–72.

Lee, Peter. 2018. "Innovation and the Firm: A New Synthesis." *Stanford Law Review* 70, no. 5: 1431–501.

"Legal Decisions in Air Brake Patent Suits." 1902. *Railway and Locomotive Engineering* 15: 51.

Lemley, Mark A., and Carl Shapiro. 2007. "Patent Holdup and Royalty Stacking." *Texas Law Review* 85, no. 7: 1991–2049.

Leonard, Devin. 2007. "Calling All Superheroes." *Fortune*, May 23, 2007.

Lerner, Josh. 1994. "The Importance of Patent Scope: An Empirical Analysis." *RAND Journal of Economics* 25, no. 2: 319–33.

Lerner, Josh. 2007. "The Governance of New Firms: A Functional Perspective." In *Financing Innovation in the United States, 1870 to the Present*, edited by Naomi R. Lamoreaux and Kenneth L. Sokoloff, 405–32. Cambridge, MA: MIT Press.

Lerner, Josh, and Robert P. Merges. 1997. "The Control of Strategic Alliances: An Empirical Analysis of Biotechnology Collaboration." National Bureau of Economic Research Working Paper Series 6014.

Leswing, Kif. 2019. "Apple Paid up to $6 Billion to Settle with Qualcomm, UBS Estimates." CNBC.com, April 18, 2019. https://www.cnbc.com/2019/04/18/apple-paid-5-billion-to-6-billion-to-settle-with-qualcomm-ubs.html.

Levin, Richard C. 1982. "The Semiconductor Industry." In *Government and Technical Progress: A Cross-Industry Analysis*, edited by Richard R. Nelson, 9–100. New York: Pergamon.

Levin, Richard C., Alvin K. Klevorick, Richard R. Nelson, and Sidney G. Winter. 1987. "Appropriating the Returns from Industrial Research and Development." *Brookings Papers on Economic Activity* 18, no. 3: 783–832.

Liebowitz, Stan J. 2016. "Paradise Lost or Fantasy Island? Voluntary Payments by American Publishers to Authors Not Protected by Copyright." *Journal of Law and Economics* 59, no. 3: 549–67.

Lilienthal, David E. 1952. *Big Business: A New Era*. New York: Harper.

Linden, Greg, and Deepak Somaya. 2003. "System-on-a-Chip Integration in the Semiconductor Industry: Industry Structure and Firm Strategies." *Industrial and Corporate Change* 12, no. 3: 545–76.

Lohr, Steve. 2017. "How Qualcomm Became Vulnerable to a Takeover Bid." *New York Times*, November 7, 2017. https://www.nytimes.com/2017/11/07/business/qualcomm-broadcom-takeover-bid.html.

Long, Clarisa. 2002. "Patent Signals." *University of Chicago Law Review* 69, no. 2: 625–79.

Lunney, Glynn S. Jr. 2004. "Patent Law, the Federal Circuit and the Supreme Court: A Quiet Revolution." *Supreme Court Economic Review* 11: 1–80.

Macher, Jeffrey T., and David C. Mowery. 2004. "Vertical Specialization and Industry Structure in High Technology Industries." *Advances in Strategic Management* 21: 317–55.

Maclaurin, W. Rupert. 1949. *Invention and Innovation in the Radio Industry*. New York: Macmillan.

MacLeod, Christine. 2007. *Heroes of Invention: Technology, Liberalism and British Identity, 1750–1914*. Cambridge: Cambridge University Press.

Mallinson, Keith. 2015. "Cumulative Mobile-SEP Royalty Payments No More Than Around 5% of Mobile Handset Revenues." IP Finance (blog), August 19, 2015. http://www.ip.finance/search?q=cumulative+mobile+SEP+royalty.

Mallinson, Keith. 2016. "Don't Fix What Isn't Broken: The Extraordinary Record of Innovation and Success in the Cellular Industry under Existing Licensing Practices." *George Mason Law Review* 23, no. 4: 967–1006.

Mansfield, Edwin. 1968. *The Economics of Technological Change*. New York: W. W. Norton.

Mansfield, Edwin. 1986. "Patents and Innovation: An Empirical Study." *Management Science* 32, no. 2: 173–81.

Marcus, Philip. 1945. "Patents, Antitrust Law and Antitrust Judgments through Hartford-Empire." *Georgetown Law Journal* 34, no. 1: 1–63.

Markham, Jesse W. 1962. "Inventive Activity: Government Controls and the Legal Environment." In *The Rate and Direction of Inventive Activity: Economic and Social Factors*, 587–608. Princeton, NJ: Princeton University Press.

Marvel Enterprises Inc. 2005. Form 8-K. Filed with the Securities and Exchange Commission, August 30, 2005.

Marvell Technology Group. 2019. Form 10-K. Filed with the Securities and Exchange Commission, March 28, 2019.

Maskus, Keith E., Kamal Saggi, and Thitima Puttitanun. 2005. "Patent Rights and International Technology Transfer through Direct Investment and Licensing." In *International Public Goods and Transfer of Technology under a Globalized Intellectual Property Regime*, edited by Keith E. Maskus and Jerome H. Reichman, 265–81. New York: Cambridge University Press.

Mayers, H. R. 1959. "The United States Patent System in Historical Perspective." *Patent, Trademark and Copyright Journal of Research and Education* 3, no. 1: 33–52.

McAfee, R. Preston, and John McMillan. 1995. "Organizational Diseconomies of Scale." *Journal of Economics and Management Strategy* 4, no. 3: 399–426.

McCracken, Todd. 2012. "Patent Reform Bill Hurts Small Businesses." *Westlaw Journal of Intellectual Property*, January 11, 2012.

McKinsey & Company. 2011. *McKinsey on Semiconductors*, no. 1.

McManis, Charles R., and Brian Yagi. 2014. "The Bayh-Dole Act and the Anticommons Hypothesis: Round Three." *George Mason Law Review* 21, no. 4: 1049–92.

Merges, Robert P. 2004. "A New Dynamism in the Public Domain." *University of Chicago Law Review* 71, no. 1: 183–203.

Merges, Robert P. 2005. "A Transactional View of Property Rights." *Berkeley Technology Law Journal* 20, no. 4: 1477–520.

Merges, Robert P., and Richard R. Nelson. 1990. "On the Complex Economics of Patent Scope." *Columbia Law Review* 90, no. 4: 839–916.

Methe, David, Anand Swaminathan, and Will Mitchell. 1996. "The Underemphasized Role of Established Firms as the Sources of Major Innovation." *Industrial and Corporate Change* 5, no. 4: 1181–203.

Metrick, Andrew, and Ayako Yasuda. 2011. *Venture Capital and the Finance of Innovation*. 2d ed. Hoboken, NJ: John Wiley.

Mill, John Stuart. (1848) 1909. *Principles of Political Economy with Some of Their Applications to Social Philosophy*, edited by W. J. Ashley. 7th ed. London: Longmans, Green.

Mock, Dave. 2005. *The Qualcomm Equation: How a Fledgling Telecom Company Forged a New Path to Big Profits and Market Dominance*. New York: AMACOM.

Mönch, Lars, Reha Uzsoy, and John W. Fowler. 2018. "A Survey of Semiconductor Supply Chains Models Part I: Semiconductor Supply Chains, Strategic Network Design, and Supply Chain Simulation." *International Journal of Production Research* 56, no. 13: 4524–45.

Morgan Lewis. 2018 PTAB Digest: The Latest Trends and Developments in Post-Grant Proceedings. https://www.morganlewis.com/-/media/files/publication/report/2018-ptab-digest-june-2018.ashx?la=en&hash=B5C0D4875DE370DB6338B835402F3B2610945E7F.

Moser, Petra. 2005. "How Do Patent Laws Influence Innovation? Evidence from Nineteenth-Century World's Fairs." *American Economic Review* 95, no. 4: 1214–36.

Mossoff, Adam. 2009. "Exclusion and Exclusive Use in Patent Law." *Harvard Journal of Law and Technology* 22, no. 2: 321–79.

Mossoff, Adam. 2011. "The Rise and Fall of the First American Patent Thicket: The Sewing Machine War of the 1850s." *Arizona Law Review* 53, no. 1: 165–212.

Mossoff, Adam. 2014. "A Brief History of Software Patents (and Why They're Valid)." *Arizona Law Review* 56, no. 4: 65–80.

Mossoff, Adam. 2019. Testimony on "The State of Patent Eligibiltiy in America" before the Senate Judiciary Committee, Intellectual Property Subcommittee, June 4, 2019.

Mourdoukoutas, Panos. 2017. "Qualcomm's Business Model at Risk." *Forbes*, April 20, 2017.

Mowery, David C. 1981. "The Emergence and Growth of Industrial Research in American Manufacturing, 1899–1945." PhD diss., Stanford University.

Mowery, David C. 1995. "The Boundaries of the U.S. Firm in R & D." In *Coordination and Information: Historical Perspectives on the Organization of Enterprise*, edited by Naomi R. Lamoureaux and Daniel M. G. Raff, 147–83. Chicago: University of Chicago Press.

Mowery, David C. 2009. "What Does Economic Theory Tell Us about Mission-Oriented R&D?" In *The New Economics of Technology Policy*, edited by Dominique Foray, 131–47. Cheltenham, UK: Edward Elgar.

Mowery, David C. 2011. "Federal Policy and the Development of Semiconductors, Computer Hardware, and Computer Software: A Policy Model for Climate Change R&D?" In *Accelerating Energy Innovation: Insights from Multiple Sectors*, edited by Rebecca M. Henderson and Richard G. Newell, 159–88. Chicago: University of Chicago Press.

Mowery, David C., and Nathan Rosenberg. 1989. *Technology and the Pursuit of Economic Growth*. Cambridge: Cambridge University Press.

Mowery, David C., and Nathan Rosenberg. 2000. "Twentieth Century Technological Change." In *The Cambridge Economic History of the United States*, Vol. 3: *The Twentieth Century*, edited by Stanley L. Engerman and Robert E. Gallman, 803–926. Cambridge: Cambridge University Press.

Mueller, Willard F. 1962. "The Origins of the Basic Inventions Underlying Du Pont's Major Product and Process Innovations, 1920 to 1950." In *The Rate and Direction of Inventive Activity: Economic and Social Factors*, edited by National Bureau of Economic Research, 323–58. Princeton, NJ: Princeton University Press.

Mueller, Willard F., and Larry G. Hamm. 1974. "Trends in Industrial Market Concentration 1947 to 1970." *Review of Economics and Statistics* 56, no. 4: 511–20.

Munari, Federico, Maria Cristina Odasso, and Laura Toschi. 2011. "Patent-Backed Finance." In *The Economic Valuation of Patents: Methods and Applications*, edited by Federico Munari and Raffaele Oriani, 309–36. Cheltenham, UK: Edward Elgar.

Myers, Mark B. 2015. "Xerography: An Invention That Became a Dominant Design." *OSA Century of Optics*, edited by Paul Kelley, Govind Agrawa, Mike Bass, Jeff Hecht, and Carlos Stroud, 57–63. Washington, DC: Optical Society.

Nathan Associates. 2016. "Beyond Borders: The Global Semiconductor Value Chain." Semiconductor Industry Association. https://www.semiconductors.org/wp-content/uploads/2018/06/SIA-Beyond-Borders-Report-FINAL-June-7.pdf.

National Association of Manufacturers. 1946. *Patents and the Manufacturer.* New York: NAM.

National Commission on New Technological Uses of Copyrighted Works. 1978. Final Report.

Nellis, Stephen. 2019. "Apple, Allies Seek Billions in U.S. Trial Testing Qualcomm's Business Model." Reuters, April 15, 2019. https://www.reuters.com/article/us-apple-qualcomm-trial/apple-allies-seek-billions-in-u-s-trial-testing-qualcomms-business-model-idUSKCN1RR10V.

Nellis, Stephen. 2020. "Apple Pays $1 Billion for Intel Unit in Push for Chip Independence." Reuters, July 25, 2020. https://www.reuters.com/article/us-intel-divestiture-apple/apple-pays-1-billion-for-intel-unit-in-push-for-chip-independence-idUSKCN1UK2X3.

Nelson, Richard R., Merton J. Peck, and Edward D. Kalachek. 1967. *Technology, Economic Growth and Public Policy: A Rand Corporation and Brookings Institution Study*. Washington, DC: Brookings Institution.

Nicholas, Tom. 2003. "Why Schumpeter Was Right: Innovation, Market Power and Creative Destruction in 1920s America." *Journal of Economic History* 63, no. 4: 1023–58.

Nicholas, Tom. 2009. "Spatial Diversity in Invention: Evidence from the Early R&D Labs." *Journal of Economic Geography* 9: 1–31.

Noam, Eli M. 1993. "Assessing the Impacts of Divestiture and Deregulation in Telecommunications." *Southern Economic Journal* 59, no. 3: 438–49.

Noam, Eli M. 2009. *Media Ownership and Concentration in America.* Oxford: Oxford University Press.

Noll, A. Michael. 1987. "Bell System R&D Activities: The Impact of Divestiture." *Telecommunications Policy* 11, no. 2: 161–78.

Olson, Thomas F. 1959. "Patent Rights in Department of Defense Research and Development Contracts." *California Law Review* 47, no. 4: 721–39.

Orozco, David, and James G. Conley. 2011. "Friends of the Court: Using Amicus Briefs to Identify Corporate Advocacy Positions in Supreme Court Patent Litigation." *University of Illinois Journal of Law, Technology and Policy* 2011, no. 1: 107–29.

Oxley, Joanne E. 1999. "Institutional Environment and the Mechanisms of Governance: The Impact of Intellectual Property Protection on the Structure of Inter-Firm Alliances." *Journal of Economic Behavior and Organization* 38, no. 3: 283–309.

Peck, Merton J., and Frederic M. Scherer. 1962. *The Weapons Acquisition Process: An Economic Analysis.* Boston: Division of Research, Graduate School of Business Administration, Harvard University.

Pellens, Maikel, and Antonio Della Malva. 2018. "Corporate Science, Firm Value, and Vertical Specialization: Evidence from the Semiconductor Industry." *Industrial and Corporate Change* 27, no. 3: 489–505.

Peterson, Kristina. 2009. "Proposed Change in Patent Policy Pits Big Firms vs. Small." *Wall Street Journal*, November 4, 2009. https://www.wsj.com/articles/SB125728918217026407.

Petroski, Henry. 2010. *The Essential Engineer.* New York: Knopf Doubleday.

Pisano, Gary P. 1991. "The Governance of Innovation: Vertical Integration and Collaborative Agreements in the Biotechnology Industry." *Research Policy* 20, no. 3: 237–49.

Pisano, Gary P. 2006. *Science Business: The Promise, the Reality, and the Future of Biotech.* Boston: Harvard Business School Press.

Pisano, Gary P., and David J. Teece. 2007. "How to Capture Value from Innovation: Shaping Intellectual Property and Industry Architecture." *California Management Review* 50, no. 1: 277–96.

Plant, Arnold. 1934. "The Economic Aspects of Copyright in Books." *Economica* 1, no. 2: 167–95.

Plehn-Dujowich, Jose M. 2013. "Product Innovations by Young and Small Firms." Report prepared for the Small Business Administration, Office of Advocacy. https://www.sba.gov/sites/default/files/files/rs408tot.pdf.

Pollack, Andrew. 1984. "Bell System Breakup Opens Era of Great Expectations and Great Concern." *New York Times*, January 1, 1984. https://www.nytimes.com/1984/01/01/us/bell-system-breakup-opens-era-of-great-expectations-and-great-concern.html.

Popper, Ben. 2016. "YouTube to the Music Industry: Here's the Money." *The Verge*, July 13, 2016. https://www.theverge.com/2016/7/13/12165194/youtube-content-id-2-billion-paid.

Posner, Richard A. 1970. "A Statistical Study of Antitrust Enforcement." *Journal of Law and Economics* 13, no. 2: 365–419.

Priest, George L., and Benjamin Klein. 1984. "The Selection of Disputes for Litigation." *Journal of Legal Studies* 13: 1–56.

Pursell, Carroll. 1990. *Technology in America: A History of Individuals and Ideas.* Cambridge, MA: MIT Press.

Qualcomm. 2018. Form 10-K. Filed with the Securities and Exchange Commission, November 7, 2018.

Radomsky, Leon. 2000. "Sixteen Years after Passage of the U.S. Semiconductor Chip Protection Act: Is International Protection Working?" *Berkeley Technology Law Journal* 15, no. 3: 1049–94.

Rampton, John. 2015. "Why VCs Don't Sign NDAs and You Shouldn't Worry about It." *Entrepreneur*, April 14, 2015. https://www.entrepreneur.com/article/245023.

Rantanen, Jason. 2012. "Why Priest-Klein Cannot Apply to Individual Issues in Patent Cases." University of Iowa Legal Studies Research Paper 12-15.

Rathmann, George B. 1993. "Biotechnology Case Study." In *Global Dimensions of Intellectual Property Rights in Science and Technology*, edited by Mitchell B. Wallerstein, Mary Ellen Mogee, and Roberta A. Schoen, 319–28. Washington, DC: National Academy Press.

Raymond, Eric S. 1999. *The Cathedral and the Bazaar: Musings on Linux and Open Source by an Accidental Revolutionary*. Sebastopol, CA: O'Reilly.

Reich, Leonard S. 2002. *The Making of American Industrial Research: Science and Business at GE and Bell, 1876–1926*. Cambridge: Cambridge University Press.

Rhoads, Christopher. 2005. "AT&T Inventions Fueled Tech Boom, and Its Own Fall." *Wall Street Journal*, February 2, 2005. https://www.wsj.com/articles/SB110729925236542968.

Rich, Giles S. 1964. "The Vague Concept of 'Invention' as Replaced by Sec. 103 of the 1952 Patent Act." *Journal of the Patent Office Society* 46, no. 12: 855–76.

Rimmer, Matthew. 2002. "Genentech and the Stolen Gene: Patent Law and Pioneer Inventions." *Bio-Science Law Review* 5, no. 6: 198–211.

Riordan, Michael. 2005. "The End of AT&T." *IEEE Spectrum*, July 1, 2005. https://spectrum.ieee.org/tech-history/dawn-of-electronics/the-end-of-att.

Risch, Michael. 2012. "Patent Troll Myths." *Seton Hall Law Review* 42, no. 2: 457–500.

Robinson, Glen. 1988. "The Titanic Remembered: AT&T and the Changing World of Telecommunications." *Yale Journal on Regulation* 5, no. 2: 517–45.

Roman, David. 2014. "Replica Ferraris Raise Ire of Auto Maker." *Wall Street Journal*, January 8, 2014. https://www.wsj.com/articles/replica-ferraris-raise-ire-of-auto-maker-1389238865.

Rooney, Kate. 2019. "Venture Capital Spending Hits All-Time High in 2018, Eclipsing Dotcom Bubble Record." CNBC, January 10, 2019. https://www.cnbc.com/2019/01/09/venture-capital-spending-hit-all-time-high-in-2018-eclipsing-the-dot-com-era-record.html.

Rothaermel, Frank T. 2001. "Incumbent's Advantage through Exploiting Complementary Assets via Interfirm Cooperation." *Strategic Management Journal* 22, no. 6/7: 687–99.

Roumeliotis, Greg, and Diane Bartz. 2018. "Broadcom Unveils $121 Billion 'Best and Final' Offer for Qualcomm." Reuters, February 5, 2018. https://www.reuters.com/article/us-qualcomm-m-a-broadcom/broadcom-unveils-121-billion-best-and-final-offer-for-qualcomm-idUSKBN1FP1KX.

Schacht, Wendy H. 2000. "Federal R&D, Drug Discovery, and Pricing: Insights from the NIH-University-Industry Relationship." Congressional Research Service, RL32324.

Scherer, F. M. 1965. "Firm Size, Market Structure, Opportunity and the Output of Patented Inventions." *American Economic Review* 57: 524–31.

Scherer, F. M. 1977. *The Economic Effects of Compulsory Licensing*. New York: NYU Graduate School of Business Administration, Center for the Study of Financial Institutions.

Scherer, F. M. 1980. *Industrial Market Structure and Economic Performance*. 2nd ed. Boston: Houghton Mifflin.

Scherer, F. M. 1984. "Technological Change and the Modern Corporation." In *The Impact of the Modern Corporation*, edited by Betty Bock, Harvey J. Goldschmid, Ira M. Millstein, and F. M. Scherer, 270–97. New York: Columbia University Press.

Scherer, F. M. 1991. "Changing Perspectives on the Firm Size Problem." In *Innovation and Technological Change: An International Comparison*, edited by Zoltan J. Acs and David B. Audtresch, 24–38. Ann Arbor: University of Michigan Press.

Scherer, F. M., Sigmund E. Herzstein Jr., Alex W. Dreyfoos, William G. Whitney, Otto J. Bachmann, Cyril P. Pesek, Charles J. Scott, Thomas G. Kelly, and James J. Galvin. 1959. *Patents and the Corporation: A Report on Industrial Technology under Changing Public Policy*. 2nd ed. Boston: Patents and the Corporation.

Schiff, Eric. 1971. *Industrialization without National Patents: The Netherlands, 1869–1912, Switzerland, 1850–1907*. Princeton, NJ: Princeton University Press.

Schnaars, Steven P. 1994. *Managing Imitation Strategies: How Later Entrants Seize Markets from Pioneers*. New York: Free Press.

Schumpeter, Joseph. (1911) 1934. *The Theory of Economic Development: An Inquiry into Profits, Capital, Credit, Interest and the Business Cycle*. Cambridge, MA: Harvard University Press.

Schumpeter, Joseph. 1928. "The Instability of Capitalism." *Economic Journal* 38, no. 151: 361–86.

Schumpeter, Joseph. 1939. *Business Cycles: A Theoretical, Historical and Statistical Analysis of the Capitalist Process*. Vol. 1. New York: McGraw-Hill.

Schumpeter, Joseph. (1942) 1950. *Capitalism, Socialism, and Democracy*. New York: Harper & Row.

Schwartz, David L., and Jay P. Kesan. 2014. "Analyzing the Role of Non-Practicing Entities in the Patent System." *Cornell Law Review* 99, no. 2: 425–56.

Schwartz, Evan I. 2002. *The Last Lone Inventor: A Tale of Genius, Deceit and the Birth of Television*. New York: HarperCollins.

Schwartz, Herbert F. 1964. "Injunctive Relief in Patent Infringement Suits." *University of Pennsylvania Law Review* 112, no. 7: 1025–48.

Seaman, Christopher B. 2016. "Permanent Injunctions in Patent Litigation after *eBay*: An Empirical Study." *Iowa Law Review* 101, no. 5: 1949–2019.

Senate Committee on the Judiciary. 1960. Patents, Trademarks, and Copyrights Subcommittee. *Report on Compulsory Patent Licensing under Antitrust Judgments*, 86th Cong., 2d sess., 1960.

Shan, Weijan, Gordon Walker, and Bruce Kogut. 1994. "Interfirm Cooperation and Startup Innovation in the Biotechnology Industry." *Strategic Management Journal* 15, no. 5: 387–94.

Sharma, Siddharth. 2007. "Financial Development and Innovation in Small Firms." World Bank Policy Research Working Paper 4350.

Shephard, William G. 1964. "Trends of Concentration in American Manufacturing Industries, 1947–1958." *Review of Economics and Statistics* 46, no. 2: 200–212.

Sichelman, Ted. 2010. "Commercializing Patents." *Stanford Law Review* 62, no. 2: 341–413.

Sichelman, Ted. 2014. "The Vonage Trilogy: A Case Study in 'Patent Bullying.'" *Notre Dame Law Review* 90, no. 2: 543–78.

Sichelman, Ted, and Stuart J. H. Graham. 2010. "Patenting by Entrepreneurs: An Empirical Study." *Michigan Telecommunications and Technology Law Review* 17: 111–80.

Sidak, J. Gregory. 2016. "What Aggregate Royalty Do Manufacturers of Mobile Phones Pay to License Standard-Essential Patents?" *Criterion Journal of Innovation* 1: 701–19.

Simonite, Tom. 2017. "Apple Becomes a Chipmaker to One-Up Smartphone Foes." *Wired*, September 20, 2017. https://www.wired.com/story/apple-becomes-a-chipmaker-to-one-up-smartphone-foes/.

Smarzynska, Beata Javorcik. 2004. "Composition of Foreign Direct Investment and Protection of Intellectual Property Rights: Evidence from Transition Economies." *European Economic Review* 48, no. 1: 39–62.

Smith, David. 1965. "Technological Innovation and Patents." In *Patents and Progress: The Sources and Impact of Advancing Technology*, edited by Wroe Alderson, Vern Tepstra, and Stanley J. Shapiro, 245–51. Homewood, IL: R. D. Irwin.

Smith, Pamela J. 2001. "How Do Foreign Patent Rights Affect US Exports, Affiliate Sales, and Licenses?" *Journal of International Economics* 55, no. 2: 411–39.

Somaya, Deepak, David Teece, and Simon Wakeman. 2011. "Innovation in Multi-Invention Contexts: Mapping Solutions to Technological and Intellectual Property Complexity." *California Management Review* 53, no. 4: 47–79.

Sterling, Christopher H., ed. 2011. *The Biographical Encyclopedia of American Radio.* New York: Routledge.

Sterling, Christopher H., and Michael C. Keith. 2008. *Sounds of Change: A History of FM Broadcasting in America.* Chapel Hill: University of North Carolina Press.

Stuart, Toby E., Salih Zeki Ozdemir, and Waverly W. Ding. 2007. "Vertical Alliance Networks: The Case of University-Biotechnology-Pharmaceutical Alliance Chains." *Research Policy* 36, no. 4: 477–98.

Stylianou, Konstantinos. 2011. "An Innovation-Centric Approach of Telecommunications Infrastructure Regulation." *Virginia Journal Law and Technology* 16, no. 2: 221–52.

Tamilla, Robert D. 2016. "History of Channels of Distribution." In *The Routledge Companion to Marketing History,* edited by D. G. Brian Jones and Mark Tadajewski. New York: Routledge.

Taylor, C. T., and Z. A. Silberston. 1973. *The Economic Impact of the Patent System: A Study of the British Experience.* Cambridge: Cambridge University Press.

Taylor, David O. 2019. "Patent Reform: Then and Now." *Michigan State Law Review* 2019: 431–509.

Teece, David J. 1986. "Profiting from Technological Innovation: Implications for Integration, Collaboration, Licensing and Public Policy." *Research Policy* 15, no. 6: 285–305.

Teece, David J. 1988. "Capturing Value from Technological Innovation: Integration, Strategic Partnering, and Licensing Decisions." *Interfaces* 18, no. 3: 46–61.

Temporary National Economic Committee. 1941. Investigation of Concentration of Economic Power, Final Report and Recommendations of the Temporary National Economic Committee, 77th Cong., 1st sess., 1941.

"Third Report of the National Patent Planning Commission." 1945. *American Bar Association Journal* 31, no. 11: 602–3, 607.

Tilley, Aaron. 2017. "Apple Is Reportedly Working on Another iPhone Chip and This Tiny Company's Stock Is Reeling." *Forbes,* April 11, 2017. https://www.forbes.com/sites/aaron-tilley/2017/04/11/apple-is-reportedly-working-on-another-iphone-chip-and-this-tiny-companys-stock-is-reeling/#f7280644ae46.

Tilton, John E. 1971. *International Diffusion of Technology: The Case of Semiconductors.* Washington, DC: Brookings Institution.

Tripsas, Mary. 1997. "Unraveling the Process of Creative Destruction: Complementary Assets and Incumbent Survival in the Typesetter Industry." *Strategic Management Journal* 18, no. 1: 119–42.

TSMC. 2018. Annual Report. https://www.tsmc.com/download/ir/annualReports/2018/english/pdf/e_all.pdf.

Tufano, Peter. 1989. "Financial Innovation and First-Mover Advantages." *Journal of Financial Economics* 25, no. 2: 213–40.

Tufano, Peter. 2003. "Financial Innovation." In *Handbook of the Economics of Finance,* Vol. 1a: *Corporate Finance,* edited by George M. Constantinides, Milton Harris, and Rene M. Stulz, 307–36. Amsterdam: Elsevier.

Tuomi, Ilkka. 2009. *The Future of Semiconductor Intellectual Property Architectural Blocks in Europe,* edited by Marc Bogdanowicz. Luxembourg: Office of the Official Publications of the European Communities.

Unified Patents. 2019. "Q3 2019 Patent Dispute Report." September 30, 2019. https://www.unifiedpatents.com/insights/2019/9/30/q3-2019-patent-dispute-report.

United Nations Economic Commission for Europe. 1968. "Aspects of the Diffusion of Technology in the United States." In *Policies and Means of Promoting Technical*

Progress: Papers Presented to the Fifth Meeting of Senior Economic Advisers to ECE Governments, 89–104. New York: United Nations.

U.S. Congress, House. 1964. Select Committee on Government Research. *Federal Research and Development Programs, First Progress Report of the Select Committee on Government Research*, 88th Cong., 2nd sess., 1964.

U.S. Congress, Senate. 1942. *Hearings before the Committee on Patents, on S. 2303, a Bill to Provide for the Use of Patents in the Interest of National Defense or the Prosecution of War, and for Other Purposes*, 77th Cong., 2nd sess., 1942.

U.S. Congress, Senate. 1967. Subcommittee on Patents, Trademarks and Copyrights of the Committee on the Judiciary. *To Promote the Progress of Useful Arts, Report of the President's Commission on the Patent System*, 90th Cong., 1st sess., 1967.

U.S. Department of Commerce. 1953. *Statistical Abstract of the United States*. Washington, DC: U.S. Department of Commerce.

U.S. Department of Justice. 1997. "Justice Department Approves Proposal for Joint Licensing of Patents Essential for Meeting Video Technology Standard Used in Electronics and Broadcast Industries." June 26, 1997.

U.S. Department of Justice. 2017. "Assistant Attorney General Makan Delrahim Delivers Remarks at the USC Gould School of Law's Center for Transnational Law and Business Conference." November 10, 2017.

U.S. Department of Justice and Federal Trade Commission. 1995. "Antitrust Guidelines for the Licensing of Intellectual Property."

U.S. Department of Justice and U.S. Patent and Trademark Office. 2013. "Policy Statement on Remedies for Standards Essential Patents Subject to Voluntary F/RAND Commitments." January 8, 2013.

U.S. Department of Justice, U.S. Patent and Trademark Office, and National Institute of Standards and Technology. 2019. "Policy Statement on Remedies for Standards-Essential Patents Subject to Voluntary F/RAND Commitments." December 19, 2019.

U.S. Patent and Trademark Office. 1987. Notice, Animals—Patentability, 1077 Off. Gaz. Pat. Office 24.

U.S. Patent and Trademark Office. 2000. "A USPTO White Paper: Automated Financial or Management Data Processing Methods (Business Methods)."

U.S. Patent and Trademark Office. 2015. "Biotechnology: All Classified Utility Patents, Number of Patents Granted as Distributed by Year of Patent Grant, Breakout by Country of Origin," https://www.uspto.gov/web/offices/ac/ido/oeip/taf/data/biotech.htm#PartA1_1a.

U.S. Patent and Trademark Office. 2019. Annual Report, Patent Public Advisory Committee.

U.S. President. 1938. *Strengthening and Enforcement of Antitrust Laws: Message Transmitting Recommendations Relative to Strengthening and Enforcement of Antitrust Laws*, 75th Cong., 3rd sess., 1938.

Usselman, Steven W. 1991. "Patents Purloined: Railroads, Inventors, and the Diffusion of Invention in 19th-Century America." *Technology and Culture* 32, no. 4: 1047–75.

Usselman, Steven W. 1999. "Patents, Engineering Professionals, and the Pipelines of Innovation." In *Learning by Doing in Markets, Firms, and Countries*, edited by Naomi R. Lamoreaux, Daniel M. G. Raff, and Peter Temin, 61–102. Chicago: University of Chicago Press.

Usselman, Steven W. 2002. *Regulating Railroad Innovation: Business, Technology and Politics in America, 1840–1920*. Cambridge: Cambridge University Press.

Vaughan, Floyd L. 1956. *The United States Patent System: Legal and Economic Conflicts in American Patent History*. Norman: University of Oklahoma Press.

Villard, Henry H. 1958. "Competition, Oligopoly, and Research." *Journal of Political Economy* 66, no. 6: 483–97.

Von Burg, Urs. 2001. *The Triumph of Ethernet: Technological Communities and the Battle for the LAN Standard*. Stanford, CA: Stanford University Press.

Walsh, John P., Ashish Arora, and Wesley M. Cohen. 2003. "Effects of Research Tool Patents and Licensing on Biomedical Innovation." In *Patents in the Knowledge-Based Economy*, edited by Wesley M. Cohen and Stephen A. Merrill, 285–340. Washington, DC: National Academies Press.

Watson, Donald Stevenson, and Mary A. Holman. 1967. "Concentration of Patents from Government Financed Research in Industry." *Review of Economics and Statistics*. 49, no. 3: 375–81.

Watson, Thomas J. Jr., and Peter Petre. 1990. *Father, Son & Co.: My Life at IBM and Beyond*. New York: Bantam.

Watzinger, Martin, Thomas A. Fackler, Markus Nagler, and Monika Schnitzer. 2020 (forthcoming). "How Antitrust Enforcement Can Spur Innovation: Bell Labs and the 1956 Consent Decree." *American Economic Journal: Economic Policy*.

Waxman, Sharon. 2007. "Marvel Wants to Flex Its Own Heroic Muscles as a Moviemaker." *New York Times*, June 18, 2007. https://www.nytimes.com/2007/06/18/business/media/18marvel.html.

Webbink, Douglas W. 1977. "The Semiconductor Industry: A Survey of Structure, Conduct, and Performance." Staff Report to the Federal Trade Commission.

Wessner, Charles W., ed. 2008. *Capitalizing on Science, Technology, and Innovation: An Assessment of the SBIR Program*. Washington, DC: National Academies Press.

White, Lawrence J. 1971. *The Automobile Industry since 1945*. Cambridge, MA: Harvard University Press.

Wigmore, John H. 1942. Foreword. In *Patents and Antitrust Law*, by Laurence I. Wood, vii–viii. New York: Commerce Clearing House.

Wilcox, Joe. 2000. "IBM to Spend $1 Billion on Linux in 2001." CNET, December 12, 2000. https://www.linux.co.cr/oem-support/review/2000/1212.html.

Wiley, John D., and Laura A. Dunek. 2017. "Serving the Public Good by Utilizing Scientific Patents to Incentivize Economic Growth." In *Challenges in Higher Education Leadership: Practical and Scholarly Solutions*, edited by James Soto Antony, Ana Mari Cauce, and Donna E. Shalala, 95–104. New York: Routledge.

Williams, Pamela Hawkins, Dotcy Isom III, and Tiffini D. Smith-Peaches. 2003. "A Profile of Dolby Laboratories: An Effective Model for Leveraging Intellectual Property." *Northwestern Journal of Technology and Intellectual Property* 2, no. 4: 81–98.

Williamson, Oliver E. 1975. *Markets and Hierarchies, Analysis and Antitrust Implications: A Study in the Economics of Internal Organization*. New York: Free Press.

Williamson, Oliver E. 2005. "Transaction Cost Economics." In *Handbook of New Institutional Economics*, edited by Claude Ménard and Mary M. Shirley, 41–65. Dordrecht: Springer.

Wilson, Bruce B. 1972. Deputy Assistant Attorney General, Antitrust Division. "Remarks before Annual Joint Meeting of Michigan State Bar Antitrust Law Section and Patent, Trademark and Copyright Section." Reprinted in 4 Trade Reg. Rep. (CCH) ¶ 13,126, September 21, 1972.

Winter, Sidney G. 1984. "Schumpeterian Competition in Alternative Technological Regimes." *Journal of Economic Behavior and Organization* 5, no. 3/4: 287–320.

Wise, Thomas A. 1966. "IBM's $5,000,000,000 Gamble." *Fortune*, September 1966.

Wood, Laurence I. 1942. *Patents and Antitrust Law*. New York: Commerce Clearing House.

Xerox. 1999. "The Story of Xerography." https://www.xerox.com/downloads/usa/en/s/Storyofxerography.pdf.

Yap, Xiao-Shan, and Rajah Rasiah. 2017. "Catching Up and Leapfrogging in a High-Tech Manufacturing Industry: Towards a Firm-Level Taxonomy of Knowledge Accumulation." *Knowledge Management Research and Practice* 15, no. 1: 114–29.

Young, McGee. 2008. "The Political Roots of Small Business Identity." *Polity* 40, no. 4: 436–63.

Zenger, Todd R., and Sergio G. Lazzarini. 2004. "Compensating for Innovation: Do Small Firms Offer High-Powered Incentives That Lure Talent and Motivate Effort?" *Managerial and Decision Economics* 25, no. 6/7: 329–45.

Zhao, Minyuan. 2006. "Conducting R&D in Countries with Weak Intellectual Property Rights Protection." *Management Science* 52, no. 8: 1185–99.

Ziedonis, Rosemarie Ham. 2003. "Patent Litigation in the US Semiconductor Industry." In *Patents in the Knowledge-Based Economy*, edited by Wesley M. Cohen and Stephen A. Merrill, 180–219. Washington, DC: National Academies Press.

Ziedonis, Rosemarie Ham, and Bronwyn H. Hall. 2001. "The Effects of Strengthening Patent Rights on Firms Engaged in Cumulative Innovation: Insights from the Semiconductor Industry." In *Entrepreneurial Inputs and Outcomes: New Studies of Entrepreneurship in the United States*, Vol. 13 of *Advances in the Study of Entrepreneurship, Innovation and Economic Growth*, edited by Gary D. Libecap, 133–87. Bingley, UK: Emerald Group.

Judicial Opinions and Administrative Rulings

Alice Corp. Pty Ltd. v. CLS Bank Int'l, 573 U.S. 208 (2014)

American Axle & Manufacturing, Inc. v. Neapco Holdings LLC et al., 939 F.3d 1355 (Fed. Cir. 2019), modified by *American Axle & Manufacturing, Inc. v. Neapco Holdings LLC et al.*, Appeal No. 2018-1763 (Fed. Cir. July 31, 2020)

American Hoist & Derrick Co. v. Sowa & Sons, Inc., 725 F.2d 1350 (Fed. Cir. 1984)

Amgen, Inc. v. Chugai Pharmaceutical Co., 927 F.2d 1200 (Fed. Cir. 1991)

Apple, Inc. v. Motorola, Inc., 757 F.3d 1286 (Fed. Cir. 2014)

Apple, Inc. v. Motorola, Inc., 869 F. Supp. 2d 901 (N.D. Ill. 2012)

Apple, Inc. v. Samsung Electronics Co., Ltd., Case No. 12-CV-00630-LHK (N.D. Cal. Jan. 18, 2016)

Apple, Inc. v. Samsung Electronics Co., Ltd., 809 F.3d 633 (Fed. Cir. 2015)

Apple, Inc. v. Samsung Electronics Co., Ltd., 2014 WL 749610 (N.D. Cal., Aug. 27, 2014)

Apple, Inc. v. Samsung Electronics Co., Ltd., 909 F. Supp. 2d 1147 (N.D. Cal. 2012)

Association for Molecular Pathology v. Myriad Genetics, 569 U.S. 576 (2013)

AT&T Corp. v. Excel Communications, Inc., 172 F.3d 1352 (Fed. Cir. 1999)

Atlantic Works v. Brady, 107 U.S. 192 (1883)

Atlas Powder Co. v. IRECO Chemicals, 773 F.2d 1230 (Fed. Cir. 1985)

Author's Guild et al. v. Google Inc., 804 F.3d 202 (2d Cir. 2015)

Author's Guild Inc. v. HathiTrust et al., 755 F.3d 87 (2d Cir. 2014)

Bement v. National Harrow Co., 186 U.S. 70 (1902)

Berkheimer v. HP, Inc., 881 F.3d 1360 (Fed. Cir. 2018)

Bilski v. Kappos, 561 U.S. 593 (2010)

Buono v. Yankee Maid Dress Corp., 77 F.2d 274 (2d Cir. 1935)

Capital Records, L.L.C. v. Vimeo, L.L.C., 972 F. Supp. 2d 500 (S.D.N.Y. 2013)

ChargePoint, Inc. v. SemaConnect, Inc., 920 F.3d 759 (Fed. Cir. 2019)

Chicago & N.W. Railway. Co. v. Sayles, 97 U.S. 554 (1878)

Columbus Auto. Corp. v. Oldberg Mfg. Co., 264 F. Supp. 779 (D. Colo. 1967)

Continental Paper Bag Co. v. Eastern Paper Bag Co., 210 U.S. 405 (1908)

Continental T.V., Inc., et al. v. GTE Sylvania, 433 U.S. 36 (1977)

Cuno Engineering v. Automatic Devices, 314 U.S. 91 (1941)

Dann v. Johnston, 425 U.S. 219 (1976)

Davoll v. Brown, 7 F. Cas. 197 (C.C.D. Mass. 1845) (No. 3,662)

Desny v. Wilder, 299 P.2d 257 (Cal. 1956)

Diamond v. Diehr, 450 U.S. 175 (1981)

Diamond v. Chakrabarty, 447 U.S. 303 (1980)

Dubuit v. Harwell Enterprises, Inc., 336 F. Supp. 1184 (W.D.N.C. 1971)

eBay Inc. v. MercExchange, L.L.C., 547 U.S. 388 (2006)

Edison Phonograph Co. v. Pike, 116 F. 863 (C.C.D. Mass. 1902)

Edward Katzinger Co. v. Chicago Metallic Mfg. Co., 329 U.S. 394 (1947)

Federal Trade Commission v. Qualcomm Inc., 411 F. Supp.3d 658 (N.D. Cal. 2019)

Federal Trade Commission v. Qualcomm Inc., 935 F.3d 752 (9th Cir. 2019)

Federal Trade Commission v. Qualcomm, Inc., Case No. 19-16122 (9th Cir. Aug 11, 2020)

General Talking Pictures Corp. v. Western Electric Co., 304 U.S. 175 (1938)

Gottschalk v. Benson, 409 U.S. 63 (1972)

Graver Tank & Manufacturing Co. v. Linde Air Products Co., 339 U.S. 605 (1950)

Hartford-Empire Co. v. United States, 323 U.S. 386 (1945)

Heaton-Peninsular Fastener Co. v. Eureka Specialty Co., 77 F. 288 (6th Cir. 1896)

Henry v. A. B. Dick Co., 224 U.S. 1 (1912)

H. H. Robertson Co. v. United Steel Deck, Inc., 820 F.2d 384 (Fed. Cir. 1987)

Hotchkiss v. Greenwood, 52 U.S. 248 (1850)

In re Alappat, 33 F.3d 1526 (Fed. Cir. 1994)

In re Johnston, 502 F.2d 765 (C.C.P.A. 1974)

In re Prater, 415 F.2d 1378 (C.C.P.A. 1968)

In re Recombinant DNA Technology Patent and Contract Litigation, 850 F. Supp. 769 (S.D. Ind. 1994)

International News Service v. Associated Press, 248 U.S. 215 (1918)

Jack Winter, Inc. v. Koratron Co., 375 F. Supp. 1 (N.D. Cal. 1974)

Jefferson Parish Hospital District No. 2 v. Hyde, 466 U.S. 2 (1984)

Jungersen v. Ostby & Barton Co., 335 U.S. 560 (1949)

Key Pharmaceuticals, Inc. v. Lowey, 373 F. Supp. 1190 (S.D.N.Y. 1974)

Leeds & Catlin Co. v. Victor Talking Machine Co., 213 U.S. 325 (1909)

MacGregor v. Westinghouse Elec. & Mfg. Co., 329 U.S. 402 (1947)

Mallinckrodt, Inc. v. Medipart, Inc., 976 F.2d 700 (Fed. Cir. 1992)

Mandel Bros. v. Wallace, 335 U.S. 291 (1948)

Mayo Collaborative Services v. Prometheus Labs, Inc., 566 U.S. 66 (2012)

Microsoft Corp. v. i4i Ltd. Partnership, 564 U.S. 91 (2011)

Microsoft Corp. v. Motorola, Inc., 795 F.3d 1024 (9th Cir. 2015)

Microsoft Corp. v. Motorola, Inc., 2013 WL 5373179 (W.D. Wash. Sept. 24, 2013)

Microsoft Corp. v. Motorola, Inc., 963 F. Supp. 2d 1176 (W.D. Wash. 2013)

Morgan Envelope Co. v. Albany Paper Co., 152 U.S. 425 (1894)

Morton Salt Co. v. G. S. Suppiger Co., 314 U.S. 488 (1942)

Motion Picture Patents Co. v. Universal Film Mfg. Co., 243 U.S. 502 (1917)

Motorola Mobility LLC & Google Inc., FTC File No. 121-0120, Docket No. C-4410 (July 24, 2013)

Mowry v. Whitney, 81 U.S. (14 Wall.) 620 (1871)

Oil States Services, LLC v. Greene's Energy Group, LLC, 138 S. Ct. 1365 (2018)

Parker v. Flook, 437 U.S. 584 (1978)

Perfect 10, Inc. v. Amazon.com, Inc. et al., 487 F.3d 701 (9th Cir. 2007)

Picard v. United Aircraft Corp., 128 F.2d 632 (2d Cir. 1942)

Polaroid Corp. v. Eastman Kodak Co., 641 F. Supp. 828 (D. Mass. 1986)

Realtek Semiconductor Corp. v. LSI Corp., 946 F. Supp. 2d 998 (N.D. Cal. 2013)

Robert Bosch GmbH, FTC File No. 121-0081, Docket No. C-4377 (Apr. 23, 2013)

Rubber Tire Wheel Co. v. Milwaukee Rubber Works Co., 154 F. 358 (7th Cir. 1907)

Rupp & Wittenfield Co. v. Elliott, 131 F. 730 (6th Cir. 1904)

Smith International v. Hughes Tool Co., 718 F.2d 1573 (Fed. Cir. 1983)

Sola Elec. Co. v. Jefferson Electric Co., 317 U.S. 173 (1942)

Sonobond Corp. v. Uthe Technology, Inc., 314 F. Supp. 878 (N.D. Cal. 1970)

Standard Oil Co. v. United States, 283 U.S 163 (1931)

Standard Sanitary Mfg. Co. v. United States, 226 U.S. 20 (1912)

Stanford University v. Roche Molecular Sys. Inc., 563 U.S. 776 (2011)

State Street Bank & Trust Co. v. Signature Financial Group, Inc., 149 F.3d 1368 (Fed. Cir. 1998)

Tubular Rivet & Stud Co., 93 F. 200 (C.C.D. Mass. 1898)

UMG Recordings, Inc. v. Shelter Capital Partners, LLC, 718 F.3d 1006 (9th Cir. 2013)

UMG Recordings, Inc. v. Veoh Networks, Inc., 665 F. Supp. 2d 1099 (C.D. Cal. 2009)

United Shoe Machinery Corp. v. United States, 266 F. Supp. 328 (D. Mass. 1967)

United States v. Aluminum Co. of America, 91 F. Supp. 333 (S.D.N.Y. 1950)

United States v. Bausch & Lomb Optical Co., 321 U.S. 707 (1944)

United States v. General Electric Co., 272 U.S. 476 (1926)

United States v. National Lead Co., 332 U.S. 319 (1947)

United States v. United Shoe Machinery Corp., 391 U.S. 244 (1968)

United States v. United Shoe Machinery Corp., 110 F. Supp. 295 (D. Mass. 1953)

United States v. Univis Lens Co., 316 U.S. 241 (1942)

United States v. Western Electric Co., 1956 Trade Cases (CCH) ¶ 68,246 (D. N.J. 1956)

Viacom International, Inc. v. YouTube, Inc., 940 F. Supp. 2d 110 (S.D.N.Y. 2013)

Viacom International, Inc. v. YouTube, Inc., 676 F.3d 19 (2d Cir. 2012)

Victor Talking Mach. Co. v. The Fair, 123 F. 424 (7th Cir. 1903)

Waring v. Dunlea, 26 F. Supp. 338 (E.D.N.C. 1939)

Waring v. WDAS Broadcasting Station, Inc., 194 A. 631 (Pa. 1937)

Windsurfing International Inc. v. AMF, Inc., 782 F.2d 995 (Fed. Cir. 1986)

Xerox Corp., 86 F.T.C. 364 (1975)

Zenith Radio Corp. v. Hazeltine Research, 395 U.S. 100 (1969)

Index